Student Companion to
Nathaniel
HAWTHORNE

Student Companion to

Nathaniel
HAWTHORNE

Melissa McFarland Pennell

Student Companions to Classic Writers

Greenwood Press
Westport, Connecticut • London

Library of Congress Cataloging-in-Publication Data

Pennell, Melissa McFarland.
    Student companion to Nathaniel Hawthorne / Melissa McFarland
Pennell.
        p.   cm.—(Student companions to classic writers, ISSN
1522–7979)
    Includes bibliographical references and index.
    ISBN 0–313–30595–1 (alk. paper)
    1. Hawthorne, Nathaniel, 1804–1864—Criticism and interpretation—
Handbooks, manuals, etc.   I. Title.   II. Series.
PS1888.P46   1999
813′.3—dc21   98–54111

British Library Cataloguing in Publication Data is available.

Library of Congress Catalog Card Number: 98–54111
ISBN: 0–313–30595–1
ISSN: 1522–7979

First published in 1999

Greenwood Press, 88 Post Road West, Westport, CT 06881
An imprint of Greenwood Publishing Group, Inc.
www.greenwood.com

Printed in the United States of America

The paper used in this book complies with the
Permanent Paper Standard issued by the National
Information Standards Organization (Z39.48–1984).

10 9 8 7 6 5 4 3 2 1

For my family,
without whose encouragement and support
this would not have been written,
and especially for Steve

Contents

Series Foreword

This series has been designed to meet the needs of students and general readers for accessible literary criticism on the American and world writers most frequently studied and read in the secondary school, community college, and four-year college classrooms. Unlike other works of literary criticism that are written for the specialist and graduate student, or that feature a variety of reprinted scholarly essays on sometimes obscure aspects of the writer's work, the Student Companions to Classic Writers series is carefully crafted to examine each writer's major works fully and in a systematic way, at the level of the non-specialist and general reader. The objective is to enable the reader to gain a deeper understanding of the work and to apply critical thinking skills to the act of reading. The proven format for the volumes in this series was developed by an advisory board of teachers and librarians for a successful series published by Greenwood Press, Critical Companions to Popular Contemporary Writers. Responding to their request for easy-to-use and yet challenging literary criticism for students and adult library patrons, Greenwood Press developed a systematic format that is not intimidating but helps the reader to develop the ability to analyze literature.

How does this work? Each volume in the Student Companions to Classic Writers series is written by a subject specialist, an academic who understands students' needs for basic and yet challenging examination of the writer's canon. Each volume begins with a biographical chapter, drawn from published sources, biographies, and autobiographies, that relates the writer's life to his or her work. The next chapter examines the writer's literary heritage, tracing the literary influences of other writers on that writer and explaining and discussing the literary genres into which the writer's work falls. Each of the following chapters examines a major work by the writer, those works most frequently read and studied by high school and college students. Depending on the writer's canon, generally between four and eight major works are examined, each in an individual chapter. The discussion of each work is organized into separate sections on plot development, character development, and major themes. Literary devices and style, narrative point of view, and historical setting are also discussed in turn if pertinent to the work. Each chapter concludes with an alternate critical perspective from which to read the work, such as a psychological or feminist criticism. The critical theory is defined briefly in easy, comprehensible language for the student. Looking at the literature from the point of view of a particular critical approach will help the reader to understand and apply critical theory to the act of reading and analyzing literature.

Of particular value in each volume is the bibliography, which includes a complete bibliography of the writer's works, a selected bibliography of biographical and critical works suitable for students, and lists of reviews of each work examined in the companion, both from the time the literature was originally published and from contemporary sources, all of which will be helpful to readers, teachers, and librarians who would like to consult additional sources.

As a source of literary criticism for the student or for the general reader, this series will help the reader to gain understanding of the writer's work and skill in critical reading.

Preface

The *Student Companion to Nathaniel Hawthorne* provides a critical introduction to the fiction of one of America's major writers. Beginning with Hawthorne's life and his career, the discussion places him within the context of his times, attempting to highlight for readers the ways that Hawthorne interacted with and reacted to the culture around him. The chapters on Hawthorne's fiction address both his short stories and his novels. Two chapters on the short stories address the best-known and most frequently anthologized tales. Chapters on the romances treat *The Scarlet Letter, The House of the Seven Gables, The Blithedale Romance,* and *The Marble Faun.*

Each chapter offers the student and the general reader background that will assist in understanding and interpreting Hawthorne's work. The biographical chapter provides an overview of Hawthorne's life, including his years in Salem and in Concord, Massachusetts. The chapter on his career traces Hawthorne's development as an author, his contributions to the genres of the short story and the romance, and his influence on contemporaries and later writers. In examining the fiction itself, the chapters that follow feature close readings of texts that include analysis of setting, plot development, character development, and themes. In addition, discussion of point of view, symbolism, and historical contexts or background appears where appropriate. The chapters on the novels also feature alternate readings that introduce critical approaches to fiction, among them feminist criticism, new historicism, and Marxist criticism. These alternate readings demonstrate how varied approaches highlight greater richness in Hawthorne's work. Lastly, the bibliography provides information on Hawthorne's published works, biographies, contemporary reviews, and recent critical studies.

I wish to thank Nancy Houghton, Registrar of the Grolier Club, for her assistance. I also wish to acknowledge the University of Massachusetts Lowell for support of my research. Thanks, also, to the students in my courses there, whose questions and insights helped to shape this volume.

Student Companion to

Nathaniel
HAWTHORNE

1

Life of Nathaniel Hawthorne

In 1804, Salem, Massachusetts, was a prosperous seaport that had built its reputation on foreign trade. Over the next decade, the town declined through the effects of the Embargo Act of 1807 and the War of 1812. The Embargo Act prohibited trade with England and France in an attempt to punish those countries for interfering with neutral trading vessels. Meant to protect American ships, the embargo brought an end to valuable foreign trade and severely hampered related industries, especially shipbuilding. A small port whose commerce depended on trade and the sea, Salem never recovered as a shipping center, especially when the war brought additional embargoes and enemy attacks on seagoing vessels. As a boy growing up in Salem, Nathaniel Hawthorne witnessed this decline and the precarious nature of livelihoods dependent on the sea. He directly experienced the vulnerability of a seafarer's family.

Born in Salem on July 4, 1804, Hawthorne was the second child and only son of Nathaniel and Elizabeth Manning Hathorne. He was just four when his father died of yellow fever while serving as captain of a ship that had sailed to Surinam. Left with three children and few financial resources, Mrs. Hathorne moved into her parents' home and from then on was dependent on the Mannings for financial as well as emotional support. Profoundly grief stricken by the death of her husband, Elizabeth Hathorne secluded herself in her family home, seldom venturing beyond her room. In spite of this, she had a maternal bond with her children, reflected in their deep affection for her and for each other. Young Nathaniel also benefited from the attention of his extended family.

Admitting later in life that he had not been fond of attending school, Hawthorne took advantage of an injury received while playing ball to remain at home and be tutored. While he recovered from his injury, Hawthorne developed the habit of what his sister Elizabeth called "constant reading," returning again and again to Bunyan's *Pilgrim's Progress* (Part I, 1678; Part II, 1684) and later to Montaigne's *Essays* (1580, 1588), as well as work by Spenser and Shakespeare (Miller, *Salem* 49). These authors had significant influence on Hawthorne's style as a writer, but he also absorbed much from his attention to the world around him. In Salem, Hawthorne saw the reminders of his family's history, one that was notable but troubling.

Near his family home was the Charter Street Burying Point, where many of his ancestors were buried. Of these, the figure most unsettling to Hawthorne was his great-great-grandfather John Hathorne, a presiding judge during the Salem witch trials. Judge Hathorne, a stern and severe man, meted out judgment; legend had it that "one of the victims, before her execution on Gallows Hill, had placed a curse on Judge Hathorne and his descendants" (Mellow 11). John's father, William Hathorne, a Puritan, had been one of the founders of the Massachusetts Bay colony in the 1630s. William Hathorne held various offices in the colonial government. He led colonial troops in campaigns against the Indians and as a magistrate dealt out harsh punishment to those convicted of offenses or those who threatened the order of the settlement, including Quakers. The severity with which these ancestors responded to the failings and supposed sins of their fellows troubled Hawthorne, who looked upon these figures with a mixture of awe and dread. The burial ground itself made a profound impression upon him, and he used it as a setting in his last, unfinished work, *The Dolliver Romance*.

For a brief period in 1818, Hawthorne moved with his mother and sisters to Raymond, Maine, where the Mannings owned property. He was sent to school in Portland but also enjoyed exploring the woodlands around the family home. In 1819 Hawthorne returned by himself to Salem to continue his education and prepare for college. During this period, he studied classical languages and also read more widely, including among his favorites the novels of Sir Walter Scott and the Gothic novels of Ann Radcliffe and William Godwin. He also produced a newspaper distributed to members of his family, *The Spectator*, containing his prose and verse compositions (Miller, *Salem* 57).

Hawthorne enrolled at Bowdoin College in Brunswick, Maine, in 1821. By his own accounts not the most diligent of students, he graduated eighteenth in a class of thirty-five. But during his years at Bowdoin, Hawthorne continued to write fiction, working on drafts of a novel as well as short stories. More important to him than his academic studies were his interactions with classmates, including future poet Henry Wadsworth Longfellow, and the close friendships he cultivated with future president Franklin Pierce, future congressman Jonathan Cilley (who later died in a duel), and the man who became Hawthorne's lifelong friend, source of financial assistance, and mainstay of professional and personal encouragement, Horatio Bridge.

When he graduated from Bowdoin in 1825, Hawthorne returned to the Manning household in Salem, where his mother and sisters were once again in residence, to occupy the attic room that had been his in boyhood. At this time, he also changed the spelling of his family name, inserting the *w* to revive the spelling that had been common in the sixteenth century. In Salem, he began in earnest to establish himself as an author. In notebooks he recorded his observations of the life around him, including the darker aspects of urban life that he discovered as he roamed his old hometown. He also spent time reading books from the Athenaeum, a private lending library, learning more about New England's past and his family's role in it. The work he wrote for publication, however, was not well received by editors. Discouraged by their responses, he burned some of his manuscripts, including the stories he had collected as "Seven Tales of My Native Land."

In 1828 he published the novel *Fanshawe* at his own expense, contracting with the Boston firm Marsh and Capen. Published anonymously, it received favorable mention in Boston periodicals but also revealed the weaknesses of a first novel, including stock characters and a predictable outcome. Embarrassed by what he felt were the novel's failings, Hawthorne destroyed his own copy and refused to acknowledge the book in later years. The unsold copies were destroyed in a bookstore fire in Boston in 1831, and the novel was not republished during his lifetime. During these years of "apprenticeship," Hawthorne began to cultivate the persona of an observer, one who stands apart from the action and views the behaviors and motives of others. He preferred to dress in black and often said little at social gatherings. He did, however, enjoy socializing with a small circle, including Susan Ingersoll, a cousin who lived in the House of the Seven Gables. He also accompanied his uncle Samuel Manning, only thirteen years his senior, on business travels throughout New England and into Canada.

In the early 1830s some of Hawthorne's stories began to appear in local publications, such as the *Salem Gazette*. An important break came in 1831 when Samuel Goodrich accepted his story "Sights from a Steeple" for *The Token and Atlantic Souvenir*, a gift book published annually. The following year Goodrich took "The Gentle Boy," "The Wives of the Dead," "My Kinsman, Major Molineux," and "Roger Malvin's Burial." Encouraged by these early signs of progress, Hawthorne began working on a piece he called "The Story Teller," inspired by his travels through Vermont and New Hampshire. Throughout the decade, Hawthorne continued to write short stories and sketches for *The Token* and other periodicals. To supplement his income, he accepted a position as editor of the *American Magazine of Useful and Entertaining Knowledge*, moving to Boston to carry out his duties. The publisher, however, soon went bankrupt, and Hawthorne received only a fraction of the salary he had been promised.

The year 1837 marked a turning point for Hawthorne. That year he published his first collection of stories, *Twice-Told Tales*. It was the first of his publications to include his name along with the title of his work. The volume consisted of eighteen stories that had previously appeared in magazines. Unknown to Hawthorne, his college friend Horatio Bridge underwrote the cost of publication. Longfellow wrote a positive review of the collection for the *North American Review*. Hawthorne's own ambivalence toward the step he had taken and the merit of his stories was revealed in his comment to Longfellow: "I do not think much of them—neither is it worthwhile to be ashamed of them" (Miller, *Salem* 104). He also admitted to Longfellow, "I have another great difficulty, in the lack of materials; for I have seen so little of the world, that I have nothing but thin air to concoct my stories of, and it is not easy to give a lifelike semblance to such shadowy stuff" (Mellow 83).

In his personal life as well, Hawthorne found 1837 to be a momentous year. Returning to Salem after the failure of his Boston venture, Hawthorne pursued a relationship with Mary Silsbee, a Salem heiress, although it later soured. Late that year, Hawthorne and his sisters accepted an invitation from Elizabeth Peabody to visit her and her sisters at their neighboring family home. During his visits, he met Sophia Peabody, who eventually became the object of his affections. Hawthorne had often described himself as a recluse during this period of his life, although biographers have suggested that he exaggerated his shyness and reserve. Hawthorne recognized in Sophia a kindred spirit: She had also experienced a period of isolation brought on by illness. Even though she had traveled to Cuba with her sister Mary and had found some success as an artist, her family believed her frail. Hawthorne, however, sensed that she could help him close the distance between himself and the world. In a letter to Sophia written during their courtship, he expressed his feelings, claiming that he

found nothing in the world that I thought preferable to my old solitude, till at length a certain Dove was revealed to me, in the shadow of a seclusion as deep as my own had been. And I drew nearer and nearer to The Dove, and opened my bosom to her, and she flitted into it, and closed her wings there—and there she nestles now and forever, keeping my heart warm, and renewing my life with her own. (Stewart, *Nathaniel Hawthorne* 36)

Although his letter was steeped in the language of sentiment favored by nineteenth-century Americans, it revealed Hawthorne's hope for their life together. He was fortunate in his match with Sophia, for she saw in him the perfect artist and one to whom she could devote her energies and talents. They became secretly engaged at the end of 1838.

Sophia's sister Elizabeth, herself once attracted to Hawthorne, began to use her connections to the New England literary and political world to advance Hawthorne's career. In 1839 she helped Hawthorne secure an appointment at the Boston Custom House, which provided him with a steadier income. Assigned to measure salt and coal, Hawthorne found work at the Custom House monotonous and less rewarding financially than he had expected. He resigned his position in 1841. Hoping to find a surer source of income from literary work, Hawthorne began to write historical and biographical pieces for children but found that this, too, did not produce the results he anticipated.

Americans in the 1840s responded to the idealism and religious liberalism of philosophers like Ralph Waldo Emerson. Numerous groups influenced by Romantic beliefs in human potential and/or the desire to resist the influence of industrialization founded experimental, utopian communities. One such was Brook Farm in West Roxbury, Massachusetts, established to explore the possibility of returning to a simpler life that blended farming with conduct based on mutual support and cooperation. Many participants also hoped to further their intellectual and artistic endeavors. Looking for a change in his life, Hawthorne joined this community in April 1841 but left after eight months. He found that the demands upon his time and energy prevented him from writing, and he was skeptical about the long-term potential of the community. His investment of time and money there ultimately proved valuable, since his experience at Brook Farm provided background for his novel *The Blithedale Romance* (1852).

On July 9, 1842, after a prolonged engagement, Hawthorne married Sophia Peabody and moved with her to Concord, Massachusetts, where they rented the Old Manse, a home owned by the Emerson family. Remaining at the Manse for three years, Hawthorne expressed a profound sense of happiness in his life with Sophia. On an anniversary he wrote, "We were never so happy as now . . . and find a more infinite ocean of love stretching out before us" (Stewart, *Nathaniel Hawthorne* 64). While in Concord, Hawthorne became even better acquainted with the members of the Transcendentalist circle that included Ralph Waldo Emerson, Henry David Thoreau, Bronson Alcott (father of Louisa May Alcott), and Margaret Fuller. Hawthorne often found himself disagreeing with their ideas and arguments, especially their understanding of human nature and the possibility of human perfectibility.

This period was a productive one for Hawthorne, as he published twenty more stories and sketches and produced a second edition of *Twice-Told Tales* that contained seventeen previously uncollected stories. During their years at the Manse, the Hawthornes also had their first child, a daughter Una, born in 1844. Unfortunately, neither his publication in magazines nor sales of his book brought in much money, and the Hawthornes found they could no longer pay rent to remain in Concord. They left the Manse in 1845 and returned to Salem, where they moved in with Hawthorne's mother and sisters.

Until Hawthorne was able to secure a position as surveyor in the Custom House at Salem, a political appointment, he depended on his friend Bridge for financial support. During his tenure as surveyor, Hawthorne published *Mosses from an Old Manse*, which contained twenty-one previously uncollected stories, many of which are now considered among his best. The Hawthornes also had a second child, son Julian, born in 1846. The family, in need of more space, rented a larger house in Salem that included a separate apartment for Hawthorne's mother and sisters. Hawthorne discovered the temporary nature of political appointments in 1849: He was removed from office at the Custom House when Zachary Taylor, a Whig, was elected president. His dismissal was controversial, and a group of friends, including Longfellow and the poet James Russell Lowell, raised a subscription for his support. In July of that year, Hawthorne experienced another loss, one that affected him far more profoundly. His mother died, which Hawthorne called his "darkest hour" (Miller, *Salem* 272).

Although 1849 was a year of turmoil for Hawthorne, he also began work on what was to be the first of his successful romances, *The Scarlet Letter*. The book appeared the following year, published by James T. Fields, and received positive reviews in the *New York Tribune, Graham's Magazine*, and the *Literary World*. Though many reviewers reacted favorably to the book, the residents of Salem were offended, particularly by "The Custom-House," a preface that depicted Salem and its residents as dry and doddering. In 1850, Hawthorne left Salem, a city he associated with loss, and moved to Lenox, Massachusetts, a town in the Berkshire region not far from New York. There he was part of a summer community that included James Russell Lowell, jurist Oliver Wendell Holmes, actress Fanny Kemble, and others. That summer Herman Melville brought his family to the Berkshires as well. Melville, then a young author striving to establish his reputation, admired Hawthorne's work and wrote favorably about it in "Hawthorne and His Mosses," published in the *Literary World*. For a time the two became fast friends, supportive of each other's efforts as authors. By the end of his stay in Lenox, however, Hawthorne had begun to cool in his feelings toward Melville, finding his emotional outpourings and desire for greater intimacy unsettling. During his stay in the Berkshires, Hawthorne wrote *The House of the Seven Gables*, published in 1851, and *A Wonder-Book for Girls and Boys*, published in 1852. In addition, he assembled a third collection of stories, *The Snow-Image*, also published in 1852, which he dedicated to his friend

Bridge. His earnings from his writings had finally become substantial enough to support his family, and in the last year of their stay in the Berkshires, the Hawthornes had their second daughter, Rose, born in May 1851.

In 1852 the Hawthornes decided to return to Concord, which they remembered fondly from their years there as newlyweds. Hawthorne purchased The Wayside, former home of the Alcotts, and had renovations made to the house. The return to Concord had promised to be a happy one, but shortly after moving into The Wayside, Hawthorne received news that his sister Louisa, on her way to visit the family at the conclusion of a trip to New York, had died in a steamboat mishap on the Hudson River. Hawthorne was grief stricken by his sister's death, a grief intensified by the close proximity of this loss to the anniversary of his mother's death. He could not retreat into mourning, however, since he had writing deadlines to meet. Hawthorne had offered to assist his friend, Franklin Pierce, nominated for the presidency by the Democratic Party, by writing his campaign biography. His work on this project angered some friends and acquaintances, for Pierce was a Democrat who did not hold strong antislavery views. Many of Hawthorne's neighbors in Concord were sympathetic to the abolitionist position and criticized Hawthorne's seeming acceptance of the Compromise of 1850, which had allowed the expansion of slave territory. Following Pierce's victory in the presidential elections, Hawthorne was rewarded with an appointment in 1853 as American consul at Liverpool, England.

Hawthorne served as consul at Liverpool until October 1857. Liverpool in the 1850s was one of the busiest ports in Europe, and Hawthorne hoped his position there would allow him to earn enough money to permit a tour of the Continent before returning home. He also hoped to save a substantial amount so that his family would enjoy economic stability when his government appointment ended. During this period, he wrote little for publication but kept notebooks in which he recorded scenes of English life. He also learned more about the experiences of sailors serving on commercial vessels and wrote letters recommending reforms in the U.S. Merchant Marine. In October 1855 Sophia, with Una and Rose, traveled to Lisbon for the winter, a trip occasioned by Sophia's bouts of ill health. She remained there until the following June, leaving Julian in her husband's care. Sophia found the separation from her husband difficult, since the death of her own parents had made her feel more dependent upon him emotionally. The stress of their life abroad made certain strains in their marriage more evident, although the Hawthornes did not acknowledge their difficulties to outsiders, nor directly to themselves.

When Pierce did not win renomination in 1856, Hawthorne realized his consular appointment would end. He submitted his resignation to the new president, James Buchanan. The Hawthornes remained in England through

1857 and in January 1858 traveled to France, then Italy. The family settled in Rome, where Sophia explored the churches and galleries. While there, Hawthorne again recorded in notebooks his impressions of life and of the expatriates, writers, and artists that he encountered. While in Italy, he saw the American poet William Cullen Bryant, the English poets Robert and Elizabeth Barrett Browning, and the American sculptor William Wetmore Story. He also visited with lesser-known artists, including Cephas Thompson, Harriet Hosmer, and Hiram Powers. Like his wife, Hawthorne took advantage of the artistic and architectural riches that surrounded him, visiting museums, churches, and even the catacombs. Although he was often moved by the art he encountered, he expressed his reservations about the degree of nudity that prevailed in painting and in sculpture. His New England reserve and the lack of early exposure to the traditions of European art clearly influenced his responses. While exploring Rome and the Italian countryside, Hawthorne began work on another romance, published in America as *The Marble Faun: Or, The Romance of Monte Beni* (1860), that makes use of the Italian scene. Though Hawthorne enjoyed his surroundings, his family was unsettled by daughter Una's bout with malaria, which lasted for about six months and left her permanently afflicted.

On the eve of the Civil War, after another sojourn in England, Hawthorne returned to America, meeting on his voyage Harriet Beecher Stowe, whose novel *Uncle Tom's Cabin* had aided the abolitionist cause. Hawthorne did not seek out Mrs. Stowe's company, but his wife found she shared Mrs. Stowe's interest in spiritualism and other popular issues of the day. The Hawthornes returned to The Wayside, in Concord, where Hawthorne attempted to work on various romances, none of which he was able to complete. The strains caused by Sophia's and Una's ill health added to the family's difficult readjustment to life in Concord. To distract himself, Hawthorne began renovations on the house, adding to it a tower that became his study and retreat from the world. As the war erupted and dragged on, Hawthorne's health continued to decline. He had consulted physicians while still in Rome, never having fully recovered his energies after his burst of productivity in the early 1850s. Seeking relief from his malaise, Hawthorne often traveled with old friends to various familiar locations in New England. In 1864, he agreed to take a trip with Franklin Pierce in an attempt to regain his energies. Shortly after the trip began, Hawthorne weakened noticeably and died in his sleep on May 19, 1864, in Plymouth, New Hampshire. He was buried along what became known as Author's Ridge in Sleepy Hollow Cemetery in Concord, Massachusetts.

Hawthorne's Career and Contributions to American Literature

In the middle decades of the nineteenth century, authorship as a profession changed substantially. Prior to the 1820s, authors depended upon the patronage of wealthy benefactors or the income produced through another profession, such as law or printing, to support themselves. Authorship was still considered an avocation rather than a profession by many. When Hawthorne decided while in college to pursue a career as a writer and to attempt to support himself by his earnings from publication, he was embarking upon a risky venture. The challenges he faced as he attempted to establish his reputation and find an audience provide insights into the changing nature of authorship and the role of literature in American culture.

HAWTHORNE'S CAREER

Hawthorne understood the need to establish connections with editors and publishers in order to get his work before the public. He discovered, however, that this was not always an easy task. Fortunate to be near Boston, one of the three major publishing centers of the early nineteenth century, Hawthorne sent his earliest collection of tales to a publisher there. After unexplained delays, he recalled the manuscript of "Seven Tales of My Native Land," burning a portion of it in disappointment. His first novel, *Fanshawe* (1828), begun while Hawthorne was a student, was published at his own expense.

In *Fanshawe*, Hawthorne draws upon his college experience to create the setting of Hartley College under the direction of Dr. Melmoth, its headmaster. Melmoth and his wife, who have a difficult marriage and no children of their own, have been guardians to Ellen Langton, daughter of an old friend. Two students at the college, Edward Walcott, handsome and dashing, and Fanshawe, quiet and scholarly, are in love with Ellen. Various complications ensue, including the supposed death of Ellen's father and her abduction by one of his enemies. After many twists and turns, Ellen is delivered from her captivity by Fanshawe, but she loves Walcott. Fanshawe accepts her love for Walcott, relinquishes any claim to her affections, and dies a short time later.

Fanshawe attracted the attention of a few critics, but their responses were mixed. One encouraged readers to buy it to support the efforts of an American writer. Others labeled it a trite love story, filled with predictable episodes, or criticized the author for lack of confidence in his presentation. Although the novel contains the defects identified by critics, it reveals characters, themes, and techniques that Hawthorne develops more fully and successfully in his later fiction. Ellen Langton's affectionate disposition and ability to make herself useful anticipate aspects of Phoebe in *Seven Gables*. Walcott's fear that Ellen has been involved sexually in a secret liaison raises issues about women and sexual knowledge that Hawthorne explores in his treatment of Zenobia in *Blithedale* and Miriam in *Marble Faun*. The novel also reveals Hawthorne's ability to create comic scenes, as in the discussion between Dr. and Mrs. Melmoth at breakfast and their near collision on the stairway a short time later. Distressed by the critical and financial failure of his novel, Hawthorne turned his attention to shorter forms of fiction for the next two decades.

About the time of *Fanshawe*'s publication, Hawthorne planned a second collection, "Provincial Tales," and a third, "The Story Teller," both of which featured stories with an American setting. Neither of these collections appeared. Instead, Hawthorne revised some of the tales for later publication, published some of them separately in gift books, and destroyed others. These early efforts reflected Hawthorne's growing interest in the potential of America's historical past to provide a context for fiction. Hawthorne was not alone in this view, for many American writers from the 1820s on depicted events from colonial history in fiction, especially the witchcraft trials and Indian wars. Besides his efforts in the short story, Hawthorne began to write imaginative sketches of individuals from New England's past.

From the mid-1830s until the end of the decade, Hawthorne wrote allegorical tales and historical sketches, among them "The May-Pole of Merry Mount" and "The Minister's Black Veil." He also began to experiment with sketches that reveal the lighter side of his nature. These, such as "Sights from a Steeple," are usually told from the point of view of an observer commenting on details of daily life. The fiction produced during this period appeared in annuals and gift books like *The Token*. Hawthorne was not identified as the author of the selections he published in such volumes. In 1837, Hawthorne collected eighteen of his stories and sketches in *Twice-Told Tales*. The stories were praised by reviewers for their careful observations and vivid impressions, their purity of style, and the genius of the author. Sales of the collection were only moderate and did not end Hawthorne's financial struggles.

The direction of Hawthorne's career paralleled the changes occurring in American publishing in the 1840s. As the emerging American middle class enjoyed more leisure time, its appetite for literary entertainment increased. Although prohibitions against fiction still sounded from the pulpit, more readers, especially women, looked to fiction to articulate the roles and values that shaped American life. The number of magazines that published fiction increased in number and in circulation during the 1840s and 1850s. Hawthorne hoped to find a market for his work through magazines and in the 1840s published frequently in *The Democratic Review*. In 1846, he assembled another collection of his work, *Mosses from an Old Manse*. The reviews of this volume commented on Hawthorne's wide sympathy, evanescent grace, and perceptions of tragedy. Despite positive reviews, this collection, too, did not produce the income that would allow Hawthorne to live by his writing alone.

By the end of the decade, Hawthorne had serious doubts about his career. He "considered himself a failure as a writer because *Mosses from an Old Manse* was selling poorly," and his publisher, Putnam, expressed little interest in new manuscripts (Madison 43). Fortunately, Hawthorne changed publishers and came under the influence of James T. Fields of Ticknor and Fields. Fields convinced Hawthorne to publish *The Scarlet Letter* as a separate work rather than as part of a collection. *The Scarlet Letter* marked a return to longer prose fiction for Hawthorne, and in rapid succession he wrote *The House of the Seven Gables* (1851) and *The Blithedale Romance* (1852). To take advantage of Hawthorne's increased public visibility, Fields issued a new collection of stories, *The Snow-Image, and Other Twice-Told Tales* (1852), and reissued both *Twice-Told Tales* (1851) and *Mosses from an Old Manse* (1854). By the mid-1850s, all of Hawthorne's major work was in print.

During the mid-nineteenth century the market for books written explicitly for children also grew dramatically. Hawthorne had found some success in this line during the 1840s, publishing *Grandfather's Chair: A History for Youth*, a history of Massachusetts for children in 1840–1841. He followed this with *Biographical Stories for Children* in 1842. In the 1850s, these two works were reissued in a single volume, and Hawthorne wrote two new, well-received collections for children. *A Wonder-Book for Girls and Boys* (1852) and *Tanglewood Tales for Girls and Boys* (1853) present well-known stories from classical myth and legend rewritten for children. In the first volume, Hawthorne's narrator, Eustace Bright, a student at Williams College, recounts stories of Hercules, Pandora, and King Midas, among others. Interspersed between the legends are brief descriptions of the interactions between Eustace and his young cousins, the "audience" for these stories. In the second collection, Bright returns as author of another group of stories that are introduced by Hawthorne. These include legends of the Minotaur and the Golden Fleece, as well as the myth of Ceres and Proserpina (Demeter and Persephone). More than one reviewer indicated that the volumes appeal to adults as well as children.

After five years of intense productivity, Hawthorne's career changed direction. Finally enjoying the reputation he had long sought, Hawthorne accepted an appointment as the American consul in Liverpool. He published no new works while he held this appointment, but he did meet English authors and poets. While serving as consul and later touring the Continent, Hawthorne continued to record his observations and impressions, as well as ideas for stories and romances. Before he returned to America in 1860, he published *The Marble Faun* under the title *Transformation* in England. This was the last romance that Hawthorne completed.

While traveling Hawthorne had begun drafts of various romances, hoping to use material recorded in his notebooks to depict life in England. Both *The Ancestral Footstep* (1883) and *Dr. Grimshawe's Secret* (1883) depict Americans in England, especially their interests in genealogy and their attempts to claim English estates. In his treatment of the American abroad, Hawthorne hoped to explore the confrontation between Old World culture and New. In addition, Hawthorne began *Septimius Felton; or, The Elixir of Life* (1872), based on a story heard from Thoreau of a young man of Concord who thought he would never die. It and *The Dolliver Romance* (1876) focus on the possibility of discovering the elixir of life, a topic that may have had personal appeal for the aging Hawthorne. These unfinished works were published, along with Hawthorne's notes for revisions and additions, after his death. Unable to complete any of the romances, Hawthorne did publish material from his English notebooks as essays in the *Atlantic Monthly*, later collected in *Our Old Home: A Series of English Sketches* (1863). Aware that his creative powers were failing along with his physical health, Hawthorne observed that the "Actual" weighed too heavily upon him. He could no longer find that "neutral territory" between imagination and reality out of which his fiction grew.

HAWTHORNE'S CONTRIBUTIONS TO THE SHORT STORY

During the first half of the nineteenth century, the short story emerged as a genre. Edgar Allan Poe, a critic as well as author of fiction, defined the nature and scope of the short story. He emphasized the importance of brevity and focus. He claimed that a writer must strive for a single, unifying effect. To accomplish this, the writer must quickly identify characters and their attributes, initiate action that will lead to the climax, and pare away any detail that does not contribute to the overall unity of the story. Free to choose the point of view and whether to emphasize character or plot, the author must always have in mind the ending of the tale. Poe praised some of Hawthorne's stories for meeting these requirements. The two men are often credited with establishing the short story as an American art form.

As his notebook entries reveal, Hawthorne's "unity of effect" often derives from the idea that stands behind the writing of the tale. For example, Hawthorne writes in his notebook, "A snake, taken into a man's stomach and nourished there from fifteen years to thirty-five, tormenting him most horribly. A type of envy or some other evil passion" (*American Notebooks* 22). Although he modifies the details and chooses a different negative passion, Hawthorne has already considered this idea as he composes "Egotism; or, The Bosom-Serpent" (1843). In developing his short fiction, he draws on familiar literary forms, including the allegory, the parable, and the fable. These forms appeal to Hawthorne because they are associated with morality and values, allowing him to explore the complications of the human condition in his own day. Working with these traditional forms, Hawthorne uses their basic structure but transforms them, placing his own stamp upon each tale. His ability to evoke the contexts and atmosphere of New England's past, to use New England as a setting for fiction, help to legitimize the claims of an emerging "American" literary tradition.

Although many of his stories are read as allegories, Hawthorne often resists the one-to-one correspondence between image or character and abstract idea that strict allegory demands. Instead, he prefers to draw more heavily upon symbolism that allows him to create multiple possibilities of meaning. In some stories, the use of a dominant symbol, as in "The Minister's Black Veil" (1836) or "The Birth-mark" (1843), allows Hawthorne to explore the preoccupation with meaning and abstraction that severs an individual from his community or loved ones. In other stories such as "Young Goodman Brown" (1835) or "Rappaccini's Daughter" (1844), a series of related symbols contributes to the ambiguity that Hawthorne uses to convey the difficulties of knowing for certain or interpreting absolutely. His use of symbols and significant images also reveals aspects of character and adds depth to the best stories without undermining their unity or coherence.

In the prefaces to his collections, Hawthorne links his short stories to "the meditative habit" (*Tales and Sketches* 1151) and to "the spell of a tranquil spirit" (*Tales and Sketches* 1145). Such comments suggest a passive quality, yet Hawthorne's plots are often important components of the tales. His experiments with plot development provide another significant contribution to the genre. Hawthorne does not follow a single narrative pattern. Some stories contain a plot line taken from drama that becomes a standard for the short story. It entails exposition, followed by rising action, a crisis, falling action, and a resolution that provides closure. Other stories, however, reveal innovations that include placing the crisis at the end, alternating scenes that advance the action with those that impede or modify it, and dividing the narrative into two or more sections to allow for more extensive character development.

HAWTHORNE AND THE ROMANCE

The novel as a genre was also a fairly new literary form in Hawthorne's day, having emerged at the beginning of the eighteenth century. Early novels used a variety of approaches to narrative in their attempts to represent life and experience within fiction. Some novels were written in the third person using a narrator closely identified with the author. Others followed the epistolary form, consisting of letters exchanged between characters, through which an author could provide insights into the characters' thoughts and states of mind. As the genre developed, distinctions were made by writers and critics between the novel and the romance.

The novel represented the realities of life for its characters, capturing their mannerisms and behaviors as they interacted with those around them. It emphasized the nature of the social structure in which characters lived and explored their life in time present. It attempted to achieve verisimilitude, the "semblance of truth" or a "lifelike" quality in its characters, setting, and events. These qualities contributed to the emergence of the novel of manners in the early nineteenth century and to the emphasis on social realism in later decades.

In contrast, the romance may include details that make the characters and setting believable and even realistic, but it does not strive toward verisimilitude. Instead, the romance presents events and situations that are improbable or unlikely, often set in the distant past or in a remote place. The writer of romance incorporates elements of the supernatural or mysterious within the narrative to expand the possibilities of fiction beyond the everyday. He or she may also explore the nature of both the imagination and the unconscious through the use of dreams, symbols, and myths. Today many critics downplay the differences between the novel and romance, indicating that the terms are often used interchangeably during the early nineteenth century.

In prefaces to his longer works, Hawthorne draws distinctions between the nature of his fiction and the novel. He explains in *Seven Gables* that he wishes "to claim a certain latitude" for his work in terms of its material and style of presentation. He states that the novel must be minutely faithful to the daily realities that people see around them, whereas Hawthorne seeks freedom to go beyond the everyday, to consider possibilities as well as probabilities. In Hawthorne's view, the romance allows a writer to enter into what he calls in *The Scarlet Letter* a "neutral territory." In that realm, the writer can "mingle" or merge the actual and the ideal. Calling his work "romance" allows Hawthorne to acknowledge that it is a product of the imagination while asserting the validity of the connections it makes between the tangible and the abstract.

Aware that earlier writers had distinguished the romance from history, drawing a line between fiction and fact, Hawthorne seeks ways to suggest that truth stands behind fiction, even though fiction is the product of the imagination. He also wants his readers to be aware that fiction may draw upon the record of history but is not limited by it. Hawthorne questions whether the historical romance can go beyond a simple retelling of history. In an 1846 review, he writes, "[W]e cannot help feeling that the real treasures of [William Gilmore Simms's] subject have escaped the author's notice. The themes suggested by him, viewed as he views them, would produce nothing but historical novels, cast in the same worn out mould that has been in use these thirty years, and which it is time to break up and fling away" (Stewart, "Contributions" 331). Three years later, Hawthorne puts himself to the test as he writes *The Scarlet Letter*. Drawing upon the New England past as he has come to understand it, Hawthorne uses his narrative to explore issues such as the nature of passion, revenge, and guilt, as well as the power and meaning of symbols. Such concerns go beyond what the historical record alone can reveal.

The three romances that Hawthorne writes after *The Scarlet Letter* make less use of the distancing effect of time, although *The Marble Faun* does take advantage of the remoteness of location in its Italian setting. In the preface to *Seven Gables*, Hawthorne states that he wishes to link the present with a "by-gone time" whose "legendary mist" will contribute to a "picturesque effect" for the reader (351). His reference to "mist," which can cloud or interfere with vision, suggests his desire to leave the reader with impressions of truth rather than precise renderings of fact. He also cautions that romances do not teach direct lessons but work upon the reader "through a far more subtle [*sic*] process" (352). Likewise, in the preface to *The Blithedale Romance*, Hawthorne admits that he has drawn upon his experiences at Brook Farm to "give a more lifelike tint" to his narrative but that he is not writing its history. He asserts that romancers in America lack access to a culturally accepted mythic past or "Faery Land" in which to set their works to take advantage of "strange enchantment" (633). Therefore, they must create their own enchantment through the treatment of material.

When he writes of the advantages of the Italian setting in *The Marble Faun*, Hawthorne again makes reference to the challenge that faces the romancer in America. He claims that in America there "is no shadow, no antiquity, no mystery, no picturesque and gloomy wrong, nor anything but a common-place prosperity, in broad and simple daylight" (854). Yet his own tales and romances contribute to the shaping of a mythic American past with its shadows, wrongs, and mysteries as well as its simple daylight. While he claims that it will be "very long" before American writers of romance will find "congenial and easily handled themes . . . in the annals of our stalwart republic" (854), Hawthorne paves the way and provides direction for doing so.

HAWTHORNE'S USE OF THE GOTHIC

The Gothic tradition in fiction emerged in the eighteenth century through the work of writers such as Horace Walpole and Ann Radcliffe. The term *Gothic* was applied to their fictions because they were set during the medieval era. The focus of their novels was not historical romance but the creation of a plot and atmosphere that would inspire terror on the part of readers. The plots often hinged on the creation of mystery and suspense, impelling the reader to continue reading in spite of the terrors to come. These novels, such as Walpole's *The Castle of Otranto*, were set in dark castles that featured hidden passageways and dungeons. They often included encounters with the supernatural, innocent maidens in distress, and devilish villains. The authors of early Gothic novels were attracted to such fiction as a means of rebelling against the emphasis on rationality and order that dominated the Age of Reason. Their novels often exploited the irrational and inexplicable, suggesting that there was more to human experience than could be determined by empirical evidence.

By the nineteenth century the term *Gothic* was applied to fiction that inspires terror or horror even though not set during the Middle Ages. These narratives draw upon the supernatural or irrational, suspense, a sense of foreboding, and an atmosphere of gloom. Although he does not write Gothic romances or stories comparable to those of Poe, Hawthorne frequently draws upon the elements of the Gothic tradition, especially in his settings and in his use of the supernatural. In *The House of the Seven Gables*, the most Gothic of the romances, Hawthorne depicts a haunted house that contains secret passages, ghosts who make their presence known through music, a family curse, a hidden vault, and tales of mesmerism that leave victims powerless. When he explores the significance of witchcraft in New England, Hawthorne again draws on elements of the Gothic through the use of haunted or bedeviled forests, inexplicable events, and characters who appear to have Satanic connections. Even his urban tales make use of some aspects of the Gothic, including the mazelike streets of "My Kinsman" (1832) and "Wakefield" (1835). Frequently Hawthorne makes use of the Gothic within his fiction as a means of exploring the psychological states of his characters, to suggest the power of the unconscious in their behaviors and perceptions.

HAWTHORNE'S INFLUENCE

The critics who reviewed Hawthorne's early work identified in it the potential for literary success. Although that success was longer in coming than Hawthorne would have liked, with the publication of *The Scarlet Letter*, he was identified as a significant American voice writing representative works of a national literature. Through the promotional activities of James T. Fields, Hawthorne came to be identified as a major American writer. Fields capitalized on the relative success of *The Scarlet Letter* by reprinting earlier works by Hawthorne to keep his name before the public. He also recognized the importance of creating a public image of Hawthorne that would attract readers' interest and enhance his prestige. By the mid-1850s, Hawthorne was identified as a significant contributor to an American tradition in letters that also included Longfellow, Whittier, and Emerson, among others. While critical regard for some of them altered as the nineteenth century drew to a close, Hawthorne and Emerson retained their centrality in the American tradition.

Many contemporaries read and reviewed Hawthorne's work, including Margaret Fuller, Edgar Allan Poe, Henry Wadsworth Longfellow, and Elizabeth Peabody. None was more profoundly influenced by him, however, than Herman Melville. Through Hawthorne's writings and in personal encounters with him, Melville perceived the greater possibilities for American fiction and for the serious American author. In his famous review "Hawthorne and His Mosses," Melville praised Hawthorne's tenderness and sympathy but also called attention to the darker aspects of Hawthorne's work. He saw in Hawthorne's stories evidence of the Calvinist legacy of New England that made Hawthorne mindful of man's sinfulness and failure.

Believing that in Hawthorne he had discovered someone who shared his own dark vision of human experience, Melville sought a personal acquaintance when Hawthorne moved to the Berkshires. They spent much time together, conversing on topics of importance to both, including the nature of human experience and the tension between faith and doubt. Through these encounters, Melville found the direction he wished to pursue in his own fiction. Substantially altering and revising *Moby-Dick*, from a narrative of whaling adventures to a deep philosophical exploration of human nature and evil, he dedicated the book to Hawthorne. Unfortunately, nineteenth-century readers did not respond to Melville's work as they had to Hawthorne's. He continued to struggle to find an audience and to support his family. Eventually fading from the literary scene, Melville was not to be rediscovered until the twentieth century. His intense personal relationship with Hawthorne also ended when Hawthorne retreated, finding the demands of Melville's friendship beyond what he could sustain.

The generation that emerged in the post–Civil War era acknowledged the importance of Hawthorne's work to their own. Writers as diverse as Rebecca Harding Davis, Hamlin Garland, and Louisa May Alcott remarked on the significance of Hawthorne and of their encounters with his work. Themes, character types, and/or narrative techniques introduced by Hawthorne are evident in the work of Sarah Orne Jewett, Mary Wilkins Freeman, and George Washington Cable. When William Dean Howells, an author and major influence on American literature from 1870 to 1910, made his literary pilgrimage to New England from Ohio in 1860, he sought out Hawthorne in Concord. Later he wrote about the profound effect reading Hawthorne's romances had upon him. Among these writers, Henry James was the most substantially influenced by Hawthorne's work.

James recalled encountering *A Wonder-Book* and *Twice-Told Tales* in childhood, but it was his adult reading of Hawthorne's romances that made a profound impression on him. In his critical biography *Nathaniel Hawthorne* (1879), James valued Hawthorne's reflections of New England life and his recognition of the powerful hold place can have on an individual. He also saw in Hawthorne's life and work the constraints that the American economy and the lack of a literary culture placed upon him. To James, this contributed to a narrowness or limitation in Hawthorne's thinking, a narrowness that affected the fiction. In stating this about Hawthorne, James reaffirmed his own decision to live abroad in order to write and to achieve the career he desired. James's comments also reflected a need to distance himself from direct comparisons with Hawthorne, in effect to make room for his own fiction to stand alone.

Throughout James's fiction, a reader discovers echoes of Hawthorne. James reflects upon the problems an artist faces in a culture that emphasizes business success and practicality when Spencer Brydon returns to America in "The Jolly Corner" (1908). In "The Beast in the Jungle" (1903) he examines the fate of a man who sacrifices human connections and love for an abstract idea. *The Bostonians* (1886) reveals the tendency of reformers to exploit or manipulate others to satisfy personal ambitions, an issue Hawthorne treats in *Blithedale*. Both novels also explore the attempts to redefine women's place within the culture. For James the American encounter with European culture forms a continuous thread in his fiction, from *Daisy Miller* (1879) to *The Portrait of a Lady* (1881) to *The Wings of the Dove* (1902). Like Hawthorne's characters in *The Marble Faun*, James's Americans must learn to read and interpret this different culture. In some instances, their mistakes in doing so initiate crises in the novels. Like Hawthorne, James recognizes the power of symbols to expand the possibilities of meaning and to suggest facets of character. James values Hawthorne's abilities as an observer who sees the suggestive possibilities in small things, a quality evident in James's own attentiveness to detail in his narratives.

During the twentieth century, Hawthorne has continued to be a significant influence on American writers. The southern novelist William Faulkner transforms southern history into mythology much as Hawthorne had done for colonial New England. Both investigate the weight of the past and the burden of guilt. For Hawthorne this was connected to the witchcraft trials and other persecutions of dissent or difference in New England. For Faulkner, the legacy of slavery and the defeat of the South in the Civil War form intertwined components of a historical legacy. Like Hawthorne, Faulkner explored the significance of the family past and its impact on identity. He was particularly concerned with social definitions of identity in light of miscegenation. He, too, witnessed the tensions between tradition and change as the South was transformed from an agricultural to a commercial economy. These tensions are often expressed through conflicts over class status and the social hierarchy. Like Hawthorne, Faulkner also used elements of the Gothic tradition and symbolism as a means of representing the psychological states of his characters.

Hawthorne's presence as a standard or "canonical" writer whose work is required reading in most schools has exposed millions of Americans to his fiction. Some American writers treat Hawthorne's work as texts against which to develop their own fiction. By inviting direct comparison between Hawthorne's work and their own, these authors explore the cultural influence of Hawthorne's fiction, while simultaneously critiquing its assumptions and assertions. An example of this approach to Hawthorne, specifically to *The Scarlet Letter*'s meaning and function as a cultural icon, can be found in the work of John Updike. His series of novels known as "The Scarlet Letter Trilogy" reflects not only his familiarity with Hawthorne's novel but the assumed familiarity of Updike's readers as well.

Updike's trilogy consists of *A Month of Sundays* (1978), *Roger's Version* (1986), and *S.* (1988). Each of these novels presents a story line similar to that of *The Scarlet Letter* told through the point of view of a character who embodies aspects of one of the central figures of Hawthorne's novel. In *A Month of Sundays*, the narrative form is that of a diary kept by a minister, Thomas Marshfield, who has engaged in adulterous relationships with members of his congregation. His character plays off that of Arthur Dimmesdale, and Marshfield must undergo a process of treatment designed to help him confront his sin and purify himself to be fit again for ministry. *Roger's Version* is told from the point of view of an unreliable first-person narrator, a suitable choice for a text influenced by the character of Roger Chillingworth from Hawthorne's novel. The main character, Roger Lambert, is a learned man, a Doctor of Divinity at a New England college. In the course of the novel, he manipulates a young graduate student, Dale Kohler, who has offended Lambert by attempting to approach God through science rather than faith. Kohler has also had an affair with Lambert's young wife, Esther, so that in this novel Updike also interweaves the issue of adultery and its impact on relationships. The last of the novels, *S.*, is told through a set of letters representing the point of view of Sarah Worth. Sarah, a housewife who lives on the North Shore in Massachusetts, rebels against her rigid New England heritage and the expectations that govern her world. She leaves a difficult marriage and journeys to an ashram in Arizona, a type of wilderness experience, in search of freedom and fulfillment. This novel makes frequent use of the letter *A* and words that begin with *A* to emphasize its connections to Hawthorne's novel.

In all three of these novels, Updike treats themes that are found in Hawthorne's work, including the relationship between an individual and the community, the tension between passion and repression, and the impact of adultery. Updike also captures the boredom that affects late twentieth-century life. It is this boredom, more than a restrictive culture, that characters attempt to counteract through their acts of passion and rebellion. While the trilogy obviously reflects Hawthorne's importance for Updike's work, other novels and stories by him are also influenced by Hawthorne's concerns and techniques. In *The Witches of Eastwick* (1984), Updike presents a modern-day exploration of witchcraft, a topic that preoccupied Hawthorne. This dark comedy, in which three witches discover the Satanic nature of their new neighbor, satirizes American popular culture. Updike, like Hawthorne, also makes use of symbols to expand the range of meaning within his fiction, taking as symbols the objects and images found in his characters' daily lives. In stories such as "The A & P" (1962) and "Still of Some Use" (1987), Updike invests the attire of a grocery clerk or the board games stored away in a family's attic with meaning beyond their usual significance.

Another writer who acknowledges Hawthorne's significance as a voice in the American tradition to which she responds is Nobel laureate Toni Morrison. Like Hawthorne, Morrison often employs ambiguities in her fiction to move readers to question accepted truths. She favors complex symbols that convey multiple meanings and frequently incorporates myth and allusion in her fiction. Morrison also explores the dangers inherent in denying the past, both personal and cultural. While Hawthorne's treatment of this past often focuses on the Puritan attempt to preserve a homogeneous culture of belief and identity through repression and persecution, Morrison examines the ways in which concepts of race and the construction of racial difference govern the past and

influence the present. She also focuses on the nature of the individual's relationship to community, but for Morrison this relationship is made more complex by the presence of a dominant white culture. While Hawthorne can
position himself within the mind-set of that dominant culture, Morrison, as an
African American woman, positions herself against it and invites the reader to
perceive its power and influence.

In appraising her early fiction, critics have highlighted issues in Morrison's
work that are similar to those in Hawthorne's. Her novel *Beloved* (1987) has
elicited the most pointed comparisons to Hawthorne's work, particularly *The
Scarlet Letter*. In *Beloved*, the central character Sethe is haunted by the past. A
former slave, Sethe ran away from the Sweet Home plantation in Kentucky,
crossing into the free state of Ohio before the Civil War and Emancipation.
Fearing that she was to be captured and returned to slavery, she killed her
daughter Beloved to prevent her from growing up as a slave. When the novel
opens, Sethe is living on the outskirts of Cincinnati with her daughter Denver
in a house "124" haunted by the ghost of her dead child. Like Hester and Pearl,
Sethe and Denver live as outcasts, and the pain of isolation has weighed heavily
on Denver. Like Pearl, she is a source of both pain and comfort to her mother.
While Hester wears a fabric letter as a sign that carries multiple meanings,
Sethe is marked by a "tree" scarred into her body from a whipping. Although
elements of Sethe's story contain parallels to Hester's, Caroline Woidat argues
that Morrison's "reinterpretation" of *The Scarlet Letter* offers a "counter-
narrative" to the vision of American identity offered in Hawthorne's novel
(529–530). Morrison does not want her character to quietly submit to the expectations of a dominant culture, as Hester does. Through Sethe's actions,
Morrison invites the reader to confront the vision of the past and its legacy as
perceived by an African American woman.

In his study of Hawthorne's career and influence, Richard Brodhead
(*School*) refers to the "school of Hawthorne" to describe a tradition in American fiction that originates with Hawthorne's work. Students and aspiring writers still read Hawthorne's fiction, and the school of Hawthorne continues to
provide inspiration and challenges to new generations.

3

Short Stories I: The New England Tales

In the 1830s and 1840s, Hawthorne devoted his writing efforts to the short story and the sketch, producing nearly 100 pieces that appeared in magazines and gift books. Many of these were later republished in his collections *Twice-Told Tales* (1837), *Mosses from an Old Manse* (1846), and *The Snow-Image, and Other Twice-Told Tales* (1852). Fascinated by the history of New England and the legacy of its Puritan founders, Hawthorne drew on that history as the context for much of his short fiction. Often he looked critically at this past, focusing on the failures as well as achievements of America's and his own Puritan forebears. Especially troubled by Puritan rigidity and prejudice, Hawthorne called into question beliefs and actions that led to self-righteousness and the easy persecution or rejection of others.

A frequent reader of New England histories, Hawthorne used terminology and images that had currency in the colonial era, enhancing the impression of that past. He sometimes chose a well-known conflict, such as the witchcraft episode in Salem, to shape his plot and setting. His view of the Puritans is never single-minded, for Hawthorne frequently sees positive as well as negative aspects in individual characters. Some tales reflect a sympathetic view of central characters, whereas in others they are presented as the sources of their own turmoil. The richness of his stories is evident in the variety of interpretations that continue to be offered of each.

The stories discussed in this chapter are among the best known of Hawthorne's New England tales. They explore the consequences of Puritan rigidity and prejudice for both communities and individuals. They consider the costs of personal inflexibility shaped by a demanding moral or religious code, including isolation and disconnection. Some treat rites of passage or the process of transition from innocence to knowledge, testing whether the process results in integration or separation from the community.

"THE GENTLE BOY" (1832, 1837)

One of Hawthorne's most popular early tales, "The Gentle Boy" was reprinted in *Twice-Told Tales* in 1837 and as a separate publication in 1839, accompanied by his future wife Sophia's drawing of Ilbrahim. In this tale set in Puritan times, Hawthorne explores the emotional and sentimental power of the mother-child bond, a relationship idealized by Hawthorne's nineteenth-century culture. He also examines the effects of religious prejudice and persecution, on both the perpetrators and the victims. Hawthorne's own era was not free from religious intolerance and suspicion, so his tale speaks to tensions in his own day as well.

SETTING AND PLOT

Set in Boston, "The Gentle Boy" begins in 1659, when the persecution of Quakers in the Massachusetts Bay colony has reached its height with the execution of two Quaker men. In this tale, the sociocultural setting plays a more important role than does the physical. Hawthorne conveys the Puritan intolerance for those who are perceived as different, especially those who are perceived as disruptive and a threat to order. The Quakers are perceived as threats to Puritan stability because they respond to the inner voice of the spirit, rather than depending upon public interpretation and instruction by a recognized clergy. Their willingness to follow a religious mission that entails abandoning family life, along with their public outbursts of enthusiasm, troubles the Puritans, who see social and moral order reinforced by family relationships. Hawthorne underscores the judgmental nature of many of the Puritans, who read others' misfortunes, such as the death of the Pearsons' children, as a punishment for sinful motives, if not sinful deeds.

Within this context, Hawthorne traces the effects that the Quaker child Ilbrahim has on individuals and on the community. His discovery by Tobias Pearson, a Puritan of military rank traveling home from Boston, initiates the action of the story. Moved by the child's plight and the sweetness of his character, Pearson takes the child home. This decision initiates not only the Pearsons' relationship with Ilbrahim but also Tobias's gradual conversion to Quaker beliefs.

The story proceeds through a series of events that provide the rising action, culminating in a double crisis, the assault on Ilbrahim by other children and Tobias's realization that he must heed the inner voice of the spirit. Through the rising action, Hawthorne further elaborates the hostility of the Puritans toward the Quakers, in contrast to the growing affection that the Pearsons feel toward Ilbrahim. While the Pearsons have custody of Ilbrahim, his mother returns, moved to speak out at a Puritan worship service. Knowing the hard life she faces and committed to the demands of her faith that require the sacrifice of earthly ties for heavenly reward, Catherine gives her child to the Pearsons. Never accepted by others as part of the community, Ilbrahim's betrayal comes at the hands of another child whom Dorothy Pearson tends following an injury. Set upon by a band of vicious children whose brutality matches that of their Puritan parents, Ilbrahim is struck down by the one he thought his friend. The violence of this blow, as severe emotionally as physically, marks the beginning of Ilbrahim's decline. It also foreshadows the rejection that his adoptive father Tobias will experience.

Having accepted Quaker doctrines, Tobias has become a pariah in the Puritan community, suffering all the punishments inflicted on outsiders and troublemakers. He feels the severity of his sacrifices and questions what his faith asks of him. While he voices his doubts, Ilbrahim's mother returns, bringing news of the king's edict that prohibits Quaker persecutions. She announces these "glad tidings" only to discover that her son is on his deathbed. This news draws forth Catherine's motherly feeling, suppressed earlier in the tale. She fears this is a test beyond her strength and faith, accusing both God and Pearson of having abused her trust.

Catherine's final moment with Ilbrahim, in which he comforts her with the words "Mourn not, dearest mother. I am happy now" (137), uttered with his dying breath, captures a scene popularized through the sentimental tradition. Evoking the belief in a loving child's spiritual influence, especially at the time of death, this moment anticipates the more famous death scene of Little Eva in Harriet Beecher Stowe's *Uncle Tom's Cabin* (1852). In both instances, spiritually gifted children about to die work a converting ordinance upon the adults present. The epilogue reveals Ilbrahim's continuing influence upon his mother as she finds a "true religion," one more in keeping with nineteenth-century norms of decorum for women.

CHARACTERS

In a community that stresses conformity, the title character of "The Gentle Boy" stands apart. Distinguished from those around him by name, religion, and demeanor, Ilbrahim serves as a figure of innocence destroyed by a corrupt world. A loving child who seeks affection, Ilbrahim becomes a part of the Pearson household, accepting them as his foster parents. Despite his bond with them, he retains a strong sense of connection to his mother, and the sound of her voice has the power to stir his emotions. Ilbrahim does not develop as a rounded character, even though he plays a central role within the story. Many of his traits, including his meekness and his refusal to use violence against those who attack him, distinguish him as a Christ figure. In this role, he operates as a redemptive influence on Tobias Pearson and on Catherine.

Having questioned the direction of the English Revolution under Cromwell, Tobias Pearson has come to New England to make a new life for himself and his family. His neighbors hold a dim view of him, believing he is motivated by economic rather than religious reasons. Ironically, his conversion to Quaker beliefs results in the loss of his material comforts and well-being. He also goes from being a man of war and violence to a man of peace who no longer fends off the blows directed against him. Ilbrahim serves as a model for what becomes Tobias's behavior, although Tobias struggles against his old feelings of resistance in a way that Ilbrahim never does.

Hawthorne labels Dorothy Pearson, Tobias's wife, a figure of "rational piety," whose actions speak of her toleration and compassion for others. She has suffered the loss of all her own children, yet willingly accepts another child into her home. Dorothy embodies aspects of womanhood valued by the Puritans and by nineteenth-century culture. She welcomes the duties of motherhood and of her domestic role. Honest with Catherine, she explains that she cannot promise to raise Ilbrahim according to beliefs she does not accept, but Catherine realizes that in her sincerity and kindness Dorothy will be a good mother to him. When her husband espouses beliefs that cost them their position in the community, as well as their material wealth and comfort, Dorothy does not repudiate him. Because a high rate of infant mortality continued well into the nineteenth-century, women readers especially identified with Dorothy's sense of loss over her own children and at the death of Ilbrahim. Her situation adds to the sentimental power of the story.

In contrast to Dorothy, Catherine violates all of the expectations the Puritans held for women. Her willingness to abandon her child undermines her maternal identity. Even though she follows the dictates of her conscience and principles in doing so, such abandonment is viewed with horror. The narrator reflects the nineteenth century's judgment toward her behavior when he claims that in leaving Ilbrahim she was "neglectful of the holiest trust which can be committed to a woman"(130). Moreover, Catherine has pursued a life of extremes, provoking the hostile responses of others through outrageous behaviors that defy social convention as well as religious beliefs. She responds with as much intolerance and vindictiveness as do her opponents, and she seems no better than her Puritan tormentors. The epilogue records her transformation after Ilbrahim's death, which softens her nature and allows her to live as part of the community. The community's new view of Catherine anticipates the way the community's view of Hester Prynne alters and redefines her place in their world.

THEMES

In "The Gentle Boy" Hawthorne examines the meaning of toleration, which has implications not only for the Puritans and Quakers of the seventeenth century but for his own day. New England in the first half of the nineteenth century saw the rise of intolerance toward Roman Catholics who were immigrating in larger numbers. Anxieties about Catholic influences led to the burning of the Ursuline convent near Boston during the 1820s and eventually contributed to the emergence of the Know-Nothing movement of the 1840s and 1850s. Hawthorne frames the narrative proper of "The Gentle Boy" with a prologue and epilogue that provide historical background for his tale. The prologue traces the course of persecutions while highlighting differences between Puritan and Quaker outlooks. The epilogue returns to the historical record, noting the king's mandate and indicating that over time "a spirit of forbearance" emerged regarding the Quakers. This spirit of forbearance leads to changes in the way the community treats Catherine, contributing to her own transformation.

Besides the issue of civil toleration, Hawthorne also focuses on the nature of a "true religion" that involves the power of genuine feeling as well as doctrine and rules. Essentially he sets up a contrast between those who live by the "letter of the law" and those who embrace its spirit. In his role as a redemptive child, Ilbrahim embodies this true religion and draws others toward it.

"MY KINSMAN, MAJOR MOLINEUX" (1832, 1852)

In this tale of eighteenth-century New England, Hawthorne presents a story of initiation, a coming into awareness of the larger world and its conflicts. His main character, Robin Molineux, comes to new realizations about himself by the end of his first night in the city. He also confronts issues of class, power, and his position as an outsider in a changing environment.

SETTING AND PLOT

"My Kinsman" is often associated with the American Revolution because Hawthorne depicts individuals who have disguised themselves to engage in political protest and mischief as occurred at the Boston Tea Party. The story takes place years earlier in the Boston of 1730. Hawthorne structures his story around the motif of the journey. Robin Molineux, the central character, initially believes that his journey is a simple trip to the city to seek his uncle, but it evolves into a journey of self-discovery and growth. The narrative can be divided into two sections. The first follows Robin as he walks the streets of Boston, encountering the various individuals who make up the diversity of city life. The second begins when he seats himself on the steps of the church to await the arrival of his uncle. During this portion of the story, Robin witnesses and participates in a scene both grotesque and carnivalesque. What he sees and does causes him to reassess his sense of self and his expectations for the future.

Robin arrives in the city at night and immediately experiences the confusion of being in a strange place without guide or direction. An evening arrival itself is out of the ordinary and has cost him extra fare. The city, now grown beyond a small settlement, has become as much a symbol of moral wilderness as the forest had been to earlier generations of New England. Robin feels a sense of displacement as he wanders the streets, seeking the home of his uncle, Major Molineux, who has promised to help him establish himself. The more Robin tries to find his way, the darker things become. As lights are extinguished around him, Robin feels his isolation increase.

Because his uncle holds a position of authority, Robin assumes that others will be happy to serve him. Instead, Robin finds that he is an object of scrutiny and derision. The ferry man examines him by the light of his lantern, concerned that Robin, whose wallet is thin, might not make the promised payment. The old gentleman of the periwig and tapping cane denies knowing the Major and warns Robin off with the threat of punishment. Robin finds this encounter particularly distressing because he hears the chorus of laughter from the barbers who have witnessed the scene. His experience at the tavern parallels this encounter when the innkeeper's "superfluous civility" turns to hostility as Robin admits that he cannot pay. Again, Robin hears a chorus of laughter as he departs. Only the young woman who wears the "scarlet petticoat," a sign of prostitution, seems happy to welcome Robin into her precincts. When the night watchman warns him to go home, Robin hears the young woman's laughter from the window above. Disheartened by his series of failures, Robin makes a last attempt to inquire for his uncle, stopping the man of the strange visage he had noticed earlier. This figure, too, attempts to rebuff him, finally telling him to wait where he is to see his uncle pass by him.

Hawthorne uses the night setting, the twisting streets and narrow lanes, and the individuals in strange attire to create an atmosphere conducive to the nightmarish situation in which Robin finds himself in the second half of the story. Hawthorne has dropped hints of what awaits Robin earlier in the tale, mentioning the "smell of tar" and the murmuring sound of laughter and activity that hovers in the background. But Robin, so intent on his own course, has failed to notice what is happening around him, depending on his own rationalizations to explain each situation.

In the second half of the story, Robin sits on the steps of a church, an important reconnection to his home values and identity, since he is the son of a clergyman. This reconnection lulls him into a more reflective state, where he thinks about home and the effect of his absence on the household. His journey continues its inward turn as Hawthorne makes references to the "dreamy sound" and "sleep-inspiring sound" of the dark night. Robin finds his "mind kept vibrating between fancy and reality" (80), adding to the ambiguity of his situation. During this pause in Robin's search, he meets the "gentleman" who will serve as his guide during the action that leads to the climax of the story.

The increasing noise of the approaching mob procession attracts Robin's attention and signals the movement toward crisis. The crisis itself hinges on a sequence of three moments of recognition, each of increasing significance. The first occurs as Robin recognizes once again the figure seated on the horse, the man with the painted face, whose military attire now mocks the rank and authority of the Major. He eyes Robin with a "fiery" look engendering the "indefinite but uncomfortable idea" that Robin will become part of the event. The second moment of recognition occurs when Robin sees the tarred and feathered figure of his uncle in the open cart. The Major has been reduced to a panic-stricken, animalistic figure, foaming at the mouth, struggling to maintain some shred of control. His eyes also meet Robin's, evoking both pity and terror in his nephew.

Rather than identify with his uncle, Robin becomes one with the crowd. As he hears the laughter build around him, he recognizes the sounds of those he had encountered on his earlier wanderings. Having been the object of their derisive laughter in the past, Robin seeks the safety of being part of the crowd, and his laughter joins with theirs, his shout becoming "the loudest one there" (86). Once he has engaged in this act of rejection of his uncle and identification with the mob, the procession moves on, leaving silence in its wake. In this silence, the last moment of recognition occurs, as Robin realizes what he has done. He returns to himself, as though awakening from a dream, but he cannot dispel the knowledge his experience has brought him. Although he is ready to depart the city, his guide encourages him to remain a few days and contemplate the possibility of making his way without the help of his kinsman.

CHARACTERS

The main character, Robin Molineux, is a young man who hopes to make his way in the world with the assistance of his uncle. The son of a clergyman-farmer, Robin comes from a family that has little money to spare. Since he is the second son and his older brother will inherit the farm, Robin must find another source of work and income. He assumes that the assistance of his uncle will provide him advantages, but his naïveté and ignorance shield him from a wider picture of life. Robin sees but does not perceive.

When he arrives in the city, he believes that his innate "shrewdness" will suffice to help him on his way, a sign of his adolescent self-confidence that has yet to be tested. As his confidence wavers, he uses his "shrewdness" to explain away or rationalize the behaviors of those who reject or threaten him. His confidence in himself is not as great as he would like to believe, however, for he also carries an oak cudgel and more than once feels tempted to use it. This cudgel connects him to his rural background, where physical strength matters more than social skill.

The various minor characters that Robin meets are stock types who represent the class distinctions and the temptations of city life. As he wanders, Robin notices the physical differences between one street and the next that convey the status and reputation of those who live in each district. He also sees the stylish attire of young men in the city, especially those who have traveled to Europe, which makes him feel the inferiority of his own attire. These interactions remind Robin of his status as an outsider, especially since most of the individuals he encounters seem to know something about the night's activities that he does not. This knowledge, and Robin's lack of it, allows Hawthorne to introduce irony into the narrative.

Two of the secondary characters, the man with the painted face and the guide, play more significant roles. Robin first sees the man with the unusual face in the tavern, struck by his distinctive appearance. His features have an irregularity and fierceness that link him with the chaos. When Robin sees him again, the man's face is painted red and black, the colors of war, of fire and darkness. He represents the dark underside of civilization and of the individual, as Robin begins to grasp during the mob scene. In contrast to this figure, the "gentleman" who becomes Robin's guide during the last portion of the tale appears to be the voice of calm and rationality. His regularity of feature and his kindness to Robin reflect more positive aspects of the individual and of social life. The existence of a link between these two figures, that they may be two sides of one entity, is suggested, however, by the question the guide poses: "May not one man have several voices, Robin, as well as two complexions?" (83).

THEMES

The motif of the journey is often used to explore the process of growth and development. Removed from familiar surroundings and companions that have reflected back one image of the self, a character has the opportunity to discover new facets of the self, both good and bad. Robin believes that his growth has already transpired, that he arrives in the city ready to become part of a new world, ready to assume adult activities. Instead, his journey forces him to recognize his own limitations and lack of independence. It also allows him to learn about his own capacity for evil and cruelty. As much as he has perceived himself an outsider, he is really no different from the other individuals he has encountered. At the end, Robin's initial reaction is to leave the city, to retreat to the country and to the past, in some ways to return to his dependent role at home. The guide, however, encourages him to postpone this decision, to think about the possibility of shaping his future through his own efforts.

HISTORICAL CONTEXT

Prior to the beginning of Robin's adventure, Hawthorne offers an account of the unrest in New England that follows the surrender of the old charters during the reign of James II. Under the old charters, the colonists elected their governors and other officials, but in the new system, the king appointed governors for the colonies who brought other officials with them. The antagonism between the royal appointees and the colonists flared periodically, and mob action was often supported from behind the scenes by respectable citizens (Colacurcio, "History" 44). The unrest that forms the backdrop for "My Kinsman" relates to the rum riots of the 1730s, to which Hawthorne indirectly refers in his mention of punch introduced to the colony through the West Indies trade. Hawthorne precipitates some of the confusion about the date of the story, however, by using the name *Molineux*. The name was known to his New England contemporaries through the reputation of William Molineux, an anti-Loyalist who supposedly participated in the Boston Tea Party (Tales and Sketches 1483). His use of the open cart in the procession also calls to mind the tumbrel carts made famous in the processions to the guillotine during the French Revolution. These elements hint at the overthrow of oppressive authority that most Americans associate with the Revolutionary War.

"ROGER MALVIN'S BURIAL" (1832, 1846)

Until the ending, the narrative of "Roger Malvin's Burial" offers a study of the effects on Reuben Bourne of an unfulfilled vow and a public lie. The ending introduces the question of expiation through the death of Bourne's son Cyrus, who dies at his father's hand. Critical responses to the ending and its overall effect on the meaning of the story make this one of Hawthorne's most controversial tales.

SETTING AND PLOT

In a reversal of the "errand into the wilderness" pattern, this narrative begins in the wilderness and follows a man's journey to settlement and return to wilderness. The wilderness is the location of Reuben Bourne's initial moral dilemma, but his arrival in the settlement does not resolve it. Instead, his situation grows more complicated by the promulgation of a false version of his actions. Although he has returned home, Reuben cannot rest, and the inner battle he wages intensifies as the years pass.

Reuben's dilemma begins in 1725 during the aftermath of a battle referred to as "Lovell's Fight," a raid on Indian encampments that turned into a defeat. Two survivors of that battle, wounded during the conflict, are struggling to make their way back to the settlements. One, Roger Malvin, knows his wounds are too severe, that he will not survive the journey. His companion, young Reuben Bourne, hesitates to leave Malvin to die alone in the wilderness. Persuaded by Malvin's arguments, Reuben promises to send help or to return to bury his friend's remains. Reuben continues the journey, eventually to be rescued and returned home.

While he recuperates from his injuries, Bourne is nursed by Dorcas Malvin, Roger's daughter. She inquires about her father, and before Reuben can explain, she supplies the answer she wants to hear. She then publicizes her version of Reuben's valor and loyalty. By the time he recovers, the myth of his actions is well established, and Reuben feels he can do nothing to correct the situation. He marries Dorcas but feels haunted by his unfulfilled promise to Roger. He also chafes against the discrepancy between his public image and his true self. Believing that he is unworthy of happiness and prosperity, Reuben gradually exhausts the farm he and Dorcas inherited and alienates his neighbors. Having reached the end of his resources, Reuben returns to the wilderness to carve out a new life, with his family in tow.

During the journey back into the wilderness, Reuben believes that Heaven is guiding him to the locus of his troubles. When Dorcas reminds him of the anniversary of her father's death, Reuben's anxiety increases. Reuben wanders in the woods, raising his gun at every rustle and creak, as though he fears a ghost from the past. When he perceives motion in the bushes, he fires, felling his son. Dorcas sees Cyrus's body at the base of the rock where her father had also lain. Reuben begins to explain, but Dorcas faints beside the body of her son. Only Reuben is left standing, finally able to weep and to pray, to acknowledge the pain of loss.

Hawthorne brings the narrative full circle through both setting and action, but the narrator's comments on expiation have ignited disagreement about the implications of the ending and the tale. Some critics read "Roger Malvin's Burial" as a version of the Abraham and Isaac story in Genesis or of the relationship between God and Christ in the New Testament, attempting to establish a theological and ethical framework for the tale. Others have offered a psychological reading of the story that focuses on the nature of obsession and compulsion. They suggest that Reuben deludes himself at the end when he feels redeemed. Historicists argue that Hawthorne establishes a parallel between the omission of facts that allowed his contemporaries to recreate a heroic version of "Lovell's Fight" and the lie that Reuben lets stand, both of which are ultimately destructive (Colacurcio, "History" 48–49). All of these readings provide helpful insights, but none alone accounts for all aspects of the tale.

CHARACTERS

Life on the frontier shapes the experiences of all four characters. Roger Malvin is no stranger to hostile interaction with Indians, having been taken captive and transported to Montreal before escaping. Roger serves as a father figure to Reuben and claims a father's authority when sending him away. He also knows of his daughter's affection for Reuben and thinks about her future. He chooses to send Reuben away to secure his posterity as he expresses hopes that Reuben and Dorcas will see their children's children. His willingness to face death alone reflects an inner fortitude that Reuben lacks.

A young man at the opening, Reuben quickly makes promises that he fails to keep. Prior to leaving on the raid, he had promised Dorcas that he would defend her father's life with his own. Before leaving Roger, he promises to return, if not in rescue then to bury Roger's remains. Rather than confront painful situations honestly, Reuben makes pledges to comfort others and himself. His inability to keep his word and to correct the false impression created by Dorcas haunts him. The one positive element in Reuben's life is his son, Cyrus, whom he believes embodies all that was once good in himself.

As the only woman in the story, Dorcas serves as a counterpoint to the men. While they engage in frontier battles and clearing of land, she maintains the domestic sphere, serving as nurse, wife, and mother. She even attempts to create a homelike setting in the wilderness, a less violent means of interacting with the natural world. Yet Dorcas's life is shaped by the violence around her, including the death of her only child. Her collapse at the end suggests that she has been overcome by the violence of the frontier experience as well as her profound loss.

THEMES

In this tale, Hawthorne explores how guilt, real or imagined, can affect an individual's life and sense of self. He links this to the perpetuation of lies that ultimately undermine the future, both personal and social. Reuben engages in a pattern of self-destructive behavior that culminates in the destruction of his son, whom he sees as an extension of himself. Reuben only feels his curse has been lifted when he suffers a torment worse than his own death, a final gesture of self-inflicted punishment in search of expiation. Through his development of a story that crosses generations, Hawthorne introduces the theme of the "sins of the fathers" that he later explores in his novels. In them he suggests that only when the truth about the past is acknowledged does the destructive cycle end.

In addition to the main theme, Hawthorne also treats a secondary theme concerning the nature of "true manhood" and how it is defined in this frontier culture. All three male characters are measured against a code of masculine behavior that includes the ability to use a gun, to hunt, to track or find one's way through the wilderness, to engage in battle, and to endure pain. Cyrus especially embodies these attributes and is viewed as "a future leader in the land" (99). He has his own dreams of glory on the frontier and thinks about his "remote posterity" (101). Given the outcome of the story, however, Hawthorne questions a concept of manhood so heavily associated with violence.

SYMBOLS

The most significant symbol that Hawthorne employs is the oak sapling to which Reuben ties the bloodied cloth as a pledge as well as a marker. At this point, the tree reflects the potential of youth, as does Reuben, for the tree is "a young and vigorous sapling" (88). When Reuben returns years later, the tree has grown, but its uppermost bough has withered, much as Reuben's better self had shriveled away. The tree can also represent a family tree whose end has come, as the fragments of the withered bough fall to earth. Because it was the topmost bough, its shattering means the tree will grow no taller, just as Cyrus's death means the Bourne-Malvin line has come to an end.

"YOUNG GOODMAN BROWN" (1835, 1846)

Perhaps the most frequently anthologized of Hawthorne's New England tales, "Young Goodman Brown" presents a version of the initiation story, although it is ultimately a failed initiation. Goodman Brown, who is on the verge of acknowledging his own potential for evil, instead becomes convinced of the evil that exists all around him. He loses not only his religious faith but also his trust in and connection to his fellow beings. Like the Reverend Hooper in "The Minister's Black Veil," he ends up a lonely and isolated man, but his situation results from what he believes about others rather than what they believe about him.

SETTING AND PLOT

By setting the story in Salem Village in 1692, Hawthorne links "Young Goodman Brown" to the witchcraft hysteria that affected the Massachusetts Bay colony. Brown sets out on a night journey into the forest, as Hawthorne consciously plays upon the Puritan concept of the "errand into the wilderness," a phrase they had used to describe their journey to the New World. The forest is viewed by the Puritans as a place and symbol of moral wilderness and chaos. Entering the woods at sunset increases the threatening aspect of this setting, for night is a time when the irrational and the devil hold greater sway. The path Brown follows is narrow and gloomy, and Hawthorne builds suspense about the outcome of this journey by suggesting that the forest conceals unseen dangers. In this tale, Hawthorne relies on a more conventional plot structure as his narrative presents action gradually rising to the crisis, followed by a brief denouement.

The rising action begins as Brown enters the wood. He encounters a man who has been waiting for him, a figure who resembles the devil. In appearance Brown and his companion are likened as father and son, but the elder man has a distinctive mien about him. As they proceed, he reveals to Brown the dark side of human nature, not just speaking in abstract and general terms but personalizing his remarks by making specific reference to Brown's father and grandfather. Brown asserts that these comments cannot be true, for the Puritans are a "people of prayer, and good works" (278), yet his naive picture of his community is shaken.

Significant encounters in the forest continue the rising action while further undermining Brown's understanding of and trust in his community. While he continues on his way, he sees his catechism teacher, Goody Cloyse, having a familiar conversation with the devil. Later he thinks he overhears the minister and the deacon as they proceed toward the devil's gathering. But there is something peculiar about these encounters, for Goody Cloyse appears out of nowhere and disappears as fast, while Brown never manages to see the minister and deacon, no matter how hard he struggles to catch a glimpse. As he does later in *Seven Gables*, Hawthorne creates alternate explanations for what appears to be the supernatural, drawing upon "either . . . or" constructions. Hawthorne thus raises questions about the nature of Brown's experience, whether he perceives the actual, sees what his imagination induces, or accepts what the devil insinuates. Brown never questions the validity of the scenes and sounds that he detects, but he does begin to doubt heaven.

Brown's doubts increase when he believes his wife has succumbed to the invitation to join the devil's circle. When a pink ribbon, associated with Faith in the opening scene, drifts down before him, Brown cries out, "My Faith is gone!" (283), as Hawthorne plays upon a Faith (Brown's wife)/faith pun. As his despair deepens, the pace of Brown's journey and the tension in the narrative increase. He makes a frenzied dash through the woods toward the "heart of the dark wilderness" (283). Driven forward by an inexplicable energy, he reaches the center of the wood where he finds the devil's gathering under way.

At this gathering, Brown sees church members and disreputable individuals joined together in a shocking scene. What he sees is a representation of human-kind, high and low, good and wicked, Indian as well as English. This assembly is the final stroke that undoes his belief, as the devil states that "ye had still hoped that virtue were not all a dream. Now ye are undeceived" (287). Brown accepts this as truth, even though it is said by the Great Deceiver. His moment of crisis has arrived: Brown and his wife are to be inducted into the company and know the full wickedness of each other. Brown cries out, "[R]esist the Wicked one!" (288), and the scene before him vanishes. No evidence of the fiery circle remains, the night is calm, the forest quiet.

The falling action follows Brown's path back into town, revealing the impact his night in the woods has had upon him. He recoils from those he encounters, believing all, including his young wife, are contaminated by evil. The denouement raises the possibility that all was a dream but goes on to explain that the explanation is less important than the effect of the experience on Brown. He has become a distrustful man whose "dying hour was gloom" (289).

CHARACTERS

Goodman Brown, the main character in this story, is a young man, recently married, who believes he is about to do something momentous in his life. His hesitation in setting forth suggests that he is uneasy about the change it may work in him. Brown has a rather naive view of himself, his wife, and the Puritan community to which they belong. He has an immature trust in the history he has been taught and in the images that other people present to him. He enters the woods having accepted a picture of life that he has never questioned and seems to lack awareness of differences between appearances and realities. This makes him susceptible to the devil's influence, for just as Brown has never questioned the Puritan version of reality, he never questions the devil's. In the course of his experience, Brown swings from one extreme to the other, initially believing his community all good, then accusing it as all bad.

The devil functions as the other principal character in the story. Hawthorne presents him in normal attire but immediately hints that there is something unusual about him, mentioning that it took him only fifteen minutes to travel from Boston to Salem, a distance of about fifteen miles. His staff, carved in the image of a snake, adds a more sinister aspect to him. The devil knows a good deal about Brown and how he will react to what he sees and hears. In some ways, the devil is a consummate showman, staging scenes that he knows will provoke the desired response in his audience. This supports his role as the Great Deceiver, for like a magician or showman, he must keep the audience engaged in the performance so that they do not begin to question how the tricks are done. He contributes a strain of dark humor in the story.

The other characters play minor roles, including Faith, Brown's wife. Her exchange with Brown in the opening suggests that she has her own anxieties for him and for herself. When he returns, she is joyful, not expecting his rebuff. The other women mentioned in the story, Cloyse, Carrier, and Cory, were all tried for witchcraft during the hysteria in Salem. By making reference to them, Hawthorne invites the reader to consider the impact of accusations and the nature of evidence in proving guilt.

THEMES

Usually a story of initiation focuses on an experience that brings a character to a wider vision of himself or of the world. Often it entails a quest or a journey through which a young person proves his or her maturity and right to adult membership in the community. Brown's journey or quest aims toward a hidden or forbidden knowledge. Some critics suggest that the underlying impulse is Brown's desire for sexual knowledge, a move from innocence to experience that accompanies his newly married state. In Brown's case, however, the initiation fails. Brown ends up blind to the world as it usually presents itself, seeing only evil. He no longer wishes to look for the good or to be part of the community that surrounds him.

SYMBOLS

Hawthorne attaches symbolic import to numerous images in the narrative. In addition to the symbolic value of the forest, the night, and the journey, Hawthorne invests everyday details with greater meaning. Faith's pink ribbons best demonstrate this. Their color suggests that she is still closer to girlhood than adult womanhood. The color pink also represents the mixed nature of her being, not completely pure (white) but also not brazenly sinful (red). By incorporating everyday objects that suggest meanings beyond themselves, Hawthorne adds to the texture of his story.

HISTORICAL CONTEXT

In this story, Hawthorne uses language charged with meaning for seventeenth-century Puritans. In addition to his repetition of the word *errand*, he also mentions *covenant*, a word that identified the basis of a believer's relationship to God and the foundation for the Puritan community. Brown's claim to keep "covenant" with the devil thus has greater implications than simply keeping a bargain. Hawthorne also includes the term *persevere*, a word that Puritans associated with one of the five points of Calvinism, the "perseverance of the saints."

Hawthorne also draws on the concept of "spectral evidence," a notion given credence during the Salem witchcraft trials. People believed that the devil could assume the shape of a follower to carry out evil deeds. When those who were accused of witchcraft proved that they had been somewhere other than where an accuser placed them, accusers claimed that the devil could use the follower's specter or physical image, even if the person was elsewhere bodily. Late in 1692, the validity of this evidence was called into question as some ministers and magistrates argued that the devil could also make use of the specters of innocent persons. This challenge to the use of spectral evidence and other forms of questionable testimony brought the witchcraft trials to an end.

"THE MAY-POLE OF MERRY MOUNT" (1836, 1837)

Against the backdrop of conflict between somber Pilgrims and mirthful revelers, Hawthorne traces a young couple's transition from irresponsible youth to sober adulthood. Presenting two extremes of behavior and belief, this story is read by some as an allegory of the conflict between Old England and New, an approach fostered by Hawthorne's headnote. Others see it as an allegory of attaining maturity, as a young couple abandon childish ways for adult responsibilities.

SETTING AND PLOT

"The May-Pole of Merry Mount" takes place in 1628 at Mount Wollaston (now Quincy), Massachusetts, not far from Plymouth. Hawthorne draws upon the contrasts between Merry Mount and Plymouth to shape the setting and action of the story. He treats the Puritans as the antagonists whose introduction into the narrative initiates rising action. That action culminates in the destruction of Merry Mount and determines the fate of Edgar and Edith.

The settlement at Merry Mount has embraced a life of mirth and playfulness, even when it must be artificially maintained. Members of this community celebrate their connections to nature and the natural world, believing that they are at one with creation. Merry Mount's residents embrace color, music, and dancing. They do not see a fallen world, and their actions link them to the traditions of the "Golden Age," or Arcadia (see "Allusions," Chapter 8). They enact rituals derived from pagan times, including fashioning images of the corn-king and erecting a May-Pole. Hawthorne likens the masked dancers to figures performing in an English masque, a form of drama presented at court, often at great expense, that conveyed political overtones. Displaced in England by the growing influence of Puritanism, the inhabitants of Merry Mount have ventured to the New World to escape the changes a more restrictive culture imposes.

Ironically, the plantation at Merry Mount is near that of the Separatists at Plymouth Plantation (better known as the Pilgrims). This community places even more narrow limits on acceptable behavior and practice than do the Puritans in England. They have come to the New World to establish their own church practice and social compact, asserting that what exists in England is too corrupt to reform. Compared to the environment at Merry Mount, that of the Puritan settlement is stark and stern. Hawthorne uses diction and detail to suggest this difference, for his descriptions of life at Merry Mount are rich and full of texture, whereas those of Plymouth are spare and direct. The Separatists look with disdain upon anything frivolous, anything that reflects the vanities of earthly life. Their lives focus on work and worship, and they see the New World as a territory to be subdued and converted to godly purposes. To enforce the codes by which they live, they have brought numerous instruments of restraint and punishment with them, including the stocks and the whipping-post.

The proximity of these two settlements and their competing philosophies of life foreshadow unavoidable conflict. The clash occurs on a day of high celebration at Merry Mount, during which the community will witness the marriage of Edgar and Edith, chosen Lord and Lady of the May. The Puritans, led by Endicott, descend upon the merrymaking, scattering the participants. Endicott chops down the May-Pole, while his fellows ready punishment for those who have engaged in pagan activity. In their zeal, the Puritans wish to destroy any instrument of levity and mirth, including the dancing bear.

The Puritans view marriage as a serious commitment, labeling husband and wife "yoke-mates" who persevere together in work and in piety. The frivolity of the ceremony at Merry Mount particularly irks Endicott, who plans to teach Edgar and Edith a lesson through punishment. Only when he recognizes their genuine love and commitment does his position change, as he recognizes something in them worth preserving. He instead orders that the two be clothed according to the fashion of the Separatists as he converts them into members of the Plymouth community.

CHARACTERS

Numerous individuals from both communities participate in the action, but only Edith and Edgar from Merry Mount and Endicott among the Puritans emerge as distinctive characters.

Edith and Edgar, the Lady and Lord of the May, embody Merry Mount's emphasis upon youthful freedom and the lack of responsibility. As they face each other in the marriage ceremony, however, they realize that their love for one another has made them aware of their commitment, its responsibilities, and "troubled joys." Edith senses that the values of Merry Mount are artificial and the "mirth unreal" (363). She and Edgar are no longer at home at Merry Mount. When Endicott confronts them, each volunteers to suffer the other's punishment, an expression of their true love for one another. Ultimately they accept the new identity offered them by Endicott, supporting each other and never regretting their departure from Merry Mount.

Although he initially appears a harsh and judgmental man, the "Puritan of Puritans," Endicott reveals some humanity in dealing with Edith and Edgar. He can do so partly because Palfrey, one of Endicott's men, voices the more rigid Puritan stance. Endicott, a man of principle and authority, is looked to by the others for direction and decision. He metes out swift, severe punishment for the residents of Merry Mount, promising that even harsher penalties will follow. Most often associated with his sword, which he uses to topple the May-Pole, Endicott sees his actions as securing the fate of New England's future. When he witnesses the love Edith and Edgar have for each other, however, he pauses. They prompt in him a moment of understanding as he recalls that youthful folly does not prevent a life of meaningful service. His final words to them, in stark contrast to those by the priest who married them, remind Edith and Edgar that true happiness is never found in shirking responsibility and perpetuating childish behavior.

THEMES

In his treatment of Edgar and Edith, Hawthorne introduces the theme of love as an initiator of change and maturity. Prior to their commitment to each other, Edgar and Edith are part of Merry Mount, an Arcadian world that celebrates the freedom of childhood. The adults who inhabit this world cling to a childish vision of life, meeting any adversity with denial or avoidance. Hawthorne suggests that lack of reflection has let some at Merry Mount slip back toward a more animalistic plane as they dance in a circle with a bear. Once Edgar and Edith begin to experience mature reflection and understanding, once they see that the mirth of Merry Mount is unreal, they can no longer remain there, they cannot retreat into childhood. Their acceptance into the Puritan community with its burden of responsibility and duty represents their entry into the world of adulthood with its cares but also its more genuine satisfactions.

ALLEGORY AND SYMBOLS

When a writer presents an allegory, he or she attempts to create a story that will be both interesting in itself and, through its characters, events, and objects, also suggest meanings that pertain to something beyond the content of the narrative. In "The May-Pole of Merry Mount," Hawthorne's narrative can be read simply as a retelling of a single event that occurred early in New England's settlement. Hawthorne, however, takes great pains to link persons and events in his story to larger political and social forces. The ideas and activities at Merry Mount are tied to the court and the social customs of Old England. The actions of Endicott reflect the efforts of the reform-minded Puritans to prevent the spread of corruption and "misrule" from Old England to New. The juxtaposition of these two opposing communities allows Hawthorne to suggest both the wider conflict between two political, social, and spiritual views and the ways these views define themselves against each other.

Hawthorne also uses numerous symbols to enhance the allegorical potential of his narrative. Those associated with Merry Mount, such as the May-Pole, the flowers, and the green boughs, signify the connection to and dependence upon nature. Others, such as the fools-caps, bells, and costumes, signify play and fantasy, the underpinnings of life at Merry Mount. In contrast, those associated with the Puritans, such as iron, signify their rigidity, whereas the whipping-post signifies their use of force to subdue human impulses.

"THE MINISTER'S BLACK VEIL" (1836, 1837)

Although not one of Hawthorne's "historical tales," in the same sense as "The May-Pole of Merry Mount," "The Minister's Black Veil" depends heavily upon the beliefs and communal experience of New England Calvinism as it shaped the values and mind-set of the characters and events. Hawthorne subtitles this tale "a parable," guiding the reader toward interpretation that will reveal a lesson or general concept about human experience. The main title focuses attention on the veil itself, as Hawthorne highlights its role as a symbol that becomes invested with meaning far more substantial than its "two folds of crape [sic]" (372). Hawthorne's interest in the effect of a single powerful symbol anticipates his approach in *The Scarlet Letter*.

SETTING AND PLOT

The story begins during the religious revival known as the Great Awakening, although Hawthorne does not mention it directly. This revival stimulated intense religious fervor and introspection on the part of individuals who felt themselves called to conversion and church membership. The Great Awakening resulted from endeavors by a number of ministers who felt that people had become lax and complacent about their spiritual well-being and hoped to restore the level of commitment that had guided the initial Puritan settlers. The opening paragraph of the story presents the town of Milford on a typical Sunday morning as the community gathers for worship. The church functions as the center of activity, and the entire community is drawn together, young and old, men and women. They are accustomed to a particular routine, marked off by certain symbols, including the ringing of bells that calls them together. The routine suggests that the church in Milford has become too comfortable with its spiritual state of affairs. Into this routine their minister, the Reverend Mr. Hooper, introduces a new symbol, the black veil he wears over his face.

Initially the congregation reacts with surprise but assumes that an explanation will be forthcoming and that the veil serves a specific but temporary purpose. The remainder of the narrative focuses on the role of the veil in Mr. Hooper's life and in that of the community. Its continuing presence disrupts the habits of interaction between Mr. Hooper and his congregation. Although he performs his usual services within the community, including the funerals and weddings that are marked by ritual and symbolism, the veil predominates over all other images. The lack of explanation, the lack of a story that provides a causal relationship between a specific aspect of Hooper's life and the veil, further enhances the veil's power to set Hooper apart from the rest. Even Hooper's betrothed Elizabeth is deeply affected by the "terrors" that this unexplained symbol provokes.

At the end of his life, Hooper maintains the veil, even as those who attend him at his deathbed assume he will remove it. Only Elizabeth, steadfast in her affections, assures that his wishes will be honored. His dying words are a form of self-revelation as well as a rebuke to all those who have rejected him as somehow different from themselves. His words reveal the pain of his loneliness. Hooper accepts the veil as a sign of the common bond of sin that unites humanity, but he does not grasp that others cannot bear to see the narrow truth of human nature reflected back at them in the living mirror that he has become.

CHARACTERS

Prior to donning the black veil, the Reverend Mr. Hooper has been an ordinary man whose habits are as routine as those of his congregation. A competent but not renowned preacher, he is a mild man not given to "thunders" (373). Once he drapes the veil over his face, however, changes begin to occur. His sermons have greater impact, and he ministers more effectively to those who "were in agony for sin" (381). Although his own sympathy for and understanding of the condition of others expands, he shares only in the negative aspects of their lives. Increasingly Hooper even avoids his own reflection, for it reminds him not only of his own sinfulness but of his isolation as well. Critical reaction to Hooper indicates the challenge posed by this story, for some readers see him as noble and truthful, while others see him as selfish and foolish.

Aside from their reactions to the veil, little is revealed about the other characters. Even Hooper's betrothed, Elizabeth, emerges fully drawn in only one scene, when she and Hooper discuss the veil and its implications for their relationship, which effectively ends. She, however, remains loyal to Hooper, and her dedicated attendance at his last illness demonstrates the consolation and comfort of human connections that Hooper has sacrificed in service to his painful truth.

THEMES

In addition to examining the power of symbols in narrative and in life, Hawthorne explores the human need for connection to others. He assesses Hooper's condition when he indicates that the veil "had separated him from cheerful brotherhood and woman's love, and kept him in that saddest of all prisons, his own heart" (382). Hawthorne warns against the dangers of any exclusive pursuit that severs one's ties to others, a theme he treats extensively in many of the stories discussed in Chapter 4.

SYMBOLS

A symbol is an object or event that also suggests or means something else. Often a symbol is a concrete or tangible object used to convey an abstract or intangible idea. In some cases, symbols are invested with meaning by an individual, but many symbols are endowed with universal or community-based suggestions of meaning. These meanings are broadly recognized within a community, and such symbols contribute to the expression of unity and shared values. When evoked by a symbol, certain meanings may reaffirm an individual's membership and participation in a particular cultural group. Within the Christian tradition, the cross functions as a symbol of widely recognized and shared meaning.

In "The Minister's Black Veil," Hawthorne explores the nature and power of a symbol. The black veil, whose presence dominates the story and the lives of the characters, becomes a symbol invested with many meanings. Although some of the meanings it evokes in the beginning are those shared by the community, the veil becomes a symbol that divides rather than unifies. Initially Hooper treats the veil as a means of reminding his congregation that all individuals, even those thought good, wear masks before the world, concealing their true selves, especially those aspects that are sinful. Thus, no one presents his or her "true" face before the world. This is the topic of his Sabbath sermon, and it both moves and unsettles his congregation.

Had the veil as symbol transmitted its meaning in this instance and been removed, it might have made a deep but limited impression on the congregation. But Hooper continues to wear it, keeping before himself and his congregation a reminder of all that is negative in human nature. Once this symbol stands between them and their minister, the townspeople can see nothing else about him. It becomes, in their eyes, the symbol of Hooper himself, an inscrutable blank to which they cannot or will not relate. Instead, they begin to inscribe their own meanings upon the veil, reading in it what they need to believe to alleviate their discomfort. As the veil's possible meanings increase, so, too, does its influence. Hooper also feels the power of the symbol, as it brings home to him the isolation of "a man apart from men" (381). The veil also becomes a symbol for Hooper's obsession with the problem of human evil, an obsession that ultimately prevents him from enjoying the possibilities of human good.

Hawthorne's interest in New England's past influences the content and context of many of his stories and sketches. Other tales that make use of the colonial legacy include "The Gray Champion" (1835, 1837), "Alice Doane's Appeal" (1835), "Endicott and the Red Cross" (1838, 1842), and the "Legends of the Province-House" (1838, 1842). Hawthorne also treats the historical past in sketches such as "Mrs. Hutchinson" (1830), "Sir William Phips" (1830), "Dr. Bullivant" (1831), and "Sir William Pepperell" (1833).

4

Short Stories II: Artists, Seekers, and Solitaries

In remarks to friends and to his wife, Hawthorne often characterized himself as a man who had experienced loneliness and isolation. At times he thought of himself as an observer of the life around him rather than a full participant in it. He was given to introspection, a trait not surprising in a writer, and was intrigued by the possibilities of knowing completely oneself or another. He frequently commented on the mysteries or secrets of the human heart and believed that an author had to illuminate these in his work. However, he was disturbed by those who probed others' secrets too deeply, for he feared that such probing could destroy those left exposed and vulnerable.

In many of his short stories, Hawthorne explores the experiences of individuals who perceive themselves set apart from the community in which they live. For some this results from a unique talent or gift, such as Owen Warland in "The Artist of the Beautiful." For others, it reflects a conscious choice to separate from community to gain a vantage point from which to observe human nature. The isolated individuals in the stories that follow are all men, many of whom, like the Reverend Mr. Hooper of "The Minister's Black Veil" (Chapter 3), sacrifice opportunities for love and happiness to pursue an abstract ideal. Hawthorne, wary of the Romantic concept of self-reliance when taken to extreme, questions its effects upon his central characters. He also explores other extremes of thought and behavior in the lives of his characters, tracing the ways such extremes distort lives and relationships.

"WAKEFIELD" (1835, 1837)

In this unusual tale of a man who leaves his family for twenty years, Hawthorne presents a meditation on the anonymity of modern life. The title character Wakefield attempts a change in his life, but the change turns into his new routine. The narrator, who imagines the details of Wakefield's experience, reveals as much about his own anxieties as he does about those of the main character. The story's potential as a comment on the desire for escape from routine in modern life has impressed later writers, who offer versions of it. Some of these include "A Slip of the Leash" (1904) by Mary Wilkins Freeman and the "Flitcraft" episode in Dashiell Hammett's *The Maltese Falcon* (1930). In her novel *Ladder of Years* (1995), Anne Tyler revises the narrative by making a woman its central character.

POINT OF VIEW

Told anonymously from the first-person point of view, this tale forces the reader to question the narrator's motives and reliability. He claims that the episode is "probably never to be repeated," yet admits that he thinks about it often, highlighting its underlying appeal as a source of vicarious escape. The narrator claims that he (and the reader) would never do what Wakefield has done, establishing a bond of sympathy between himself and the reader. At the same time, the narrator attempts to distance himself from Wakefield by labeling him a "foolish man" (292) and a "crafty nincompoop" (294) who engages in a long "whim-wham" (294). This attempt to diminish Wakefield and thereby undercut what he has done suggests the narrator's own fear. He, too, desires change but fears that his efforts will produce an ironic situation like Wakefield's, the exchange of one stifling routine for another. He needs to reassure himself that his own life has not reached the same level of mundane routine and that he is a more appealing individual than the title character.

The link between this story and the problems of modern life is established at the outset. The narrator states that he only remembers the outlines of this story as reported in an old magazine or newspaper. Learning of this episode through the media rather than through conversations with others highlights the depersonalization of modern life. The narrator's own anonymity underscores this reality, as do his references to the loss of individuality as the narrative proceeds. Since the story "appeals to the general sympathies of mankind" (290), he decides to speculate on a fuller version of what occurred. The narrator, however, does everything he can to undermine any sympathy that the reader feels for Wakefield, for if his character and situation seem reasonable, then the unbearable aspects of modern life must be acknowledged.

SETTING AND PLOT

The story of Wakefield's twenty-year "disappearance" takes place in London on two adjacent streets. Hawthorne makes use of the urban setting to ensure plausibility, since in the city one can fade into the crowd. When Wakefield leaves home, he is dressed in drab and ordinary attire, so that he easily blends into the scene. He follows a mazelike path to get to his destination, a small apartment on the street next to his own.

Wakefield leaves home, takes an apartment one street over, stays away for twenty years, then returns and resumes his former life. Around this basic thread, the narrator weaves a more detailed pattern of action. He imagines Wakefield changing his appearance with the addition of a wig of reddish hair and a change of clothing. He describes Wakefield's observations of his wife and the toll his absence takes on her. He creates a moment of encounter between Wakefield and his wife, describing how he passes undetected, although he seems vaguely familiar to her. Finally, he presents the impetus for Wakefield's return, a rain shower that drenches him just as he passes by his old home. Having brought the story to an anticlimax, the narrator ends his speculation about Wakefield and asserts a moral about the role of systems and routines in shaping identity and place. His final use of hyperbole in describing Wakefield as the "Outcast of the Universe" suggests how greatly magnified this episode has become in the narrator's thoughts. It indicates that the narrator struggles to convince himself of the futility and danger in what Wakefield has done.

CHARACTERS

This tale can also be read as a character study, one that emphasizes the negative aspects of an individual. The character, named Wakefield by the narrator, remains a figure of mystery. The reader learns little about him other than details that pertain to his disappearance or his attitudes toward what he has done. No mention is made of his employment or how he maintains his livelihood during his disappearance. He interacts with no one, save the chance encounter with his wife. Ironically, his anonymity and isolation are greater than before he disappeared.

The narrator refers to him as the "hero" of the story, but the qualities he ascribes to him are anything but heroic. His attributes include sluggishness, lack of imagination, "quiet selfishness," and a "cold, but not depraved or wandering heart" (291). Wakefield easily disappears in the crowd, an ordinary man. The narrator even mocks him by calling attention to his insignificance. To his other negative qualities, the narrator adds that Wakefield is "feeble-minded" and that beneath his plans lies a "morbid vanity" (293). Wakefield's passivity shapes his experience, for he sets out with no definite plan and lets events dictate his actions. A creature of habit, Wakefield shifts from one routine path in life to another. His new existence offers no greater excitement than did the old. He has become a type of voyeur as he spies upon his old household, anticipating certain qualities of Miles Coverdale in *The Blithedale Romance*.

Is this a story of a midlife crisis, since Wakefield is at the "meridian" of life? He desperately wants to be noticed, to stand out from the background of at least his family's daily activities. He does not look for a new love and during his absence remains faithful to his wife. He does, however, choose to watch how "widowhood" and his disappearance affect her. Initially, Wakefield believes that his disappearance has not provoked a sufficient desperation in his wife. When she shows signs of fatigue and anxiety, Wakefield decides not to return home, even as he sees a doctor at the door. Has Wakefield's life reached a quiet desperation that makes any reaction, even worry and suffering, better than no reaction from others? The narrator refrains from pursuing this question, just as he refrains from any conjecture regarding what occurs when Wakefield returns.

THEMES

The narrator emphasizes the importance of routine, of "systems" that provide people with security and a sense of place in their daily lives. Especially in a modern, urban environment, this may be the only source of identity, as individuality is undermined by "the great mass" that makes up city life. Hawthorne uses the narrator's own need for security and acceptance to raise questions about their cost. He invites the reader to consider how one's place in the world is determined by connections to others as well as by physical location and cultural conditions.

"THE BIRTH-MARK" (1843, 1846)

In the early nineteenth century, science and technology assumed more dominant roles in American life, vying with religion as a source of meaning and understanding. There was uneasiness, however, about what science might attempt to do, what boundaries it might attempt to cross. In England, Mary Shelley's *Frankenstein* (1818) had explored the result of a young scientist's attempts to transfer the spark of life into an inanimate being. His experimentation resulted in success but also horrific failure as the "monster" he produced searched for acceptance and identity, wreaking destruction in its path. In "The Birth-mark," Hawthorne presents another scientist whose experimentation also produces a desired result—but with dire consequences. Aylmer, obsessed with his wife's mark of mortality and imperfection, dedicates himself to its removal, regardless of the cost.

SETTING AND PLOT

Hawthorne sets this story in the later part of the eighteenth century, at the close of what is often referred to as the Age of Reason, an era defined by the pursuit of scientific discovery through experimentation and rational analysis. The story begins in the dwelling of the scientist Aylmer and his bride, Georgiana, but shifts to his laboratory as the center of activity. This shift is significant, for it removes their relationship from the realm of the domestic, where Georgiana holds influence, to the arena of scientific endeavor, in which Aylmer dominates. He has created a "boudoir" where Georgiana will reside, an artificial environment that functions as a controlled setting for a laboratory experiment. Although this setting might be "a pavilion among the clouds" (770), it excludes sunshine, the natural light that sustains life. When Georgiana enters the laboratory proper, she is shocked by its utilitarian aspect compared to the elegance of the chamber Aylmer provides for her. She is further shocked by Aylmer's appearance there, as though his true self emerges in this close and odorous environment. His work space reveals that his science is not all of "mind," that it is not all "pure," and that he cannot guarantee what his efforts will produce.

Aylmer focuses his energies and attention on what becomes his main objective and the central action of the tale, the removal of the birthmark on Georgiana's face. Aylmer's revulsion at the sight of the birthmark has affected Georgiana's view of it as well, and she agrees to submit to his plan for its removal. Initially Aylmer attempts indirect means of accomplishing his goal, and Georgiana becomes aware of unusual sensations, although she cannot pinpoint their cause. He then informs her that her case "demands a remedy that shall go deeper" (773), as he develops an elixir that will remove the stain from her cheek. Trusting in her husband's science and desperate to please him, Georgiana drinks the liquid in the pursuit of perfection. As the mark fades from Georgiana's face, so, too, does the life energy from her body. Although Aylmer's science removes the mark, it kills Georgiana. In his attempt to impose the ideal, Aylmer destroys his chance for earthly happiness.

CHARACTERS

An intensely focused story, "The Birth-mark" revolves around the actions and interactions of the two main characters, Aylmer and Georgiana. Only one other character appears, the laboratory assistant, Aminadab.

Aylmer sees himself as the consummate man of science, a product of eighteenth-century enlightenment. Hawthorne, however, suggests otherwise. He acknowledges the methodical nature of Aylmer's work, his honesty in recording failures as well as successes, and his high ideals. However, he also links Aylmer to the tradition of alchemy and sorcery. The majority of Aylmer's experiments have been failures, but he believes he can "draw a magic circle around [Georgiana], within which no evil might intrude" (770). According to the narrator, Aylmer, like other men of science, believes that his abilities will progress step by step until he possesses the very secrets of life.

Aylmer becomes obsessed with the birthmark. It becomes the only part of his wife that he sees; it even dominates his unconscious, as his dream reveals. Determined to use his power to eradicate this mark of imperfection, he plans to refashion his wife into a perfect figure. He claims that he feels "fully competent" to remove the mark, calling it his triumph over nature. Likening himself to her creator and claiming godlike powers, he even encourages Georgiana to contemplate worshipping him, should his efforts succeed. As he initiates the process of treatment, Aylmer attempts to entertain Georgiana with little demonstrations of his abilities and inventions. Each of these fails, but Aylmer disregards them. Convinced that he can accomplish his ultimate goal of perfection, Aylmer sees nothing else. His narrowness of vision has produced a blindness toward his own human frailty as well as that of Georgiana.

Georgiana is a woman thought beautiful by many. She is sensitive, especially to her husband's feelings for her. When she realizes that his distaste for the birthmark encompasses a general feeling toward her, she begs him to remove it. Her anguish has brought her to the point of desperation, and she knows of no other means to regain Aylmer's affection. She experiences profound self-loathing, having internalized the feelings her husband has expressed toward the mark. Georgiana becomes an object in her own eyes as well as Aylmer's. When she knows she is dying, she speaks to her husband with "more than human tenderness" (780), for as her one mark of imperfection fades, she can no longer remain an earthly being. Georgiana expresses pity for him, that he "rejected the best that earth could offer" (780).

In contrast to Aylmer, who has become primarily "mind," his assistant Aminadab is earthy and earthly. He represents "man's physical nature"—little above the animal in his shaggy-haired appearance—he growls and grunts. Although Aylmer is inferior in intellect, Aminadab has a more primitive appreciation of Georgiana is charms, suggesting a sexual potency that Aylmer no longer possesses.

THEMES

In "The Birth-mark," Hawthorne explores one individual's misuse of his power over another. Aylmer's concern for perfecting his wife rather than creating a new life with Georgiana suggests the harm his science has done him. Aylmer has lost a sense of balance—he has succumbed to the danger of devoting oneself exclusively to a single principle. In doing so, he has lost the connection to his heart, the connection that would allow him to sympathize with Georgiana rather than treat her as an object in an experiment. Hawthorne does not condemn Aylmer's idealism; rather, he condemns his inability to accept the truth of human frailty and fallibility, including his own. In some ways, Hawthorne hints at the danger of making science a new religion unregulated by conscience or sympathy.

SYMBOLS

As does the veil in "The Minister's Black Veil," the birthmark becomes a dominant symbol. The narrative includes the responses of others toward it, indicating that their reactions to this mark reflect their own natures. Men who admired her saw it as a fairy's imprint, a sign of Georgiana's "magical endowments" (765) that made her desirable. Some women, jealous of Georgiana's beauty, saw the mark as a stain that impaired her appearance. Aylmer sees the mark as the one flaw that makes her imperfect and as a challenge to his own science. He has spent his life seeking the scientific ideal, and by realizing the perfect physical specimen, he believes he will achieve it. In Aylmer's dream, the mark is bound to Georgiana's heart, but Aylmer ignores the implication that to remove it removes the core of her being.

"EGOTISM; OR, THE BOSOM-SERPENT" (1843, 1846)

In stories that focus on artists and writers, Hawthorne explores the dangers inherent in their solitary pursuits, including the loss of connection to others, a tendency to become self-absorbed, and the inclination to expose the hidden secrets of other hearts. Roderick Elliston, the main character in "Egotism," is a writer who appears later as the author/narrator of "The Christmas Banquet" (1844, 1846). He is bright and talented but suffers the effects of a destructive pride and self-absorption that cost him relationships and seemingly his sanity.

The word *egotism*, defined as "the vice of thinking too much of oneself; self-conceit, boastfulness; also selfishness" (*Oxford English Dictionary*, 2nd ed.), comes into use in the early 1800s. Its usage reflects both the Romantic interest in the nature and development of the individual, including self-cultivation and self-reliance, and the concern for what happens when an individual takes self-interest to an extreme. Hawthorne explores the complexity of this problem as he demonstrates how egotism feeds upon itself. Elliston knows that his fixation is destroying him, but he is powerless to overcome it alone. In Hawthorne's story, Roderick Elliston suffers the most from his egotism, but those around him are pained by his cruelty. Only through love and forgiveness, which require connection to others, can Roderick find release from his self-absorption and return to productive wholeness.

SETTING AND PLOT

The story takes place in the unspecified hometown of Roderick Elliston, descendant of a prominent family and heir to its mansion and extensive gardens. Hawthorne provides few details about the town, and except for the central characters, no one in it is identified by proper name. All but the Elliston property recedes into the background, since Roderick Elliston himself remains cut off from any other connections to place or person.

The story has a rather simple plot. George Herkimer, Elliston's friend from days past, has arrived to see him and to deliver a message from Elliston's estranged wife. Having spent five years studying sculpture in Florence, George is shocked by the changes he witnesses in his friend. He wonders whether Elliston has suffered from mental illness or a physical disease that has produced such strange symptoms. Herkimer needs to know more about what has transpired during his absence and seeks information. Hawthorne uses this as a device to provide the reader with Elliston's history, which forms the center of the narrative. The account of Elliston's malady becomes a study of fixation and mental breakdown. It also allows Hawthorne to establish the multiple meanings associated with the bosom-serpent. Once the details of Elliston's case have been established, the narrative resumes the action of time present, as Herkimer accompanies Roderick Elliston's estranged wife Rosina to the Elliston mansion. At the moment of crisis, Elliston states what it would take to cure him, and Rosina steps forward to provide the means. The resolution presents the scene of Elliston's redemption through Rosina's love.

CHARACTERS

The main character in this tale, Roderick Elliston, is a young man from a prominent family who has become convinced that something resides within him, gnawing at his vital organs. So strong is his mental conviction that he walks with undulating motions and hisses while he talks. He has even taken on a greenish tinge, a color associated with both snakes and envy. He tries at times to exert control over the outward signs of his illness but cries out, "It gnaws me!" whenever he loses control. Listeners assume he speaks of the "snake" within biting him, but the word *gnaw* also means to afflict or trouble persistently, especially when used in a figurative sense. Thus Elliston's own words suggest the psychosomatic nature of his illness and the existence of a deep-seated emotional or moral disturbance.

Elliston's breakdown begins shortly after he separates from his wife, as a "gloom" spreads over his life. His friends attempt to discover what has happened, some focusing on physical illness, whereas others believe it is mental or moral. Elliston resents this and isolates himself within the family mansion. In desperation, he resorts to the ministration of quacks, whose outlandish claims make him an object of curiosity and gossip for the townsfolk. Elliston knows there is something profoundly wrong at his core, something he has initially nurtured there. It has grown beyond his control, and he feels powerless to rid himself of it. Elliston longs for release, yet his identity is fully bound up with his affliction, and he fears that to do away with it is to do away with himself.

Two other characters who play a part in Elliston's story, George Herkimer and Elliston's estranged wife Rosina, represent the community of which Elliston was once a part. They are sympathetic but idealized figures who play stock roles as Hawthorne keeps all attention focused on Elliston and his peculiar condition. Herkimer is a true friend to Elliston, which Elliston recognizes when he detects no serpent around Herkimer's heart. Herkimer's only motive is to help his friend and to restore happiness to Rosina. When she appears, Rosina functions as the redemptive woman who can draw Elliston out of himself and his painful isolation. Like Phoebe in *Seven Gables*, Rosina embodies the potential of love to restore wholeness. She also orients the resolution of the story toward the future, curtailing the influence of the past.

THEMES

The story reflects Hawthorne's interests in the possibilities of transformation, a theme that governs his later romance *The Marble Faun*. Through Roderick Elliston's experiences, Hawthorne traces the negative change that occurs when someone loses his connection to others and becomes totally self-absorbed. He also, in a more abrupt turn, presents the positive transformation that love accomplishes through the agency of those who are truly compassionate. Since Elliston is a writer, Hawthorne uses this tale to underscore a writer's need to maintain bonds of connection and belonging that create balance against the solitude and isolation that often mark a writer's life.

SYMBOLS

As he did in "The Birth-mark," Hawthorne creates a dominant symbol in "Egotism," one more unnerving and repulsive. Using the image of a serpent that has invaded a man's body, Hawthorne creates an unsettling tale of Elliston's obsession and isolation. The serpent, often associated with temptation and sin, represents the destructive element at Roderick Elliston's core. It also assumes other meanings as the narrative recounts the course of Elliston's illness. As his symptoms become more pronounced and his sense of superiority increases, Elliston confronts others about the serpents they harbor within, uncannily identifying the desires and resentments hidden for years. His favorite target is the heart infected with jealousy, which he describes as "an enormous green reptile, with an ice-cold length of body, and the sharpest sting of any snake save one" (788). Elliston becomes like the Reverend Mr. Hooper of "The Minister's Black Veil," as he forces people to confront daily their own sinfulness and failings. His actions, like Hooper's, do not create a sense of connectedness through human frailty, instead inspiring fear and resentment.

In a story Elliston hears from his black servant Scipio, the snake also represents a destructive family legacy. According to Scipio, a snake has lurked in the fountain on the Elliston property ever since the arrival of the first settlers. It infected Elliston's great-grandfather and tormented him. Elliston discounts the idea, but through Scipio's story, Hawthorne introduces questions about the sins of the fathers that he returns to in *Seven Gables*.

"THE ARTIST OF THE BEAUTIFUL" (1844, 1846)

Concerned by an American culture that increasingly valued the marketable and useful, Hawthorne feared it made little room for the beautiful and artistic. Given his own choice to pursue a career in belles lettres when many of his classmates were establishing themselves in business or the law, Hawthorne brings a sympathetic perspective to the efforts of the artist. Because he differs from his peers, Owen Warland, the main character in "Artist," often finds himself isolated or misunderstood. Even the woman he loves cannot respond to his dreams and goals. Some critics feel that the insignificance or narrowness of Owen's creative work qualifies or limits Hawthorne's defense of him. Owen's dedication to his art and his success in creating something beautiful, however, allow him to transcend the limits of other people's visions.

SETTING AND PLOT

Set in a nineteenth-century New England village, "The Artist of the Beautiful" reflects the culture's endorsement of the Protestant work ethic. The people of the village are hardworking and practical. They do not believe in wasting time and have little room for play, as indicated by Peter Hovenden's derogatory remarks about toys. Descendants of the Puritans, they hold suspect all things "vain and idle," such as the pursuit of creativity or the exercise of the imagination for its own sake. They view all aspects of life from a utilitarian perspective: That which is not useful has no place in their world.

The story's time period reflects an era of transition in American culture. Owen Warland gains his training as Peter Hovenden's apprentice in a production system based on small shops and master craftsmen. The early nineteenth century, however, reflects the growing presence of industrial technology in the steam engine, water power, and the "cotton-machine." By the 1830s, the factory system for mass production has been established in New England. This emerging technology will eventually displace artisans like Robert Danforth, "the man of main strength" whose blacksmith forge and "blow of hammer upon anvil" (912) tie him to an earlier era. Although his practicality is valued by his community, Danforth's own lack of creative insight will limit his ability to adapt to a new world.

Hawthorne constructs his plot in three sections. The first consists of exposition that introduces all of the main characters, establishes contrasts between them, and describes the dominant value system of the culture. Hawthorne presents this through the conversation between Peter Hovenden and his daughter Annie, their encounter with Robert Danforth, and Danforth's visit to Owen Warland's shop. At the end of Danforth's visit, Hawthorne introduces the pattern that will govern the long middle section as Owen, reacting to Robert's brute nature, crushes the object on which he has been working. From this point on, Owen endures cycles of creativity and despair. His despair often results from his feelings of failure and his dismay over rejection by others, especially Annie. Owen hopes that Annie can appreciate his gifts and dreams of winning her love.

The middle section follows Owen through these cycles. For a period, he attempts to conform to his society's values, applying himself "to business with dogged industry" (913). After another demoralizing encounter with Hovenden, however, Owen retreats to the woods, romantically seeking nature's restorative power. He returns to his creative task, only to be disheartened by Annie's inability "to comprehend him" (917) and her failure to sympathize with his endeavor. A literal change in fortune through inheritance provides Owen with material comfort. Again conforming to his culture's values, he becomes lazy and intoxicated, until he is reawakened to the ideal by the appearance of the butterfly in spring. His final crisis occurs with the news of Annie's forthcoming marriage to Danforth. Upon hearing this news, Owen falls into "a fit of illness" (922) and for a time abandons his artistic dream. Fortunately, his artistic spirit "was not dead, nor passed away; it only slept" (923).

Having suffered the vicissitudes of life and the unpredictability of the creative spark, Owen emerges as an artist in the final section. His various trials and rejections have forced him to grow and to trust his own insight. He explains,

"[T]his butterfly is not now to me what it was when I beheld it afar off, in the day-dreams of my youth" (927). He visits the Danforths and Peter Hovenden to give them the gift of the butterfly, to offer them a piece of the creativity missing from their lives, but it is a gift they cannot appreciate or accept. At the end of the story, Owen realizes that it is the process of creation that ultimately matters for him, not the product, which others may destroy.

CHARACTERS

Each of the characters in "The Artist of the Beautiful" represents a specific idea or attribute, so that the story can be read as an allegory of the Romantic ideal in a materialist age or of the struggle to realize the creative impulse in a mundane world. Hawthorne, however, fully develops his characters so that they are interesting and believable outside the parameters of allegory. He enhances their development through the contrasts that emerge among them.

The artist Owen Warland is a diminutive figure whose main interests in life are the Beautiful and the Ideal. His lack of physical presence indicates that his energy goes into thought. His resistance to his culture's emphasis on using time productively, reflected in his creative manipulation of timepieces, reinforces his desire to achieve something that stands outside of time. Owen is the only character who engages the spiritual dimension of life, and he is willing to sacrifice earthly success to do so. Owen is not immune to the range of human emotions and expresses the need for love and sympathy, although he does not find them in his community. His isolation is a source of both pain and power. When he learns of Annie's upcoming marriage, he suffers physical illness and retreats into a childlike state, regressing toward a happier time when Annie was his playmate. Some readers interpret this as a sign of Owen's fear of adult sexuality, which demands engagement with someone other than the self. While he longs for Annie's company and support, his lack of attachment and obligation to others frees him to pursue his artistic ideal. Hawthorne expresses the difficulty in finding the balance between Owen's artistic isolation and the companionship that demands the sacrifice of his ideals.

Hawthorne develops one contrast to Owen Warland through the character of Robert Danforth. A large man whose work reflects his physicality, Danforth prides himself on his prowess. He is loud and to Owen displays a "hard, brute force" (912) that overwhelms the refined and spiritual. Danforth does not dislike Warland, but he does not understand him. Danforth's vision is grounded in the practical. His questions to Warland about perpetual motion indicate that his concept of the creative is tied only to what can be made useful. Sensitive to class issues related to occupation, Danforth fears that Annie will prefer Warland's "genteeler business," since Owen's work involves greater finesse and mental acuity than his own. Once he is married to Annie, Danforth no longer perceives Warland as a threat. He dismisses Owen by claiming that Warland's labor is a "waste" (928), echoing the sentiments of his father-in-law.

Peter Hovenden offers another contrast to Owen Warland through attitude and outlook. He, too, has been a watchmaker, yet he admires the physical power of Robert Danforth and guides his daughter toward him as a husband. Hovenden is judgmental, especially toward those who hold values different from his own. A product of his culture, Hovenden values a practical sensibility, a firm grasp on reality, and a no-nonsense approach to life. He is concerned with material comfort, especially since his own failing eyesight has left him unable to continue in watch repair and "too poor to live at his ease" (908). The detrimental power of Hovenden's scorn is evident when he attempts to touch the butterfly Owen has made. It "drooped its wings" and "grew dim" as though dying (929), a reflection of the impact such scorn has had on Owen over the years. When his grandson crushes the butterfly, Hovenden "burst into a cold and scornful laugh" (930), as though this gesture proved the superiority of his ideas and values over Owen's.

During the early part of his life, Owen hopes that Annie Hovenden will recognize his love for her and respond in kind. Unfortunately, she is heavily influenced by her father, and although sensitive to Owen's feelings, she cannot appreciate him or his genius. She is attracted to the beauty and wonder in what he creates, but she, like her father and husband, does not value beauty for its power to move the soul. Annie's procreative accomplishment in the birth of her son presents a parallel to Warland's creative act in producing the butterfly. Annie sees her son as an innocent, but he has inherited his family's traits, especially those of his grandfather. He grasps at the butterfly as something to control, reducing it to "glittering fragments" (930).

THEMES

Concerned about the place of creativity in American culture, Hawthorne focuses on the struggle of the artist to realize his dream. The final scene of the story also presents the need to find a middle way between two extremes. Owen has sacrificed his connection to people to achieve his dream, whereas the Hovenden-Danforth family risk a limited future by being mired in the material and utilitarian. Hawthorne draws clear distinctions between those who see only analytically or practically and those who see imaginatively. He suggests that these two perspectives are actually complementary and necessary for a balanced life.

SYMBOLS

The butterfly, both living and created, serves as the central symbol in this tale. It is an image often associated with the soul or the spirit, so that its return to Owen Warland, especially in the spring, stimulates a resurrection of his own spirit. The butterfly that he creates symbolizes his attempt to make tangible an ideal. Its lifelike aspect suggests how close Owen has come, yet he knows that his goal is unattainable in the realm of human time and materiality. Hawthorne often used the butterfly as a metaphor for fanciful or imaginative activity (Baym, *Career* 58–59). Interestingly, the word *butterfly* is used to label an individual interested in frivolous pleasure, reflecting the way Owen's culture views him.

"RAPPACCINI'S DAUGHTER" (1844, 1846)

This tale, like many of Hawthorne's, contains strong allegorical elements. Early criticism treated it as an allegory of religion and the crisis of faith. Recent approaches explore many other possibilities. From a psychological perspective, critics explore the story's reflections of Hawthorne's personal anxieties about women in his life and about the nature of masculinity. Feminist critics have examined its treatment of the images of woman, especially in light of gender roles in the nineteenth century. Historicists have traced its connections to theological, philosophical, and scientific controversies that shape its underlying tensions. The range of possible interpretations indicates the story's richness. When considered in the company of the stories discussed earlier, "Rappaccini's Daughter" reveals Hawthorne's continuing concern over destructive aspects of human behavior, including the willingness to exploit others for one's own ends.

SETTING AND PLOT

For years readers assumed that "Rappaccini's Daughter" took place in the nineteenth century, but historical research now places the tale in the early sixteenth century. The action of "Rappaccini's Daughter" takes place in Padua, Italy, site of one of Europe's oldest universities. During the Renaissance, the University of Padua was known for its faculty's research in science and medicine. In the late sixteenth century, Galileo taught there. The city also contains a large botanical garden first cultivated in the sixteenth century. The focal point of the action in Hawthorne's story is Rappaccini's garden. Dr. Rappaccini, a man of science interested in the medicinal properties of plants, has created a garden of great physical beauty but also of grave danger. In this garden,

Giovanni experiences temptation and loss. The garden as a setting also evokes other literary gardens, including the biblical Garden of Eden and the Eden of Milton's *Paradise Lost* (1667).

The story begins with elements often found in a bildungsroman, a type of novel about a young man's growth and maturity. These elements include Giovanni's journey to the city, his encounter with a potential mentor in Baglioni, his desire for knowledge, and his experience of love (or what he calls love). Their presence reveals Hawthorne's interest in dramatizing Giovanni's transition from innocence to experience or knowledge. Hawthorne develops one side of this process through a series of episodes that reveal Giovanni's increasing intimacy with Beatrice, then his rejection of her. The opposing pattern of Giovanni's development appears as Hawthorne inserts encounters with Baglioni between each episode with Beatrice. Baglioni creates doubts and suspicions about Beatrice, becoming more dire in his warnings the more involved with her Giovanni appears.

Hawthorne uses physical proximity to convey the changes between Giovanni and Beatrice. Initially Giovanni observes Beatrice from afar, gazing down from his balcony into the garden. In their next encounter, he speaks to her from the balcony and tosses her a bouquet of flowers. Determined to pursue their relationship, Giovanni gains entrance to the garden to meet Beatrice face-to-face. Although they develop an "intimate familiarity" (995) through conversation, Giovanni and Beatrice have no physical contact, save the time she stops him from picking a flower. Her touch leaves a "purple print" upon his hand (994).

As the relationship between Giovanni and Beatrice grows, the dislike and suspicions voiced by Baglioni intensify. His first encounter with Giovanni entails a discussion of Rappaccini's science and lack of humanity. Baglioni characterizes Rappaccini in Faustian terms. He also suggests that Beatrice is unnatural because of the education her father has given her. In their next encounter, Baglioni claims that Giovanni is becoming one of Rappaccini's experiments and that Beatrice has a hand in it. Time passes before they meet again, at which time Baglioni tells the story of the poisonous woman given to Alexander the Great, then claims that Rappaccini has similarly made his daughter poisonous. Baglioni gives Giovanni an antidote to administer to Beatrice, implying that it will free her from her father's poisonous influence.

When he realizes that he has begun to absorb the poisons that allow Beatrice to function in her father's garden, Giovanni's anger drives him back to her to accuse and punish. He confronts Beatrice with mixed motives. On the one hand, he plans to reject her; on the other, he wants to convince her to drink the antidote so that he might "redeem" her and lead her "by the hand" to an "ordinary" life beyond the garden walls (1003). In his rush to shame Beatrice for her father's actions and her own, Giovanni wounds her with brutal words. The antidote he gives her compounds the damage. Like Aylmer in "The Birth-mark," Giovanni cannot accept Beatrice as she exists and insists that their love can only continue if she changes. Willing to risk anything out of love for Giovanni, Beatrice, like Georgiana, submits, and like Georgiana, she dies.

CHARACTERS

Four principal characters engage in the conflict of "Rappaccini's Daughter." The men, Dr. Rappaccini, Professor Baglioni, and Giovanni, all have ties to the academic community. While Giovanni has not yet assumed a professional career, Rappaccini and Baglioni participate in the empirical and analytical modes of science. Beatrice, on the other hand, interacts with the world of nature.

Arriving in Padua to continue his studies, Giovanni Guasconti lives for the first time away from home. On the threshold of maturity, he demonstrates aspects of naïveté and innocence. As a student, he remains easily influenced by the ideas and philosophies of others. He has come to Padua to further his academic knowledge, but Hawthorne reveals that he also needs to know more about himself, the world, and love. Giovanni also must learn to "read" or interpret the actions and words of others, since they at times conceal true motives beneath pleasant or noble surfaces. Giovanni's youth is also reflected by his pride in his appearance and his sometimes shallow, sometimes uncontrolled emotions. His loss of innocence comes not through sexual initiation or knowledge but through his complicity in Beatrice's death.

Dr. Rappaccini and Professor Baglioni are competing men of science. Rappaccini, slender and sickly, has an expression "marked with intellect and cultivation" but does not express "much warmth of heart" (978). He appears in the opening of the story tending his garden, then retreats until the end when he finds Beatrice dying. Although not a visible actor, he has manipulated the situation from behind the scenes, gradually introducing poisons to Giovanni's system that will allow him to join Beatrice. Rappaccini has a dim view of ordinary human experience and claims that he infused his daughter with poisons to make her invincible. He believes that by being "as terrible as [she is] beautiful" Beatrice can avoid a woman's weakness and vulnerability. But Rappaccini has only given her a physical armor, not anticipating that her emotions, her heart, would make her vulnerable. He, too, is like Aylmer in his inability to accept a woman's natural being.

While Rappaccini gives Giovanni physical poisons, Baglioni poisons his thoughts. He claims that he only wishes to protect the son of an old friend, but Baglioni is a professional and personal rival of Rappaccini. His jovial demeanor and "apparently genial nature" conceal his ambitious plans. He hopes to destroy Rappaccini's reputation as a scientist-physician, even if it costs Beatrice's life or happiness. Although he claims that Rappaccini lacks humanity or a moral sense, Baglioni is little better. He sees Giovanni primarily as an instrument through which he can accomplish his own ends.

The most complex character of the story, Beatrice has within her poison-tainted body a pure heart, an irony that builds tension in the story. She displays a depth of feeling that contrasts with Giovanni's shallowness. The only character to act out of genuine love for another, Beatrice suffers for others' hard-hearted behavior. She has no freedom to define herself and is subject to the barriers her father has placed around her. She also suffers from a lack of human contact, as the intensity of her conversations with Giovanni reveals. The inability to receive and show affection through touch has magnified her loneliness. Her character also reflects the dualism associated with female nature in a patriarchal culture in that she is simultaneously beautiful and pure while being a source of danger and entrapment. Highlighting this dualism, Beatrice's name links her to the heavenly guide in Dante's *Paradiso* (c. 1321) and to Beatrice Cenci, who was executed for murder (see "Allusions" in Chapter 8).

In addition to the major characters, one minor character appears, Giovanni's landlady Lisabetta. She provides information to Giovanni when he first sees the garden. More significantly, she provides him access to the garden through a secret passage, for which Giovanni pays her in gold.

THEMES

Hawthorne continues to explore issues that have been of concern to him, especially the ambiguities in human experience. Through Giovanni's quest to understand the mystery of Beatrice, he has an opportunity to learn more about himself as well. Unfortunately he engages in little introspection, spending most of his time trying to sort out the details that accumulate about her. He is not sure whom to trust, Beatrice, Baglioni, or himself. By developing the duality of the garden and of Beatrice, Hawthorne suggests that the world and human experience contain both beauty and danger, but that the greatest danger comes from a hardened and selfish heart.

SYMBOLS

When he sees it from his window, Giovanni thinks of the garden as a source of symbolic language that will "keep him in communion with Nature" (981). Many of the images in the garden convey symbolic import, but two that stand out are the fountain and the purple-flowered plant. The fountain itself, sculpted with rare art, lies shattered in ruins. It represents the heights of human creativity and the fact that all human creations or constructions are subject to time and nature. The spring that feeds the fountain continues to flow like the life force of nature, unrestricted by human contrivance. Giovanni associates the waters with an immortal spirit, as Donatello does in *The Marble Faun*. The waters feed the plants of the garden, whether or not they are poisonous. In the midst of a pool formed by these waters sits the shrub that bears magnificent purple flowers, the shrub Beatrice calls "sister." Traditionally, flowers have been used as symbols for young women, representing their beauty and their sexuality. The deadly poison of the purple flower makes it untouchable, as is Beatrice. She lavishes physical attention on the plant, since she cannot embrace even her father. Through this link between the flowering plant and Beatrice, Hawthorne heightens the presence of dangerous beauty.

"ETHAN BRAND" (1850, 1852)

Another of Hawthorne's seekers who sacrifices his connections to humanity, Ethan Brand has spent his life searching for the "Unpardonable Sin." Claiming that he has found this sin within himself, Brand returns to the limekiln where his journey began. In a tale laden with Faustian allusions, Hawthorne posits the dangers of intellectual obsession that crushes other facets of the self and other people. Like some of Hawthorne's other solitary figures, Ethan Brand has allowed his life to shift out of balance. Instead of attempting to regain that balance, Brand plunges headlong into the flames that first stimulated his intellectual pursuits.

SETTING AND PLOT

Drawing upon notes he had made from his own travels through the Berkshire Mountains of western Massachusetts, Hawthorne sets his story in the shadow of Mt. Greylock. A rural and sparsely populated area in the early nineteenth century, the location contributes to the loneliness that marks the night of Brand's return. The tale takes place before the kiln that Brand once tended. The kiln is used to reduce marble through intense heat to produce lime. The kiln provides "a fierce light" that partially illuminates the scene, its heat and bright flames associated with hellfire. This artificial brightness overwhelms the "tender" light of the half-moon, a source of illumination associated with nature and the natural. These contrasts between the natural and the artificial or manmade are significant, for Hawthorne asserts that in his quest Brand has sacrificed his natural sympathies, that his "inner lights" have led him astray rather than serving as a guiding beacon.

The plot of "Ethan Brand" presents five interrelated scenes that culminate in Brand's final "homecoming" as he follows his journey full circle, literally returning to dust at the end. Hawthorne also makes use of circle imagery as he arranges the characters before the kiln. The first circle includes Bartram and his son Joe, who are tending the kiln. The arrival of Brand enlarges the circle, as he engages in conversation with Bartram, reflecting on his journey and what he has discovered. The third scene presents an encounter between Brand and the older men from the village, each of whom shows signs of the struggle with life. In this scene and the next, the circle expands as Hawthorne delineates the range of humanity from whom Brand distances himself. The fourth scene encompasses the arrival of the village youth and a wandering German Jew. The final scene focuses upon Brand's solitary tending of the kiln and his suicide, followed by the discovery of his remains as Bartram and Joe are once again the only figures before the kiln.

CHARACTERS

Dressed to blend in with the local scene, Ethan Brand appears out of nowhere, his presence first announced by a roar of laughter. His thin face and grizzled hair indicate that he is no longer young, but the glow from his burning eyes reveals that a fierce energy, like that of the limekiln, resides within him. He has an almost gaunt aspect, as though his obsessive quest has consumed his physical substance as well as his life. His scornful laugh echoes that heard in "My Kinsman, Major Molineux" but is even bleaker.

Brand admits that he has found the unpardonable sin within himself, that it is "the sin of an intellect that triumphed over the sense of brotherhood with man, and reverence for God" (1057). But he says this with pride, rather than remorse, claiming that he would do it all again. His quest has given him an identity that sets him apart from the broken individuals he encounters on his return, but the effects of his "sin" are revealed through these encounters, for Brand has no sympathy or compassion. Life for him has become as tattered and worn out as the pictures in the diorama, and nothing moves him. His final words acknowledge the gulf that has opened between him and the world, human and natural.

In contrast to Brand, Bartram, the current tender of the kiln, is an earthy figure, "begrimed with charcoal," who spends little time in thought. Concerned with the material aspects of life, he ignores abstract and intangible issues. He views the natural world only in terms of how it will provide him with a means to make his living. He remarks at the end that his "kiln is half a bushel richer" with the addition of Brand's remains. Initially he assumes Brand is drunk or mad, trouble in either case. When alone with Brand, Bartram feels the stirrings of his own conscience but shifts his thoughts to stories of Brand's past to avoid confronting his own inner darkness. He is a man intent on surviving in his world, even if it means closing off parts of himself to avoid vulnerability.

Believing that men must shield themselves from vulnerability, Bartram rebukes his son Joe for his sensitivity and sensibility. Joe is not yet hardened by life, not yet cut off from the natural world nor from the honest expression of his emotions. He fears Brand even though he is intrigued by him and remains in the background, often hiding in his father's shadow. He also possesses a "tender spirit" that allows him to view Brand with compassion, for Joe "had an intuition of the bleak and terrible loneliness in which [Brand] had enveloped himself" (1063). That Joe is expected to harden himself to life becomes evident at the end, when his father, hearing his relief at Brand's departure, calls him up to the top of the kiln to see Brand's skeleton amid the lime. Ironically, Bartram does not see that Brand's end results from his own hardness of heart.

Life in this mountain region is harsh and takes its toll. Among the figures who join Bartram and Brand at the kiln, the stage-agent, the lawyer, and the doctor all reflect the ravages of life in an unforgiving environment. To compensate for this, the three villagers have resorted to drink and encourage Brand to do the same. They reflect one avenue of life that Brand might follow upon his return. But he rejects them for their "vulgar modes of thought and feeling" (1059), unable to look with sympathy upon their condition. Likewise, he avoids answering the question posed by the anxious old man who seeks his daughter Esther. Brand knows that he has been the agent of this daughter's exploitation but fails to express remorse.

The other figure with whom Brand interacts briefly is the German Jew who has appeared in the company of the village youth. He is an itinerant entertainer, a man viewed as an outcast in the parochial world of New England. In his treatment of this character, Hawthorne alludes to the legend of the Wandering Jew, a man who spurned Christ on the road to Calvary and was condemned to wander the earth till Judgment Day. Brand, who has spurned God and his fellow beings, realizes that he faces the destiny of a wanderer, should his life continue. The Jew's German background and his use of the diorama also link him to early versions of the Faust legend, in which Faust was a wandering magician who reputedly had supernatural powers.

THEMES

In what may be one of his bleakest tales of isolation and self-absorption, Hawthorne explores the effects of a negative quest that leads not toward wholeness but toward fragmentation. Although Brand believes he has achieved a distinction in life, having found the "Unpardonable Sin," his pride and his hardness of heart are not enough to sustain him in the world. Through Brand's failure, Hawthorne emphasizes the need for connection and for compassion. He treats Brand's homecoming as an ironic gesture: When one has lost the ability to feel for others, one no longer has a place called home.

SYMBOLS AND ALLUSIONS

To enrich this tale, Hawthorne uses many symbols and allusions. The symbolic value of circles comes into play as Hawthorne uses them to recall the cycles of life and of night and day. He draws on the image of the circle as a boundary to convey belonging and isolation, since it can define who stands inside and who is excluded. He also uses the image of a circle when he describes the dog who chases its tail in a futile exercise, suggesting that Brand's journey has been the same.

The diorama symbolizes life for Brand. A diorama is a device through which one views scenes whose depth and contours are created by the manipulation of light. For Brand, who in his intellectual quest has sought to see the light itself, the pictures are all a sham. When he looks into the diorama, he sees nothing, conveying the nihilism into which he has fallen, where moral values and life itself are meaningless.

The allusions to *Faust* reflect the popularity of the legend as retold by Goethe in 1808 and 1832. Earlier versions of the Faust legend claimed that Faust had made a pact with the devil, that in exchange for greater knowledge and magical power the devil would own his soul. In Goethe's version, Faust makes the pact and, in the course of pursuing knowledge and pleasure, destroys Gretchen, a woman who loved him, as Brand has ruined Esther. In the second portion of Goethe's work, Faust finds redemption through his connection to others, a redemption that eludes Ethan Brand.

These stories provide examples of Hawthorne's treatment of artists, scientists, and seekers. Other stories that focus on this group of characters include "The Ambitious Guest" (1835, 1842), "Dr. Heidegger's Experiment" (1837), "The Man of Adamant (1837, 1852)" "The Prophetic Pictures" (1837), and "Drowne's Wooden Image" (1844, 1846).

The Scarlet Letter
(1850)

Published in 1850, *The Scarlet Letter* was Hawthorne's first successful romance. He completed the manuscript in about six months, writing during the period immediately following his dismissal from the Salem Custom House in 1849. Drawing upon New England's history, as he had in many of his short stories, Hawthorne offered an interpretation of life in seventeenth-century Puritan society. He also examined issues pertinent to his own day, including the relationships between the individual and the state and between nature and culture. Although *The Scarlet Letter* never attained the status of a best-seller, it found a receptive audience and has never been out of print since its first appearance.

At first glance the story of *The Scarlet Letter* seems far removed from our experience, given the greater personal freedoms enjoyed in America today. Yet this sad and powerful novel continues to attract readers, as well as playwrights and screenwriters who have adapted it for stage and film. In his exploration of Hester Prynne's experience in the rigid and unforgiving atmosphere of Puritan New England, Hawthorne reveals the power of human emotions and the need for connection. He invites the reader to sympathize with Hester's plight when she is condemned by her former neighbors. He uncovers enough of Dimmesdale's inner struggle to elicit understanding for a man torn between his need to accept responsibility and his fear of punishment and rejection. He shows how the desire for revenge in Chillingworth can become all consuming, as destructive to a human being as deadly poison. As readers acknowledge the familiarity and truth of his characters' struggles, Hawthorne reveals that human conflicts and passions are not limited to one place and time.

"THE CUSTOM-HOUSE"

As a preface to *The Scarlet Letter*, Hawthorne wrote "The Custom-House," a lengthy sketch set in his own time, offering observations on the daily activities of the Salem Custom House, where he worked for approximately three years. This sketch serves multiple purposes. By allowing him to vent his frustration over the system of political appointments to government jobs, the sketch justifies Hawthorne's actions as an officer in the Custom House. He had come under fire when removed from office, accused by his political opponents of "corruption, iniquity and fraud" (Gerber 5). Hawthorne knew the criticisms leveled against him were unjust; his satirical treatment of various individuals in the sketch undercut the validity of their accusations.

But "The Custom-House" has a wider scope than Hawthorne's political grievances. He further explores the dangers of being dependent on the government or political patronage for support. Hawthorne uses the image of the eagle that rests above the door of the Custom House to introduce this theme. He explains that "many people are seeking . . . to shelter themselves under the wing of the federal eagle," not realizing that she "is apt to fling off her nestlings with a scratch of her claw" (123). Hawthorne's image suggests that the paternalism inherent in the method of political appointments creates a deceptive relationship between individuals and the state, for it implies a benevolent power when in reality the state is like the eagle who unpredictably "flings off her nestlings." As he introduces the figures in various stages of decline who people the Custom House, Hawthorne implies that this paternalism is ultimately a threat to individuality and self-realization. These comments reflect Hawthorne's uneasiness over patronage, although he, too, had relied on political connections to obtain his appointment.

Through "The Custom-House" Hawthorne also questions an author's freedom to do his (or her) best work when placed in a dependent position, always conscious of the source of financial support. At this time in his career, Hawthorne had yet to support himself and his growing family by the proceeds of his work as an author. His comments, therefore, critique the nature of an American writer's life in which he cannot survive without some type of outside assistance. He admits that since beginning work in the Custom House he finds "literature, its exertions and objects, were now of little moment in my regard. . . . A gift, a faculty, if it had not departed, was suspended and inanimate within me" (140–141). The demands of daily tasks in the Custom House leave him little energy or inclination for writing, inhibiting the very creativity that such a position was meant to enable.

In this preface, Hawthorne explores the nature of authorship and authority. He explains how he discovered the record of events that shapes his narrative and the remnant of the letter *A*. He states that the real purpose of the sketch is to establish his role as the narrative's editor. This claim of veracity for the events incorporated in the novel reflects a common practice by eighteenth- and early nineteenth-century writers of fiction. The nature of the novel (or any work of fiction) was still being debated by segments of society in Hawthorne's era. Many people distrusted narrative that was the product of the imagination or fancy, rather than based in historical fact. By reporting that some physical evidence stands behind the story, Hawthorne attempts to circumvent questions about the truthfulness of the narrative. For Hawthorne, the imagination works upon the materials presented to an author through the course of experience, and the resulting narrative contains a truth of its own.

Hawthorne also calls attention to the power of symbols to stimulate the imagination, focusing on the remnant of the letter. He claims that upon placing the letter on his breast he "experienced a sensation not altogether physical, yet almost so, as of burning heat" (146), a foreshadowing of the passion, shame, and punishment associated with the letter in the narrative to come. His sympathetic response to the power of the letter also links Hawthorne to the character of Hester Prynne, her artistry, and her role as an outsider in her community.

Lastly, Hawthorne introduces in the sketch several themes that he will explore in the romance that follows. These include the nature of civil authority and its coercive powers, the impact of isolation on the individual, and the sense of separation experienced by the artist or thinker from the rest of society. He also raises questions about the link between person and place, exploring the subconscious attraction that draws an individual back to a place of significance, even one associated with pain. Hawthorne's relationship to the town of Salem reflected this connection in his own life. He declared his departure from the town at the end of his Custom House sojourn, stating, "I shall do better amongst other faces; and these familiar ones, it need hardly be said, will do just as well without me" (157). Yet not a year later, Hawthorne returned imaginatively to Salem for the setting of *The House of the Seven Gables* (1851).

SETTING, PLOT, AND STRUCTURE

Hawthorne's choice to write a novel set nearly two centuries before his own time is a complex one. By recreating the past through fiction, Hawthorne is able to give freer play to his imagination: His narrative cannot be judged by strict comparisons to the life around him. As many source studies have shown, Hawthorne drew heavily upon the histories of New England that he had read earlier in his life. While these provided Hawthorne with the larger context for his narrative, the main characters are his own inventions.

Setting and plot development are interdependent components in this romance. Set in seventeenth-century New England, *The Scarlet Letter* depicts the era during which the Puritans were establishing their colonies. They had come to New England in hopes of establishing communities that would exemplify the religious and moral rigor that they deemed necessary for salvation. Puritans lived by strict codes of conduct that encouraged confession of sin and public repentance. They meted out severe punishment to those caught violating the laws of the community, believing that such actions threatened the cohesiveness of the settlement. The early settlers thought of themselves as founding a "city upon a hill," as John Winthrop claimed in his speech aboard the *Arabella*, convinced that the eyes of the world were upon them. This intensified both their anxieties about the success of their "errand into the wilderness" and their feelings of isolation.

Unlike many historical romances that depend upon large-scale action, changes of scene, and complicated plot lines, the narrative of *The Scarlet Letter* explores internal conflict as the main characters grapple with the implications of sin, guilt, remorse, and revenge. The action that occurs takes place in a fairly restricted area: the small settlement of Boston, its outskirts, and the forest surrounding it. Much of the action occurs indoors or in enclosed spaces, reinforcing the impression that the tensions between the characters hinge on internal struggle rather than public conflict. The scenes in the prison, in Hester's cottage, in the Governor's mansion, and in the house shared by Dimmesdale and Chillingworth also reinforce that Hester, Dimmesdale, and Chillingworth have secrets they hope to withhold from public exposure. The public settings that Hawthorne uses, the marketplace and the scaffold, are circumscribed by the other structures that define the Puritan community. Only the forest remains an unbounded space that Hawthorne links with the idea of freedom but that his characters associate with moral wilderness and danger. Hawthorne accentuates the isolation of the community and of individuals who stray beyond its bounds by describing the region that surrounds the settlement as presenting "the mystery of the primeval forest" (275).

The story of Hester Prynne begins in Chapter 2, "The Market-Place," with her public humiliation and condemnation by the community. Hester emerges from her prison cell, holding her child, the product of adultery. She mounts the scaffold, a platform that places her in clear view of those below. Separated from those around her, Hester appears an isolated figure singled out for public censure. The harsh nature of this censure is evident in the responses of the women in the crowd. Unable to deny her participation in adultery, Hester is forced to accept a punishment that will perpetually remind her and those around her of her act. She is encouraged to name the father of her child, reminded by her questioners that he, too, should bear punishment for this sin. Hester refuses. As punishment for her sin and her silence, Hester is forced to live on the outskirts of the settlement and to wear upon her clothing at all times a scarlet letter *A* to remind her and all around her of her sinful nature.

This scene on the scaffold is pivotal. All other scenes in the novel are measured against it. Hawthorne carefully structures the remainder of his narrative, bringing his main characters back to the scaffold at the center and near the end of the novel. When all four are present, the emotional and psychological impact on each is significant. Between these scaffold scenes, Hawthorne alternates chapters that focus on Hester and Pearl with those centered on Dimmesdale and Chillingworth. The contrasts between the private meeting of Hester and Chillingworth in the first half and between Hester and Dimmesdale in the second half of the narrative and the two additional scaffold scenes contribute more to character and thematic development than does plot alone.

Hawthorne creates symmetry and contrast between Hester's encounter with Chillingworth in Chapter 4 and her encounter with Dimmesdale in Chapters 16 through 18. During "The Interview," Hester must face the absent husband wronged by her act of adultery. She does so as night approaches, within the prison cell that has held her for the period of her confinement (both her punishment and her pregnancy). This setting, with its oppressive atmosphere, governs the mood of their meeting. It also reflects Hester's feelings about her marriage as a type of prison. She has been agitated, and her jailer fears that she might harm herself or her child, so he admits Chillingworth to her cell. Hester is distracted and distrustful, although her fear of Chillingworth, as her husband is now called, makes her "as still as death" (178). In the course of their conversation, she admits that she did not love him when they married but also knows that she has wronged him. Likewise, Chillingworth admits that he wronged Hester when he married someone whose youth and energy he hoped to absorb. He seeks no revenge against her but wishes to know her lover's name so that he might exact retribution on him. Hester refuses to name him but fears Chillingworth's ability to perceive the truth. Shrugging off her refusal, Chillingworth enjoins Hester to keep the secret of his identity as well. Confident that he will ultimately learn what he needs to know, Chillingworth wishes to conceal his identity to forward his purposes. His request ironically links him to Dimmesdale, who also treats Hester as a repository of secrets.

The meeting between Hester and Dimmesdale seven years later evolves into a strikingly different scene. Hawthorne develops this encounter over three chapters, the most sustained interaction between characters. The forest is described as "dismal," providing an "intense seclusion" (280), and the two meet in a moment of discomfort and "mutual dread" (281). Once they have established contact with each other through the clasp of hands, their discomfort subsides. Dimmesdale confesses his misery to Hester, and she, moved by her "still so passionate" love, reveals the identity of Roger Chillingworth. Horrified and angered by this information, Dimmesdale initially blames Hester for inflicting Chillingworth upon him but forgives her, claiming that Chillingworth's sin of revenge has been graver than their sin. As Hester pleads that "what [they] did had a consecration of its own," she and Dimmesdale are drawn together. Her continuing faith in him gives Dimmesdale hope, and he invokes Hester's strength to help them; she describes avenues of escape through the wilderness or by the sea. When Dimmesdale quakes at the possibility of venturing into the world, Hester reassures him, "Thou shalt not go alone!" (289).

The possibility of freedom from their burdens forecasts Hester and Dimmesdale's actions in the chapter that follows. Believing in the "golden light" that has created a dreamlike atmosphere around them, they further discuss plans to escape. While still in the forest, Hester removes the scarlet letter, freeing herself from its stinging weight, and removes her cap, revealing her luxuriant hair and the vitality that still exists at her core. At this moment "as with a sudden smile of heaven" (293), the sun emerges. In this light of hope Hester tells Dimmesdale that he must know their daughter, Pearl. But Pearl's entry into the scene brings with it the return of reality, for she forces her mother to resume the scarlet letter and replace the cap before approaching. Pearl unsettles Dimmesdale, asking if he will walk back into town with them (an echo of her question on the scaffold) and washing away the kiss he bestows on her.

Hawthorne develops two scenes in which Dimmesdale stands upon the scaffold, one midway through the narrative, the other near the end. "The Minister's Vigil" (Chapter 12) takes place at night when the purpose of the scaffold is controverted, becoming a place of concealment rather than exposure. Dimmesdale, unlike Hester, faces no crowd that passes judgment as he stands on the platform. Although he shrieks aloud while on the platform and imagines all the terror of a public confession, Dimmesdale engages in a "vain show of expiation" (246). Even when joined on the scaffold by Hester and Pearl, Dimmesdale cannot accept responsibility for his actions, for which Pearl accuses him, stating, "Thou wast not true!" (253). Hawthorne uses this scene to reinforce the reader's understanding of Dimmesdale's weakness and his pride. The use of *vigil* in Chapter 12's title indicates that this episode entails watching and waiting but no action that will resolve either the minister's or Hester's plight.

The final scaffold scene occurs in Chapter 23, "The Revelation of the Scarlet Letter." It follows Dimmesdale's meeting with Hester and Pearl in the forest and reveals the culmination of his inner struggle. Set within a day of public celebration rather than public punishment, Dimmesdale's exposure on the scaffold stands in stark contrast to Hester's. He stands amid all the ceremonial activity of Election Day as a man within his element, though physically weak and unsteady. He directs the movement of the other characters, summoning Hester and Pearl forward to join him on the scaffold. As he does this, "there was something at once tender and strangely triumphant" in his gesture (335). Gaining the crowd's attention, he places himself center stage. He compares his sin to Hester's and claims that her letter "is but the shadow of what he bears on his own breast" (338). The narrator then describes what follows: "With a convulsive motion he tore away the ministerial band from before his breast. It was revealed! But it were irreverent to describe that revelation" (338). Everything in this scene points to the exposure of some physical mark upon Dimmesdale, the presence of "his own red stigma" (338), but it is never directly confirmed for the reader. As Dimmesdale lies dying in Hester's arms, he beckons Pearl, who kisses him. His last words are for Hester, as he tells her all their suffering was necessary, for it served God's purpose.

The ambiguities that shape this last scene on the scaffold have troubled readers. Hawthorne reinforces this ambiguity by reporting the responses of the crowd of witnesses, among whom there is no agreement as to what has transpired. In spite of his dramatic act of self-display, Dimmesdale never states before the crowd that he is Pearl's father and Hester's partner in adultery, thus leaving open to interpretation what his final words and gestures truly mean. Hawthorne weights this scaffold scene with symbolism, especially Pearl's kiss, which seems to break "a spell" and visually demonstrates the bond that is not articulated. The reader is left to judge the sincerity and effect of Dimmesdale's confession.

The last chapter of the novel brings Hester full circle as she returns to Boston after a period in England. Upon her return, Hester voluntarily resumes wearing the scarlet letter upon her dress. Her own sorrow and loss have given her insight into the nature of human suffering, and she ministers to those who seek her counsel. When she dies, her grave adjoins that of Dimmesdale, and the two share one tombstone. The stone itself stands as an emblem for the novel, for against its dark background emerges an "ever-glowing" letter *A*.

CHARACTERS

While the novel opens with an event that highlights the relationship between the individual and the community and is almost impersonal except for the view of Hester, the remainder of the narrative focuses on the relationships and inner lives of the four main characters. Their experiences are set within the context of the larger community, but Hawthorne is more interested in their individual struggles. He paces the development of each character, at times focusing on one alone, other times presenting the character interacting with others to reveal him or her more fully. The main characters are intimately bound, but their connections are not always bonds of sympathy.

When she first appears, Hester Prynne is described as an attractive young woman. She is tall, with luxuriant hair that surrounds a face "beautiful from regularity of feature and richness of complexion" (163). Her movements reflect a natural dignity and personal strength. Standing on the scaffold, holding Pearl, she is likened to an "image of Divine Maternity" (166). Her early appearance conveys vitality and individuality, yet as Hester enters into her long period of isolation, her appearance becomes more subdued. She dresses in coarse material and drab colors, her carriage losing its buoyancy and grace. Hawthorne suggests that as Hester becomes more introspective, her life energies are withdrawn.

Taking up residence on the edge of town after her imprisonment, Hester finds that she no longer feels a part of the community. In the early years of her isolation, she is singled out for verbal abuse and scorn by the clergy, the townspeople, even the children. Those around her see Hester only in terms of the scarlet *A* she wears on her gown. She has richly embroidered the letter, revealing her artistic ability, which further incenses some who wish to see her punished. Because the birth of her child makes Hester's sin public, she openly proclaims her fault in this way, as if to own the symbol of her fall and redefine it. She also dresses Pearl in rich shades of red, reinforcing the impression that her child is a living version of the letter. Hester's ability in needlework and her quiet way of life ultimately lead to a reappraisal by the townsfolk. Her acts of charity as a "self-ordained . . . Sister of Mercy" (257) cause many in the community to reinterpret the letter, "that it meant Able; so strong was Hester Prynne, with a woman's strength" (257).

While the town's view of Hester reflects an aspect of outward change, Hester also undergoes inner changes. From the beginning of her solitude, she feels the sting of punishment inflicted upon her, so that "her imagination was somewhat affected" and she fancied that the letter "had endowed her with a new sense" that "gave her sympathetic knowledge of the hidden sin in other hearts" (192). As she spends more time in thought, Hester develops independent ways of thinking, assuming a freedom of thought that allows her to reject the world's laws. Associated by the narrator with Anne Hutchinson, another figure of rebellion, Hester questions woman's lot in life. She comes to reject the social systems that govern woman's place. Out of this thinking comes her strength, so that Hester believes herself more capable of meeting the challenges that confront her. This strength manifests itself during her meeting with Dimmesdale in the forest and in their final meeting on the scaffold.

The last view of Hester presents a figure changed yet again. Commenting on her independence of thought in Chapter 13, "Another View of Hester," the narrator claims, "The scarlet letter had not done its office" (261), implying that Hester had not submitted to the authority of the church and state, nor had she truly repented of her relationship with Dimmesdale, submitting herself to God's judgment and mercy. In the conclusion, Hester returns to Boston, finding that there is "more real life" for her there than in England. Resuming the scarlet letter of her own accord, Hester becomes a counselor to those in trouble, especially women. Her counsel advocates that change for women will come when the world is ready for it, and she has come to reject the role of "prophetess" of a new truth that she had once envisioned for herself.

Hester's partner in adultery, the Reverend Arthur Dimmesdale, is a young minister called to preach in New England. A learned, talented orator, he needs the affirmation he gains through his congregation's approval, as well as that of the elder clergy, especially Wilson. Because his self-image is dependent upon how those in the community see him, Dimmesdale conceals his relationship with Hester and his paternity of Pearl. He denies his responsibility for either of them and avoids being seen near them. Although he accuses himself inwardly and inflicts punishments on himself in secret, he cannot bring himself to do what he exhorts his congregation to do—publicly confess sin and perform acts of penitence for it. Dimmesdale fears the punishment that the laws of his society dictate for one who has sinned as he has, but even more, he fears the loss of image that he knows will accompany his downfall. Just as the Puritans feared the failure of their enterprise, so Dimmesdale fears the collapse of his ministry. He prefers to suffer privately with the knowledge that he is a hypocrite than to suffer publicly by exposing his weakness.

Because he cannot confess, Dimmesdale cannot relieve his guilty conscience. He has witnessed the relief that comes after the admission of sin, and his weakness and decline reflect the toll that his gnawing conscience takes. Ironically, while he suffers this inner turmoil, his public reputation rises, and he enjoys even greater popularity among the people. He tells his congregation that he is "altogether vile" and "the worst of sinners" (242), but these statements are always so general that no one suspects the truth. Dimmesdale tortures himself with visions of exposure, especially during his vigil on the scaffold, but he admits to Hester and to himself that he does not have the strength to endure such a scene.

Not until he meets Hester in the forest and explores with her the possibilities of escape does Dimmesdale experience a shift in his thinking. Initially, the possibility of escape unleashes a wildness in him. He contemplates uttering "blasphemous suggestions" (306) and "intensely poisonous infusion[s]" (307), held back by exertions of self-control. Only when he encounters old Mistress

Hibbins does the minister stop to question his plan for escape, admitting that it is like striking a bargain with the devil. As he enters his own study and sees the signs of his earlier activity around him, Dimmesdale gains a new perspective on himself, believing that the wisdom he has carried forth from the forest undermines his former life. The narrator suggests that Dimmesdale has experienced a changed understanding that gives him an adult view of himself and his situation. This costly but necessary knowledge allows him to make choices to accept responsibility for his actions, which he plans to do in his final appearance on the scaffold.

Not unlike Dimmesdale in his learning and his understanding of the human psyche, Roger Chillingworth is welcomed into Boston as a physician who will add to the common store of knowledge and contribute to the town's well-being. Although some people question his presence, most hope that he will treat Dimmesdale's illness. Friends encourage Dimmesdale to confer with him, creating one of the dramatic ironies of the narrative. Easily labeled a villain, Chillingworth is also a victim, primarily of his own need to take revenge. Obsessed with discovering the minister's secret, he uses his considerable skill to intensify Dimmesdale's psychic discomfort. He even effects an arrangement by which he and Dimmesdale are housed together so that he will have greater opportunity to observe his victim. The multiple implications of the title of Chapter 9, "The Leech," become plain: Not only does Hawthorne use the term commonly applied to early physicians, but he characterizes the parasitic relationship that develops between Chillingworth and Dimmesdale, as Chillingworth slowly saps his victim's strength.

Just as Dimmesdale shows through physical changes the effect of his torment, so, too, does Chillingworth undergo changes wrought by his zeal for revenge. As he begins to explore Dimmesdale's inner nature, a smile of self-satisfaction appears on Chillingworth's face. When he finds Dimmesdale in a deep sleep one afternoon, Chillingworth pulls back the vestment covering Dimmesdale's breast. The narrative conceals what Chillingworth sees, but his reaction suggests that it confirms his suspicions regarding Dimmesdale's secret. He reacts with "ghastly rapture," and his behavior is likened to "how Satan comports himself, when a precious human soul is lost to heaven, and won into his kingdom" (237). Following this discovery, the more obsessed Chillingworth becomes with revenge, the more twisted his body appears, so that what was once a minor defect becomes a pronounced malformation of his shoulders and spine. Through this physical twisting, Hawthorne reveals that Chillingworth's inner being has degenerated under the influence of his anger and his inability to forgive.

As the climax of the narrative approaches during the Election Day festivities, Chillingworth continues his attempts to control Dimmesdale's fate. But as

Dimmesdale calls Hester and Pearl up on the scaffold to stand with him, Chillingworth fears the loss of influence and control. To prevent this, he leaps forward "to snatch back his victim from what he sought to do!" (336), and as he hears the words of Dimmesdale's confession Chillingworth cries out, "Thou hast escaped me!" (338). This loss of purpose has a profound effect upon Chillingworth, for he withers away and dies within a year of Dimmesdale's death. In his own act of restitution, he leaves his property in England and America to Pearl.

In many respects, Pearl is the most complex character of the romance, though less developed than Hester and Dimmesdale. She is frequently identified as the living symbol of her parents' sin, by them, the townspeople, and the narrator. The other characters attempt to read her nature through their own anxieties about who she is and what she might be, fearing that as a product of sin she is Satan's child rather than a gift from God. Hester names her "Pearl" because she has come at great price, and Hester believes that Pearl is her only reason for living. Such feeling about her daughter explains Hester's response to the threats to take Pearl from her.

Pearl is beautiful, having a natural grace and lightness about her. However, she is also a mischievous child who tries to circumvent rules whenever she can. Her unpredictable responses and uncontrollable actions are described as those of a "sprite" and an "elf." Her mother's situation defines Pearl's world, and she, too, lives as an outcast. Her treatment by other children recalls the hostility and cruelty shown an outsider in "The Gentle Boy," although Pearl is a feisty opponent, unlike Ilbrahim. Because she suffers her mother's exile and exclusion by children her own age, Pearl often looks to the natural world for companionship, finding in the woods, sunshine, and babbling brook the company she seeks. In these instances, Pearl reflects a romantic connection to nature: She does not see herself as living an existence separate from it, nor does she see it as something she must fear and conquer. For Pearl, the natural world has not become a place of danger or the forest an emblem of moral chaos.

Growing up on the margins of the Puritan culture, Pearl has not been socialized to view life or people as it does. Thus, she does not enact the hypocrisy of her culture but is quick to recognize the hypocrisy of others. Pearl seeks the truth from her mother, from Dimmesdale, and from the natural world. She questions her mother about the meaning of the letter, she questions the minister about his connection to her. Pearl confronts the minister with the charge that he is "not true," implying not only his failure to tell the truth but also his lack of loyalty and commitment. Although it is the narrator who gives voice to the motto, "Be true! Be true! Be true!" (341), it might as easily have been said by Pearl.

At the end, the narrator reveals that Pearl has returned to England, where she enjoys a happier adulthood. Unlike Hester, who is tied to the place of her passion and her fall, Pearl has never absorbed the Puritan sensibility. She can escape it as neither Hester nor Dimmesdale can. The details of Pearl's adult life are not made known, but people believe she has married and feels fondly toward her mother, sending Hester small gifts of remembrance.

ROLE OF MINOR CHARACTERS

Three of the minor characters in the romance are drawn from history, although Hawthorne shapes them to suit his own purposes. By using figures from New England's historical past, Hawthorne creates a more realistic setting for his major characters.

Governor Bellingham represents the civil authority within the colony. Because the colony has a strong theocratic element, Bellingham exercises his power in conjunction with that of the ministers. The Governor, however, has traits that make him an unconventional Puritan. He likes elaborate dress, exemplified by the embroidered and fringed gloves that Hester delivers to him, and his house has ornate decoration. Although Hawthorne uses little historical detail about him, Bellingham had been involved in sexual controversies and charges of improper conduct (Colacurcio, "Choice" 110–111). His rigidity toward Hester's case in *The Scarlet Letter* provides another example of the hypocrisy that Hawthorne identifies with this Puritan culture.

The Reverend John Wilson represents the ecclesiastical authority within Massachusetts Bay. One of the senior clergy, he is depicted as unsympathetic to the problems faced by individuals like Hester. He focuses on God's judgment against sin rather than God's mercy toward sinners as he guides his congregation's spiritual development. Yet Wilson is described as kindly and is regarded as a devout and righteous leader. He serves as one model of the father, for he is an interpreter of the law and an authority, both in terms of his knowledge and in terms of the power he wields within the community. He takes a fatherly interest in Dimmesdale, solicitous of his well-being.

Mistress Hibbins, sister to the Governor, is an eccentric associated with witchcraft and the fears people have of evil in their midst. Like Bellingham and Wilson, Mistress Hibbins is drawn from historical record. A woman widowed in the 1650s, Hibbins was viewed by her neighbors as troublesome. She was accused of witchcraft in 1655 and executed in 1656. Hawthorne uses her as a figure who provokes admissions from Hester and discomfort in Dimmesdale. She claims secret knowledge gained by consorting with Satan, yet her activities are never depicted, only implied.

The townspeople are always in the background of the romance. During the opening scene, they serve as a chorus, providing commentary on what happens and reflecting the community's values through their judgment of Hester. They are not a sympathetic group, especially the women, who feel Hester's punishment has not been severe enough. Only one voice sounds a sympathetic note, but the narrative reveals that such tender natures are not meant for the work of settlement, since this young woman dies a short time later. The townspeople are again present for the Election Day scene, as Dimmesdale makes his confession. The responses to his admissions are less uniform than those that greeted Hester's appearance on the scaffold: Some believe they have seen the marks of his self-inflicted letter; others say there was nothing to be seen. Hawthorne uses the presence of the townsfolk at the opening and at the close to create a cultural frame around his tale. Their placement at these two points reminds the reader of the values and expectations that have shaped the lives of the main characters. Even though they may deviate from these values, the main characters all function against this backdrop.

THEMES

Hawthorne introduces numerous themes within his narrative. Many develop through a process of contrast, as Hawthorne examines two sides of a particular question. Among the themes that he considers are the relationship between the individual and the state, the difference between the private self and the public self, the consequences of passion and repression, and the tensions between nature and culture.

The relationship between the individual and the state, introduced in "The Custom-House," reappears in the opening chapter of *The Scarlet Letter*. This brief chapter explains that every new settlement inevitably recognizes the need to set aside land for a prison. Focusing on this symbol of punishment, Hawthorne asserts that one of the major roles of the state is to coerce individuals into obedience and conformity to the laws established by the social order. This may be necessary to maintain order and to ensure the survival of the community, but it also implies that little room exists for individual expression in a community as legalistic as that of the Puritans. Those who violate the laws or social codes, and even those who merely question, face ostracism and rejection. Hawthorne emphasizes this through mention of Anne Hutchinson, a woman who rebelled against the clerical authorities of the colony and who was driven into exile, where she died.

In the chapters that follow, Hawthorne links the civil authority with the power to punish in a community where minor infractions are treated as severely as gross offenses. Even a minor public official like the beadle announces this power when he proclaims, "A blessing on the righteous Colony of the Massachusetts, where iniquity is dragged out into the sunshine!" (164) as he draws Hester out of her cell. His words suggest that the state also has the power to investigate the activities of its members, who can do little to protect their privacy. When Hester approaches the scaffold, the narrator remarks that it is a device that promoted "good citizenship" and compares it to the guillotine in revolutionary France. Through these remarks, Hawthorne establishes an adversarial relationship between the individual and the state, especially any individual who threatens rebellion. This shapes Hester's view of those in authority and influences her interactions with them in the first scaffold scene, at the Governor's house, and in her forest encounter with Dimmesdale.

In light of this adversarial relationship in which open disregard for or disobedience of the law invites prosecution and censure, Hawthorne introduces a second theme related to the first: the difference between the private self and the public self. Each of his major adult characters presents one face to the world but reveals another in private.

During her period of life on the margins of the community, Hester appears as a docile and submissive woman, one who has accepted the punishment meted out to her and who will make no demands upon the community. She acts charitably toward those around her, even when they scorn her, and gradually wins over even the civil authorities. Beneath this surface, however, Hester has become an intellectual rebel who questions the authority of those who govern, the basis for the social order, the very nature of relations between men and women. Hester knows that to reveal these ideas may result in further punishment; therefore, she keeps her thoughts to herself. Her outward conformity allows her to conceal thoughts that are dangerous and thereby prevents her from suffering greater punishment, including death.

Dimmesdale also presents one self to his congregation while he reveals another in private, but his self-concealment reflects hypocrisy. He claims that it is the congregation that sees him as saintly and as the perfect husband for some village maiden. Dimmesdale, however, goes to great pains to preserve this image, even though he begins to show signs of his inner torment. He is especially proud of his voice and thinks it one "the angels might else have listened to and answered" (240). He acts in ways that are expected of him and is scrupulous in his public conduct toward Hester and Pearl, going so far as to lay his hand on Pearl's head in benediction as he would any child's in the community.

The very quality of his public image makes Dimmesdale's private self intolerable to him. He knows the truth and longs to announce it, naming himself "a pollution and a lie" (241). The narrator, however, reveals the full picture, that Dimmesdale's public posturing has insured that his confession will not be believed. Spurred on by his self-loathing, the minister privately inflicts physical tortures upon himself, but these, like his sham confessions, bring him no catharsis. Even in the final scaffold scene, when all is to be revealed, Dimmesdale's public image serves to sustain the expectations of his congregation, many of whom see no sign of his sin at the end.

Roger Chillingworth presents the most loathsome hypocrisy in the discrepancies between his public and private self. People assume he is a man who brings healing and good to the community and is genuinely concerned for the well-being of Dimmesdale. Nothing could be further from the truth. Since they do not know that he is Hester's husband, the townsfolk have no reason to suspect his intentions or motives. In the privacy of the house he shares with Dimmesdale, Chillingworth uses all of his skill and knowledge to delve into the secrets of the minister's heart and to inflict mental as well as physical suffering upon him. He becomes the agent of illness and torment, rather than the agent of healing he is thought to be.

The pattern of concealment of the private self and the hypocrisy associated with it relates to another theme that Hawthorne explores, the nature of passion and its repression. The most obvious passion to which Hawthorne refers is love, expressed through sexual feeling and desire, but he acknowledges the power of other passions as well, including anger.

While Hester does not speak her lover's name when she stands upon the scaffold, she never repudiates the bond between them. Through seven years of isolation, she accepts the distance required by Dimmesdale's wish to conceal their relationship. When she does meet him in public situations, she maintains a reserve that reveals no connection beyond their original ties as pastor and parishioner. Just as her change in outward appearance hides the vitality she still possesses, so this reserve signals the repression of her intense feeling for the minister.

Hester's self-control holds her in check until she meets Dimmesdale in the forest, when she can contain herself no longer. His anger over her revelation of Chillingworth's true role unleashes Hester's full display of feeling. Hester's sense of herself is fully bound up in her feelings for Dimmesdale, and she cannot abide his frowning upon her as the rest of the world has done. The threat of Dimmesdale's rejection shakes her to the core, for it redefines their relationship and means that their intercourse had no "consecration of its own" (286). For Hester, the repression or denial of passion amounts to a denial of truth.

Anger over his wife's rejection and betrayal sets in motion Roger Chillingworth's plan and eventual degeneration. Since he tells Hester that he will not seek retribution against her, Chillingworth focuses on the identity of her unnamed lover. That his victim's identity remains concealed forces Chillingworth to conceal his acts of redress as well. By internalizing his feelings and allowing one destructive emotion to dominate his relations with others, Chillingworth gradually loses his humanity.

In addition to developing themes that focus upon the nature of individuals and their experiences in the world, Hawthorne considers issues that reflect a wider scope, especially the tensions that exist between nature and culture. For Hawthorne, nature itself presents ambiguities. It can appear sympathetic to the human condition, such as the rose at the prison door, "a token that the deep heart of Nature could pity and be kind" (158). Nature brings solace to Pearl in her moments of loneliness, reflecting the romantic belief that nature offers a healing balm to the human spirit. But Hawthorne also describes "that wild, heathen Nature, of the forest, never subjugated by human law, nor illumined by higher truth" (293). Thus nature is never all positive or negative but manifests the very ambiguity that Hawthorne manipulates in his fiction.

The word *subjugated* reflects the attitude of Puritans (and the later American culture that endorsed westward expansion) toward nature. Nature must be brought under human control, ordered, cultivated, and tamed. The Puritans feared unregulated human nature; they held the same views toward physical nature. As long as that nature remains wilderness, it is a place of chaos and danger. Those who inhabit this wilderness are also in need of regulations and illumination, thus the missionary work of figures like Eliot. The tensions between a wild and a cultivated nature reflect the tensions between what Hawthorne sees as two sides of the self. One retains the impulses and instincts characteristic of natural beings; the other reflects the socializing power of culture and its institutions.

SYMBOLS

The Scarlet Letter can be read as a narrative about the nature of symbolism, including the symbolic role of language. Hawthorne remains acutely conscious of how symbols are invested with meaning and interpreted through personal experience as well as through cultural values. He is also aware that what symbols signify can change over time, just as words alter in meaning as they are used in speech and writing by different individuals.

Clearly the most important symbol in *The Scarlet Letter* is the red letter *A* itself. It assumes different meanings in the romance, depending upon the perspective of the individual who interprets it. The letter initially serves as a visible symbol of Hester's crime, the act of adultery. Gradually, however, Hawthorne introduces other threads of meaning associated with the letter, so that by the end of his narrative it has become as complex as the characters themselves. Some of the additional meanings read through the letter include "artist," "able," "angel," and "atonement."

Pearl is often referred to as the living version of the letter, a vital symbol of her mother's and Dimmesdale's sin. Pearl herself is fascinated by the letter, fixating upon it as an infant and questioning her mother about it as soon as she is old enough to talk. She perceives that in some way her own being is attached to the meanings behind the letter, but the nature of this attachment remains for her a mystery. The letter also signifies a visible bond between mother and child, and when Hester removes the letter in the forest, Pearl is distressed to discover it missing. She insists that it be replaced, reasserting her own claim over Hester's loyalty and affection that had so recently been offered to Dimmesdale. When Pearl makes for herself a letter *A* in imitation of her mother, she fashions it out of seaweed, signifying her own tie to the natural world, for green is the color of hope and of life.

Hawthorne manipulates the meaning behind other symbols in the romance as well. The scaffold, usually a symbol of exposure and ignominy, becomes both a place of concealment and a place of redemption. By altering this role for the scaffold, Hawthorne invites the reader to contemplate how things are invested with meaning by those who use and interpret them, rather than through their natures alone. Likewise, the forest can symbolize both freedom and danger.

The names of the characters have symbolic qualities as well. *Hester* recalls Hestia, the Greek goddess of the hearth and home, and Esther of the Old Testament, a woman who intercedes for her people and is often considered an image of inner strength coupled with beauty. Dimmesdale's given name *Arthur* is associated with the legends of Camelot, a kingdom ultimately compromised by adultery. His surname, *Dimmesdale*, suggests a valley of darkness, a clue to his inner state. Because he has chosen the name by which he will be identified in the community, Roger *Chillingworth*'s is also revealing of his nature. The reader discovers that he is a cold man, who behaves like a rogue in his secretive manipulations of Dimmesdale. Hester consciously gives *Pearl* a name that has symbolic value. Even Master *Brackett*, the jailer, supposedly a historical personage, has a name that reflects his occupational role as one who encloses others.

Other symbolic patterns in the narrative include Hawthorne's use of light and dark, his use of colors, especially shades of red and black, and his use of images that suggest the heart. All of these are used to create greater possibilities of meaning within the novel.

HISTORICAL CONTEXT

While life in seventeenth-century America forms the larger historical context for Hawthorne's romance, two issues within that context are of particular importance: the Antinomian Controversy and witchcraft in New England.

Through numerous references in the novel, Hawthorne links Hester to Anne Hutchinson, emphasizing Hester's role as a rebel who resists the authority of the clergy. Anne Hutchinson was an Englishwoman who had immigrated with her family to New England in 1634. The Hutchinsons followed their pastor, the Reverend John Cotton, who had fled England in fear for his life at a time when persecution of dissenting clergy was on the rise. As the daughter of a minister and an active member of the church, Hutchinson was well versed in religious matters and learned for a woman of her day. She often found fault with sermons she heard and began to hold meetings in her home for the religious instruction of other women. Soon men also attended these meetings, and word spread that Hutchinson was questioning the theology and teaching of the senior clergy. Her views were labeled "Antinomian," meaning contrary to the law. Her independence of thought provoked the clergy, and she was informally accused of witchcraft. Ultimately she was charged in civil court with sedition and in church court with heresy. Her trials resulted in her banishment from Massachusetts Bay. She and most of her family were killed in an Indian attack in New York in 1643. Hutchinson serves as a model of what might happen to Hester should she give voice publicly to the radical thoughts she entertains in her solitude.

The presence of Mistress Hibbins and her references to secret knowledge introduce the motif of witchcraft in the novel. The charge brought against those who violated the norms or expectations of the Puritan culture, *witchcraft* implied a conscious choice to separate oneself from the rules and authority of the community. The fear of witchcraft did not suddenly overtake the settlers of the Massachusetts Bay colony when they arrived in New England. The persecution of witches was prevalent in Europe in the decades that preceded settlement. King James I had an interest in the subject, and one of Shakespeare's famous tragedies performed for the king, *Macbeth* (1606), includes witchcraft. Witches were feared because they seemed to possess unexplained powers and dangerous knowledge. They were seen as threats to the order of society and to the spiritual well-being of communities because of their supposed relationship with the devil. Often individuals accused of witchcraft were those identified as free-thinkers or those who were perceived as troublesome by their neighbors. The famous witchcraft hysteria in Salem occurs in 1692–1693, nearly a half century after the period of *The Scarlet Letter*. (For information on Hawthorne's family and the witchcraft trials, see "Historical Context," Chapter 6.)

ALTERNATE READING: FEMINIST CRITICISM

Feminist scholars, interested in the condition of women in society, question how gender shapes an individual's relationship to power, the ability to exercise one's voice in a culture, the opportunities to engage in self-definition or self-realization. They often critique a male-centered or male-dominated culture (patriarchy) by examining how gender expectations control the ways men and women behave in society and with each other. Feminist critics raise these questions when they read literary texts, treating the texts as representations of a particular culture's values. *The Scarlet Letter* invites a feminist reading since it presents a woman's experience in the male-dominated society of the Puritans.

A feminist critic often begins by examining the treatment of female characters and their roles within the narrative. Hester is depicted as strong, self-reliant, and freethinking, but in the world of the Puritans, these are problematic traits in a woman. While Hester holds radical ideas about the need for change for women, she also accepts the way her culture has defined her. Her artistic expression through needlework reflects activity deemed appropriate for a woman of Hester's time, as opposed to painting or writing. Even though Hester holds radical views, the narrative ultimately places her romantic relationship with Dimmesdale above her intellectual or artistic aspirations. This treatment reflects conventional (patriarchal) assumptions about woman's nature, that she is more concerned with relationships to others and finds fulfillment through those relationships rather than through her own achievements.

In addition to examining the development of Hester as a character, a feminist analysis might also consider her role as a mother. In Hawthorne's day, a woman's highest calling was motherhood. She was expected to be the first teacher of her children, their first and most profound moral and spiritual guide. A woman declared an unfit mother was thus a failure in the defining role of her life, and Hawthorne projects this threat of failure back to Hester's day. Because Hester's role as a mother results from an immoral act, those around her have grave doubts about her suitability to raise a child. The fact that she does not follow the dominant child-rearing practices of her day that relied upon strict regulation and corporal punishment, instead allowing Pearl to exert her own will, increases concern. This makes Hester's anxiety over her custody of Pearl all the more pointed in her confrontation at the Governor's house.

To a feminist critic, this confrontation is most revealing. An episode that brings together the figures prominent in the first scaffold scene, the confrontation at the Governor's house has no audience. Unlike the stark and forbidding scaffold that exposes Hester to public view, the Governor's house has a "cheery aspect," illuminated by its ornate decoration. This appearance creates a pleasant impression inconsistent with what awaits Hester. She has learned that members of the community, including the Governor, wish to take Pearl from her so that Pearl will be reared according to Puritan expectations. In addition to the Governor, those present include the Reverend Wilson and the Reverend Dimmesdale. By arraying before Hester the authorities of this theocracy, Hawthorne reveals that the power of the Puritan state is exercised in the private as well as the public realm. He also visually demonstrates the link between gender and power.

During the scene that ensues, the men direct their questions not to Hester, as they had earlier, but to Pearl, attempting to discern whether she has learned some of the catechism or whether she is an "elf-child." When Pearl, despite Hester's best efforts with her, tells the questioners that she was not made by God but "plucked by her mother off the bush of wild roses" (213), Wilson feels they have all the evidence they need to take the child from Hester. This threatened loss of the one thing that provides her with a sense of purpose in life provokes an outburst from Hester in contrast to her silence on the scaffold. When Hester endured exposure on the scaffold, she asked for no help, drawing upon her own strength to sustain her. However, this assault upon her fitness as a mother forces her to acknowledge her weakness before the patriarchy. She calls upon Dimmesdale, as her former pastor, to help her make her case. He explains that God meant Pearl as a blessing and a retribution, so that Pearl serves as a complement to the scarlet letter. This makes Hester's custody acceptable to the Governor and Wilson.

The mother-daughter relationship is important to feminist critics because it provides opportunities to investigate alternatives to male-defined relationships. Pearl is the one figure upon whom Hester can lavish her affections, and she relies upon Pearl to give purpose to her life. Hester feels that her life has been marked by false steps; to lose Pearl would be the ultimate sign of her downfall. She often questions whether any part of herself has been transmitted to her daughter, especially when Pearl seems to ignore her. However, Pearl's attempts to fashion the letter *A* upon her own dress emphasize a connection through the body of mother and daughter. It also suggests that Pearl looks to her mother as a significant model of womanhood, even though Hester does not embody all of the feminine traits valued by their culture. The narrator's remarks at the end reveal that Hester's relationship with her daughter proved to be enduring and sustaining.

A feminist analysis also asks who has opportunities to be heard in public, to influence the values and ideas of the larger community. In this Puritan world, the men who hold positions of civil and church office are the speakers in the public realm, serving as articulators and enforcers of community standards and codes. Chillingworth, as a physician, can also lay claim to a voice of authority in that world. None of these men hesitate to speak in public, even though they may use their public roles to conceal their private truths. Hester does not speak publicly from her position on the scaffold, either at the beginning or at the end. Her avenues of expression remain in the private realm, whether it be in her meetings with the other characters or at the end when she counsels troubled souls. Her reluctance to speak out on any occasion reflects the impact her culture's values have had on her. Even though she feels rebellious toward that culture, she does not openly cross the gender boundaries it has set in place.

Hester's surrender to the expectations of her culture at the end of the novel poses a challenge for feminist critics. Many admire Hawthorne's sympathy for Hester and his articulation of the strictures culture places on women. His comments on the nature of a "true woman" and Hester's acceptance of the fact that she will not be an instrument of social change indicate, however, that he also shared in the gender expectations of his nineteenth-century culture. These expectations emphasized that a woman's gifts arose from her emotional sensitivity and that she was best suited to the domestic or private sphere. Thus, Hester's role at the end, as a counselor of women who have also suffered the wrongs of passion or great trouble, is consistent with the dominant values of Hawthorne's day.

6

The House of the Seven Gables (1851)

The House of the Seven Gables followed quickly after *The Scarlet Letter*. Begun in April 1850, *Seven Gables* appeared in 1851. It was immediately compared to its predecessor. Early critics identified links between the two works, especially the use of New England's Puritan past and the exploration of sin and retribution. Hawthorne, however, felt *Seven Gables* was more optimistic than his earlier romance and called it "a healthier product of [his] mind" (*The Letters* 451). This seems an unusual remark about a novel that features a haunted house, a family curse, and a hidden treasure. However, it underscores Hawthorne's attempt to achieve greater balance between light and darkness in this narrative. That he succeeded is evident in Herman Melville's appraisal: "We think the book, for pleasantness of running interest, surpasses other works of the author. The curtains are more drawn; the sun comes in more; genialities peep out more" (Melville, *Letters* 123).

Although Hawthorne interweaves humor and brings the narrative to a positive close, he continues in *Seven Gables* to explore issues of serious import. His characters struggle with the burden of the past and its implications, with the problem of human greed and deception, with the effects of isolation, and with the need for love and affirmation. Writing about the life of individuals in his day, Hawthorne reveals aspects of human behavior that are prevalent today. Do people still have an interest in their family past and the possibility of discovering long-lost relatives or property? Do they still dream of unexpected windfalls or of attaining wealth and power? Popular fiction, television dramas, and the evening news all reflect a continuing interest in uncovering true identities and family relationships, recovering lost fortunes, and even establishing family dynasties.

SETTING, PLOT, AND STRUCTURE

Seven Gables is set in Salem, Massachusetts, in the mid-nineteenth century. Although little of the town beyond the Pyncheon house and street appear, Salem is significant because of its history. Known for its association with the witchcraft hysteria of 1692, during which numerous residents were imprisoned or executed as witches, Salem in the early nineteenth century had distanced itself from that episode. Leading families preferred to ignore the dark side of Salem's past. A history of the town published in the 1840s celebrated its achievements during the colonial era while downplaying the persecutions that occurred (Emery 132–135). Hawthorne, whose ancestors had participated in the persecution of those accused as witches, was troubled both by this legacy from the past and by his contemporaries' wish to ignore or deny it.

Having read Salem history extensively, Hawthorne provides his own version of one family's part in the colonial past and the unsavory actions that contributed to their accumulation of property. Hawthorne uses the first chapter of *Seven Gables* as he does "The Custom-House" sketch of *The Scarlet Letter* but in inverse fashion. In *The Scarlet Letter*, he set the sketch in time present, creating a context for the story that unfolds in the past. In *Seven Gables*, he opens with a narrative of the past to create a context for the story that unfolds in time present. As in *The Scarlet Letter*, Hawthorne sets up discrepancies between the public image of a leading figure and his private realities.

In the first chapter of *Seven Gables*, he recounts the story of Colonel Pyncheon, a man of "iron energy of purpose" (356) who hopes to acquire a desirable piece of property held by Matthew Maule. The Colonel holds a position of high regard and authority, whereas Matthew Maule was "obscure" but obstinate in asserting his rights (356). Unable to obtain the land through legal maneuverings, Colonel Pyncheon presides over the execution of Maule for witchcraft. At his execution, Maule utters a prophecy against the Colonel. Charging that "God will give him blood to drink!" (358), Maule echoes a curse laid upon one of the judges at the witchcraft trials in Salem.

Through the actions of Colonel Pyncheon, Hawthorne begins to narrow the setting of the romance, focusing on the construction of the Pyncheon mansion. Not one to be dissuaded from his plans, Pyncheon builds his house atop the ground that had held Maule's home, a visual sign of his triumph over Maule. Further, the street on which the house stands is renamed from Maule's Lane to Pyncheon-street, Hawthorne's way of highlighting how those who hold power mark the land as their own. Only the well, whose sweet water had made the property valuable, retains Maule's name, but it turns brackish, its water dangerous to consume. On the day he opens his house to the community to celebrate its completion and the symbolic establishment of the House of Pyncheon, the Colonel dies. The blood upon his ruff, deemed by physicians the result of apoplexy, recalls the prophecy of Maule. Thus the House of the Seven Gables, as it comes to be called, is associated from its beginnings with deception and death.

Hawthorne uses the history of the house to create the context and atmosphere for his story set in time present, about 160 years later. The narrator describes the house as a repository of human stories, which had a "meditative look" and "secrets to keep" (374). He enhances the impression that the house itself is a living thing, claiming "that the very timbers were oozy, as with the moisture of a heart" (374). Even though the house as a human construction stands apart from the natural world, it has held within it a life force but one that has diminished over time. Age and decline mark the house and its current guardian, Hepzibah Pyncheon. It has become for her a type of prison similar to the literal prison that has held her brother Clifford as an inmate.

The house becomes the central stage within which the action of the novel occurs. Various chapter titles, such as "The Little Shop-window" (Chapter 2) and "Clifford's Chamber" (Chapter 16), suggest that Hawthorne takes the reader on a tour of the old mansion (Gray 98). Having set the physical parameters for his story, Hawthorne divides the narrative into two major sections. The first introduces the main characters and conflicts, whereas the second presents a series of crises that culminate in the death of Judge Pyncheon and the liberation of Hepzibah and Clifford. Throughout the novel, Hawthorne also makes use of a deliberately impeded narrative, in which the straightforward or linear progress of the plot is slowed or interrupted. This narrative form, a standard in detective fiction, sustains the underlying mystery of the family story that unfolds.

In the first section, the plot advances through the entrances of characters into the precincts of the house. The first figure to appear within the house in time present is Hepzibah Pyncheon. That she is the only character to appear by herself highlights her loneliness and her singular nature. Her circumstances indicate the declining fortunes of her branch of the family. For years isolated within the house, Hepzibah fears contact with strangers and even her neighbors. Much to her dismay, she feels compelled to open a cent-shop, a store that sells small household necessities and foodstuffs, as a means to secure income. Hepzibah sees this as the real decline in her fortunes, for as a genteel woman she resists the idea of participating in trade. The risks in her endeavor are made plain by the comment of a man on the street who explains that his wife had lost money in just such a venture. But Hepzibah feels that she has no choice and busies herself arranging the meager offerings in her shopwindow to attract customers. The plainness of her offerings stands in contrast to the opulent food and beverages served at the celebration of the opening of the house by Colonel Pyncheon, another sign of Hepzibah's failing resources. Although she holds a tenancy in the house until her death, Hepzibah barely scrapes by, living as much on her family pride as on any real nourishment.

Hawthorne uses a pattern of paired entrances for the remaining characters, which allows him to suggest greater meaning through comparisons. Hepzibah's first encounter with a "customer" introduces the second major character of the romance, her boarder Holgrave. Holgrave appears to reassure Hepzibah that her endeavor to support herself is a noble, not ignominious, choice. She refuses Holgrave's money for the purchase of some biscuits, offering them as a gesture of friendship. This interaction serves as a rehearsal for Hepzibah's encounter with an actual customer, young Ned Higgins, a schoolboy in search of gingerbread. Initially, Hepzibah treats him as a younger version of Holgrave, giving him the desired gingerbread while refusing his proffered cent. When he returns in search of more, however, Hepzibah claims his payment. In a passage tinged with ironic language, the narrator indicates the significance of this act for Hepzibah and its insignificance to the larger world: "The sordid stain of that copper-coin could never be washed away from her palm. . . . The structure of ancient aristocracy had been demolished by him, even as if his childish gripe had torn down the seven-gabled mansion!" (396).

As Hepzibah's day of business continues, Hawthorne provides the first glimpse of the antagonist of the romance, Judge Jaffrey Pyncheon. Although he does not enter the house, his appearance upsets Hepzibah and undermines her brief feeling of competence. A clever, successful man, Jaffrey always grasps for more, much as Colonel Pyncheon had done to build the initial family fortune. Juxtaposed to the turmoil Jaffrey's appearance instigates, the calm that accompanies Uncle Venner's arrival reflects his nature. Uncle Venner is a man of little means who speaks often of ending his days at the poor farm. Like Holgrave, he reassures Hepzibah about the nature of her work. He also alludes to the return of Hepzibah's brother Clifford, whose shadowy existence in Hepzibah's life has been hinted at by the narrator.

The much anticipated arrival of Clifford is delayed in the narrative by the unexpected arrival of Hepzibah's cousin Phoebe. Hawthorne brings Phoebe and Clifford into the house within hours of each other, but by strikingly different means. Phoebe arrives at the front door of the house, having used a public coach for transportation. Hepzibah initially plans to send her away after one night's lodging but discovers that she enjoys Phoebe's company and appreciates the way she makes herself useful. Meanwhile, Clifford enters the house as he enters the narrative, under the whisper of concealment. Phoebe detects his presence when she hears the "murmur of an unknown voice," senses "respiration in an obscure corner of the room," and hears "a footstep mounting the stairs" (434–435), all suggesting the presence of a ghost. Returning from years of imprisonment for a crime he did not commit, Clifford meets the world in a tentative manner. The ethereal qualities of his nature amplify the impression that he lacks substance or life force. Phoebe's first direct encounter with him occurs in the chapter "The Guest" (Chapter 7), and Hawthorne plays on a guest/ghost pun.

While Clifford enters the house unsure that he belongs, Jaffrey enters the shop as one who already owns it. He presents himself as a man of substance and readily assumes the role of antagonist, although he tries to conceal his purpose behind the mask of benevolence. Jaffrey approaches the house like one besieging a fortress, and his presence introduces the major conflict of the plot. Convinced that Clifford knows the secret to the lost family fortune, Jaffrey intends to confront him, whatever the cost. Hepzibah physically blocks his assault upon the house and upon Clifford, but the narrative makes clear that this is just his first attempt. Through Jaffrey's agency, the house becomes a space defined by contention and conflict, rather than the sanctuary Hepzibah had hoped it would be.

A form of sanctuary is available in the Pyncheon garden, which functions as a mediating space between the house and the world. This garden is not Eden, however, for at its center lies Maule's well, the pool of tainted water. In the context of the garden, Hawthorne introduces the love story subplot of Phoebe and Holgrave. Having heard a little about his radical ideas and companions from Hepzibah, Phoebe meets Holgrave with mixed feelings. But by placing their meeting in a garden that Holgrave has been cultivating, Hawthorne suggests that Holgrave is not entirely a rebellious figure. His careful tending of the garden, growing vegetables that provide nourishment for the inhabitants of the house, reflects his sense of responsibility. It also links him to an agrarian tradition based upon ties to the land and a settled way of life.

Chapter 10, "The Pyncheon-Garden," presents a moment of stasis that separates the first section of the narrative from the second. Conscious that his narrative development slows, Hawthorne admits that this chapter's effect hinges on the reader's sympathetic understanding of the garden's appeal, for it represents in miniature a pastoral existence free from worry and tension. The main characters, with the exception of Jaffrey, gather in the garden on a Sunday afternoon. Here they find peace and contentment seldom enjoyed in their daily experiences. The garden reflects the years of neglect it has withstood, yet it shows signs of becoming productive once again under Holgrave's tending. In the garden especially, Phoebe and Holgrave are shown to have nurturing qualities that have the power to transform. Unfortunately, none of the characters can stay in this garden; it offers only temporary respite. Hawthorne suggests that until the various conflicts in which the characters are enmeshed can be resolved, they cannot rest.

Disrupting the tranquility, Hawthorne impels the characters forward into a series of crises culminating in the last confrontation with Jaffrey and his death. The first crisis involves Clifford, who has functioned primarily as an observer of the action around him. While viewing a street scene from the arched window of the family home, he longs to reengage the world. He attempts to step onto the balcony, from which he might leap toward the action below. Held back by Phoebe and Hepzibah, who fear for his sanity, Clifford exclaims, "[H]ad I taken that plunge and survived it, methinks it would have made me another man!" (495). He resigns himself and Hepzibah to imprisonment within the house, which he believes they are destined to "haunt" as "ghosts" (498).

From this moment of tension, Hawthorne shifts the focus to Holgrave and Phoebe, who meet again in the garden. Holgrave reveals more of his views on the problem of the past and tells Phoebe that he has written a story based on Pyncheon family history. He hopes to sell his story to a popular magazine and invites Phoebe to hear it. He then recounts the tale of Alice Pyncheon, an earlier occupant of the House of the Seven Gables. Through this story, Hawthorne provides information about a generation of Pyncheons in the eighteenth century and the continuing conflict between the Pyncheons and Maules. He also intimates the seductive potential of art through the story's effect on Phoebe.

In Holgrave's account, Gervayse Pyncheon risks his daughter Alice's well-being in the hopes of discovering the location of documents that would enhance his fortunes. Alice is bewitched by the carpenter Matthew Maule, who plans to humble her but ultimately destroys her. Reaching the conclusion of his tale, Holgrave realizes that he has mesmerized Phoebe. He, too, can exert mastery over the spirit of another. The temptation is great, but the narrator observes that Holgrave had "the rare and high quality of reverence for another's individuality" (535). He awakens Phoebe from her trance, leaving her free to exercise her own will. Holgrave's growing regard for Phoebe has begun to work a transformation in him.

Phoebe also acknowledges changes in her nature, claiming that she has grown wiser and more sober through her interactions with Clifford and Hepzibah. She has become a mediator between them and the destructive energy of Jaffrey. Fulfilling a role popularly termed "the angel in the house" through her domestic accomplishments and spirituality, Phoebe has also become its guardian angel whose light wards off Jaffrey's darkness. Her temporary departure provides an opening for Jaffrey's final assault upon his cousins.

When Phoebe departs, Jaffrey uses the power of intimidation to overwhelm Hepzibah and insist on the confrontation with Clifford. Hepzibah dreads this meeting, not only because of its danger to Clifford but because it evokes the evils of the past associated with Pyncheon greed. She reflects that she would gladly surrender any wealth she had if it would only buy her and Clifford's freedom. In this section of the narrative, Hawthorne again slows the pace of the action, as Hepzibah delays finding Clifford and explores any avenue of potential help. When she does not find Clifford, Hepzibah panics and returns to Jaffrey, who waits in the parlor. Realizing that Jaffrey is dead and fearing Clifford's role in what has occurred, Hepzibah contemplates the horror of public exposure.

Clifford perceives the death of Jaffrey as a moment of liberation and forces Hepzibah to leave the house. Although Clifford believes they are embracing freedom, he and Hepzibah have become wanderers. They are thrust into the swirl of human activity, but their ride upon the train so long observed from a distance has no specific goal. While on the train, Clifford begins an exchange with a fellow passenger that becomes an outpouring of all the thoughts he has kept within himself. His flood of talk indicates the relief he feels at Jaffrey's death, since his only way of resisting Jaffrey's power had been to remain silent. His outburst reveals his rejection of the practicality that defines Jaffrey's vision but leaves Clifford grasping at abstractions. His impetuous behavior and the courage of his false bravado vault the two "owls" into an uninhabited area, a decaying solitude similar to the Pyncheon household before Phoebe's presence. Realizing that his own actions are futile, Clifford sinks back into his shell. Once again Hepzibah must overcome her own feelings of inadequacy to provide for her brother.

The last few chapters of the romance move toward resolution of the main and subplots. Returning to the precincts of the house, Hawthorne offers a satirical eulogy in which Jaffrey's true nature is revealed. The tone of Chapter 18, "Governor Pyncheon," is mocking, filled with questions that are taunts to the now-powerless man. Hawthorne then guides the reader out of the Judge's death chamber and onto the local street, where neighborhood residents comment on the absence of Hepzibah and Clifford. Their remarks suggest that the Pyncheons have not been as invisible to their neighbors as they believe, especially since Jaffrey has revealed that he used neighbors and customers in the shop as spies. Hawthorne also reunites Phoebe and Holgrave. Their union introduces hope for the future, and the narrator claims that in professing their love for one another "[T]hey transfigured the earth, and made it Eden again" (616). Meanwhile, Hepzibah and Clifford, worn out by their journey, return amid great relief. Hepzibah "had staggered onward beneath the burden of grief and responsibility, until now it was safe to fling it down" (617) in a gesture that echoes the relief of Christian in John Bunyan's *Pilgrim's Progress* (1678). In the last chapter, Jaffrey's deceit in planting evidence against Clifford is revealed, as is the location of the hidden vault, ironically concealed behind the portrait of Colonel Pyncheon, the source of the family's turmoil as well as its prosperity.

The conclusion of the romance has generated much debate among critics and readers. Many have objected to its happy ending, its quick resolution of conflicts, and what some see as a complete reversal of Holgrave's attitude. In the end, Holgrave claims his true identity as a Maule, and Clifford, Hepzibah, and Phoebe, as the surviving Pyncheons, inherit Jaffrey's wealth. With Holgrave, they retire to the Pyncheon country estate, leaving the House of the Seven Gables to the past. Unlike the cataclysmic ending of Edgar Allan Poe's "The Fall of the House of Usher" (1839, 1845), the House of the Seven Gables does not collapse in ruin. Having acknowledged the past and come to terms with its implications, the main characters are able to move into a new phase of life, as they "bade a final farewell to the abode of their forefathers" while the Pyncheon elm "whispered unintelligible prophecies" (626).

CHARACTERS

Hepzibah, Clifford, Phoebe, and Holgrave are well-intentioned individuals who seek wholeness in their lives. At the beginning, each exists as an isolated individual, even Phoebe, who has left her family home. Phoebe quickly reaches out to make connections with the others, and gradually they form a community. The fifth major character, Judge Jaffrey Pyncheon, functions as the source of disruption for this community.

While her family ancestors are remembered as men of temper and ire, Hepzibah Pyncheon is an "old maid" who feels powerless. She lives in the family home that once conveyed status but now reminds her and others of declining Pyncheon fortunes. Hepzibah enjoys no family life and no social life, the two spheres in which women traditionally expressed their identities and exercised influence. Because she is excluded from these activities, Hepzibah has no role in the life of the community.

The scene in which she first appears supplies details that indicate that Hepzibah's life is regulated by outmoded rules of behavior. These have become a barrier, both protective and restrictive. Hepzibah's desire to participate in life as much as her financial need motivates her plan for the cent-shop. But the act of inviting the world in provokes greater terror for her than do the "ghosts" of her aging family home. Her one hope is that with Clifford's return she will resume the role of devoted sister, embracing a relationship that will give definition to her life.

Hepzibah has, beneath her scowl and reserve, the potential to show affection. She demonstrates this in interactions with Phoebe, whose openness allows Hepzibah to reveal more of herself. Hawthorne suggests that the reader, like Phoebe, needs to see beyond Hepzibah's surface to appreciate her true nature. Although Hepzibah clings to ideas of genteel womanhood and at times expresses both pride and anxieties about class status, she needs positive connections to others. She calls upon her inner strength to preserve her independence and to defend the well-being of Clifford. When she must, she can call up her own vein of Pyncheon iron.

Clifford Pyncheon, like his sister, has been shaped by isolation, although his has been literal imprisonment. Having undeservedly spent years in jail for the murder of his uncle, Clifford must come to terms with the larger world, one that attracts and terrifies him. Hepzibah pictures her brother as he looks in the miniature portrait she treasures. When he appears, however, he is as fragile and sterile as she, his spirit diminished. His long estrangement from the world has left Clifford unable to deal with the realities of life. He withdraws, but neither the house nor his inner self can provide sustenance.

Clifford also reflects the dangers of an aesthetic sensibility denied the opportunity to mature. Although he is drawn to people and things of beauty, Clifford has little compassion. He rejects Hepzibah's attempts to please him because he finds her physical appearance distasteful. He enjoys Phoebe's company because she is young and attractive, but he is ready to absorb her energy without having any to return. He muses over questions of life and art, but as a dilettante more interested in blowing soap bubbles than in creating works of substance. Hawthorne links Clifford's refined tastes to those of his ancestors like Gervayse Pyncheon but implies that Clifford, like Gervayse, is a consumer of beauty rather than a creator. Through Clifford's signs of arrested development, Hawthorne conveys the costs of Clifford's imprisonment at a young age, that he has been robbed of an adult life.

The emotional barrenness and protective reserve that characterize Hepzibah and Clifford initially define Holgrave as well. A boarder in the House of the Seven Gables, Holgrave appears forthright, yet retains an element of mystery about him. Living apart from the family, though within the Pyncheon house, Holgrave defines himself against their world and history. While talking to Phoebe, he refers to the Pyncheon house as one of the "Dead Men's houses" that is tainted by the legacy of the past. Although he wishes to shed its influence, exclaiming, "Shall we never, never get rid of this Past!" (509), Holgrave, like the other characters, is trapped by it.

The glimpses of Holgrave's history prior to his revelations at the end suggest a man unsettled and uncertain, moving from profession to profession. Concealing his identity behind a name and philosophies not his own, Holgrave speaks with a "half-hidden sarcasm," even when he addresses Phoebe. This sarcasm allows him to maintain his distance from others, suggesting his own anxieties over intimacy and the revelation of self that it entails. He also projects the image of a progressive reformer who advocates dramatic change, but there is no indication that he attempts to put thought into action. His occupation as a daguerrotypist suggests quite the opposite: He is a recorder and preserver, even though his method is modern. This role, as well as his bond to the land through gardening, indicates the underlying thread of conservatism that is part of his nature.

Holgrave is an incomplete figure, one who has allowed his masks and barriers to become his reality. Ironically, his insight as an artist allows him to see beneath surfaces and reveal others' secrets, as in his exposure of Jaffrey's true nature in the portraits, while concealing his own. Professing his love for Phoebe and his desire to marry, he announces a change in outlook: "I have a presentiment, that, hereafter, it will be my lot to set out trees, to make fences—perhaps even in due time, to build a house for another generation" (616). This statement reveals the other side of Holgrave's nature, one that he has hidden from Phoebe and himself. Claiming the name Maule allows Holgrave to acknowledge his ties to the history of the house and to the fate of the Pyncheons. He no longer needs to reject the past but can draw upon its lessons as he plans for the future. By accepting Phoebe and a settled life, he appears to repudiate his critical voice and to abandon a career in art. His change has troubled readers who feel this turnabout is artificial or undermines his credibility as an artist (Baym, "Holgrave" 595–597).

Phoebe, as her name suggests, is the source of light in the darkened world of the Pyncheon household. She is the most frequently criticized of Hawthorne's heroines, seeming too good and simple to be true. Hawthorne anticipates this reaction within his narrative as he cautions the reader against a superficial glance at Phoebe. He suggests that Phoebe has not been unduly influenced by the modern world she inhabits. She finds spiritual devotions a natural part of her life and is linked to the natural world through images of light and association with flowers. Phoebe is one with her environment, and as she draws brightness from the natural world, she radiates it to the human world around her.

This brightness continues in the narrative, as Phoebe becomes an integral part of the Pyncheon household. She strikes a unique balance between the physical and the spiritual and demonstrates her talent in the "gift of practical arrangement," which empowers her to "exorcise the gloom" from her own chamber and from Pyncheon lives. Daily chores assume a new dimension under her care, and she represents the artist of the domestic sphere. Phoebe's world is one of unity and grace; her natural tendencies bring things and people into order and harmony. Her lack of sophistication and intellectual curiosity may trouble the modern reader, but Hawthorne seems more interested in developing Phoebe as an emblem of goodness rather than as a fully rounded character.

Phoebe's innocence and animation establish her as a vehicle of transformation for others. Holgrave, in describing the effect of light in photography, describes Phoebe's effect as well, for she "actually brings out the secret character with a truth no painter would ever venture upon, even could he detect it" (430). Phoebe's relationships with Hepzibah and Clifford demonstrate this effect, but her relationship with Holgrave becomes most significant for his and her future. Phoebe draws forth from Holgrave submerged aspects of his character, helping him achieve a wholeness that makes him suitable as a marriage partner. Through Phoebe's influence and the light she provides, Holgrave more fully sees and accepts himself.

In his treatment of Jaffrey Pyncheon, Hawthorne not only provides an antagonist for Hepzibah and Clifford, but reveals a cynical portrait of a politician. Jaffrey cultivates goodwill in public but can be ruthless in pursuing his own ends in private. Jaffrey most resembles the Pyncheons of old and attempts to conceal his iron will behind the smile of false benevolence. Hawthorne depicts this in the daguerreotype of Jaffrey. Despite Holgrave's attempts to compose a pleasing likeness, Jaffrey's true nature shines forth. Bruce Michelson compares Jaffrey to the traditional shapeshifter of American folklore whose real nature can only be glimpsed when he is caught off guard (81). The portrait links him to his ancestor the Colonel, whose scowling visage still unsettles the inhabitants of the house. His manner with others confirms that link, especially in his comments to Hepzibah, in which he calls her "Woman" in an attempt to put her in her place for refusing to do his bidding.

The hardness of Jaffrey's heart is conveyed through his own family's disintegration. His wife died in the third or fourth year of their marriage. It was rumored that her death was hastened by Jaffrey's demand that she demonstrate "fealty to her liege-lord and master" (458) even in the small gestures of life. He had cast off an "expensive and dissipated son," refusing to forgive him for his failings until the hour of the son's death. Another son, who receives only brief mention, has been out of the country. He dies of cholera just as he is about to return. He may have been the heir named in Jaffrey's will, but he never appears in Jaffrey's thoughts.

Hawthorne also implies that there is something rotten at Jaffrey's core. Seen as a man of "eminent respectability" by his contemporaries, Jaffrey has dark secrets that should weigh on his conscience. But Jaffrey believes the public image of himself. In a metaphorical tale that alludes to the early Pyncheon-Maule history, Hawthorne likens Jaffrey to a man who has built a magnificent palace that deceives both the builder and the public. A decaying corpse lies buried in the palace, ultimately poisoning the whole. The description of the dead judge sitting at the center of the house near the end of the novel recalls this metaphor of secret guilt (Gray 93). Jaffrey also embodies six of the seven deadly sins, conveying the extent of his evil. The only deadly sin he does not manifest is sloth. Hawthorne mentions instead that Jaffrey has developed a nervousness that does not let him rest. These "deadly" sins forecast Jaffrey's fate in the novel.

ROLE OF MINOR CHARACTERS

In addition to the main characters who are the focus of the narrative, Hawthorne creates minor characters who contribute in significant ways to his romance.

Uncle Venner, a neighborhood handyman, uses the resources available to him to sustain himself. He has slowed over time but still has an energetic manner. He collects kitchen scraps from local housewives to feed his pig, chops wood in exchange for kindling, tends gardens, and performs other menial but necessary tasks that keep the community functioning. Thought to be "deficient" in his wits, Venner dispenses homely wisdom. His references to retiring to his "farm" are a euphemism for his anticipated end at the poor farm. That he too was part of an old family of Salem that had seen better days allows Hawthorne to highlight the effects of social and economic instability. Venner also stands in contrast to Jaffrey, since Venner performs necessary tasks and uses only the resources he needs to get by, whereas Jaffrey exploits others and consumes more than his share.

Another minor character who plays a role throughout is Alice Pyncheon. Her presence in the novel is felt indirectly, as she or memory of her haunts the House of the Seven Gables. She is associated with the posies, the garden, and the harpsichord's mystic tunes. Holgrave tells her tragic story to Phoebe, who is often linked to Alice. Her continuing presence in the house suggests that as a victim of Pyncheon greed and Maule vengeance she will not find peace until the conflict is resolved. At the end of the romance, Uncle Venner thinks he hears music from within the house and guesses that Alice's spirit has given one last touch to her harpsichord before floating "heavenward" to a lasting rest.

In *Seven Gables*, voices of various townsfolk are heard, and they express the values and expectations of the time. Through these figures, Hawthorne provides a wider scope for issues of class status and gender expectations, as well as greater detail about the activities of daily life. These voices help to place his narrative in time present. They are necessary to establish that link since the inhabitants of the House of the Seven Gables have little interaction with the world around them. The most entertaining of these figures is the young Ned Higgins, who devours as much gingerbread as he can obtain.

THEMES

Conscious that many readers look for a "moral" or theme that reflects the central principle of a novel, Hawthorne states one in his preface. He indicates that he will explore how the "wrong-doing of one generation lives into successive ones" (352). Sin and retribution emerge as one thematic thread of *Seven Gables*, but Hawthorne addresses a wider range of issues. Preoccupied with the burden of the past, Hawthorne examines how his characters relate to the past, individual, familial, and cultural. He considers the conflicts between the values of the past and present, especially between aristocracy and democracy. He raises questions about the influences of heredity. To create balance in his narrative, Hawthorne also explores the transforming power of love in lives that have been marked by isolation and fear.

The selfish wrongdoing of individuals often results in the breakdown of community and family. Hawthorne develops this theme as he recounts acts of Pyncheons that have benefited some members of the family but destroyed others. Beginning in the first generation of the Pyncheon "dynasty," powerful individuals have been willing to sacrifice others, family members or neighbors, to obtain greater wealth or property. This pattern continues through succeeding generations, as revealed in the story of Alice Pyncheon and in Jaffrey's willingness to have Clifford unjustly imprisoned. Each of the perpetrators suffers punishment for his "sin," whether it be the untimely deaths of the Colonel and the Judge or Gervayse's loss of his daughter. Hawthorne suggests that evildoers ultimately pay for their wrongs, but he sees human nature and history as more complex than this single pattern can encompass.

Hawthorne's greater concern is the relationship of the individual to history. Through Holgrave, Hawthorne articulates the philosophy of human progress and the desire to turn one's back on the past to escape its influence. Likewise, Clifford's pronouncements on the train suggest that the past is inferior to the present. Hawthorne asserts, however, that this is an incomplete picture, for to deny the influence and truth of the past has costs. One cost is the loss of identity, a problem with which Clifford and Holgrave/Maule have had to cope. The larger cost comes, however, in the danger of repeating the errors of the past. The tragedy of the Pyncheons results from their denial of responsibility, personal and familial. Each generation, it seems, must repeat the errors of its predecessors and suffer similar consequences. Holgrave, too, faces such danger in the vengeance of the Maules, but he has learned a crucial lesson from the story of Alice Pyncheon. His choice not to enthrall Phoebe in his power allows him to break a pattern from the past. Ultimately, Hawthorne suggests that human experience is mixed, reflecting both progress and repetition as generations pass.

At the heart of the conflict between the Pyncheons and Maules lie the issues of class and privilege. Hawthorne expands this to examine the competing interests of aristocracy and democracy. Through Hepzibah and Clifford, Hawthorne presents a fading aristocracy, still bound by form but unable to function in the world of the present. Hepzibah's concerns with being a "lady" and the importance of having an old, respected name cut her off from interaction with her neighbors. They nearly cost her the companionship of Phoebe, who, in Hepzibah's opinion, cannot be a "lady." Clifford also exhibits an aristocratic mien, yet he is incapable of dealing with the life around him. Even Alice Pyncheon is brought to her doom through her pride and aristocratic sense of entitlement that provoke the carpenter Maule to humble her. In contrast, Phoebe can function successfully in both the house and shop because she is not preoccupied with status. Holgrave, too, reflects a more democratic perspective. His associates are viewed as a mixed lot, and he judges individuals by their values and actions, not by their names or social positions. He has ventured forth on his own, not expecting family status or patronage to provide the way.

The importance of family lineage pertains to Hawthorne's questions about heredity. The efficacy of the Pyncheon curse hinges on the belief that heredity dominates, even though it may involve transmission of a physical malady rather than a supernatural one. Physical resemblance plays a crucial role in identifying Jaffrey's true nature and the link to his founding ancestor. Hepzibah also focuses on the importance of family traits, trying to decipher how much "Pyncheon" shows up in Phoebe. Associating Phoebe's competence with traits she inherited from her mother, Hepzibah firmly believes that the plebian Phoebe is no Pyncheon. Likewise, Holgrave's ability as a mesmerist appears to be an inherited talent, linked to elements of wizardry associated with his family background. In Holgrave's case, however, Hawthorne suggests that some family influences are escapable and that in a democratic culture one can be self-made.

To balance his exploration of negative aspects of human action and the past, Hawthorne also explores the transforming power of love. Through Phoebe's presence and her interaction with the other characters, Hawthorne traces a redemptive and regenerative force at work. Her ability to bring light into the dim recesses of the Pyncheon house serves as an effective metaphor for her impact on its inhabitants. Hepzibah finds new warmth and energy in Phoebe's company, and Clifford becomes young again and more amiable in her presence. Even Holgrave is drawn out of his separate apartment in the house and becomes part of the community once Phoebe arrives. Hawthorne creates in Hepzibah, Clifford, and Holgrave self-defensive reserves and barriers that Phoebe overcomes.

This transformative power of love supports a secondary theme that Hawthorne interweaves, the search for home. The main characters, including Hepzibah, are looking for a place to call home, with the comfort and security that such a place provides. Ultimately the characters discover that home is not a structure, for they leave the Seven Gables behind, but the community they have formed supported by their commitments to each other.

SYMBOLS AND ALLUSIONS

One of the striking differences between *Seven Gables* and *The Scarlet Letter* rests in Hawthorne's use of metaphors and symbols. In *Seven Gables*, Hawthorne uses many metaphors, and some images assume symbolic import, but none emerges as the dominant metaphor of the novel (Dauber 127). Two images that provide a frame for the narrative and assume symbolic import are the Pyncheon mansion (discussed above) and the Pyncheon elm. The Pyncheon elm not only denotes a living part of nature but also connotes a "family tree" or lineage. The contrast between the two is striking, for the elm is still "strong and broad," whereas the Pyncheon family has declined to a small remnant. Another symbol, Maule's well, the sweet spring turned sour, reflects the effect of revenge on the Maule family. That this spring sits at the center of the Pyncheon garden emphasizes the interdependency of these two family stories.

A humorous symbol for the Pyncheon family, the Pyncheon chickens resemble their human namesakes. The attempt to preserve the chickens' purity by avoiding interbreeding with other stock has left the remnant only a shadow of their former glory. Through this, Hawthorne emphasizes that the Pyncheon attempt to preserve an "aristocratic" lineage has similarly left them only an echo of their founding fathers. The birds have been reduced in number and, like Hepzibah and Clifford, must scratch out their meager existence with little to sustain them until Phoebe arrives. She cares for the birds as she does her aging cousins, sympathetic to the needs of both.

In *Seven Gables*, Hawthorne uses numerous allusions as well, but those to the Garden of Eden resonate profoundly. Associated in Genesis with the story of man's fall from grace, Eden is also a place of beginnings. Although Hawthorne admits that it is impossible to regain the perfect innocence and happiness of Eden, he sees possibilities for redemption for human beings and their world. His frequent references to Adam and Eve when speaking of Holgrave and Phoebe suggest that their growing relationship offers the potential for a fresh start. They, too, will experience the fall into knowledge of their world and each other, but Hawthorne implies that it is not an entirely unfortunate fall.

THE SUPERNATURAL

As in many of his short stories, Hawthorne draws on elements of the supernatural in shaping *Seven Gables*. He uses an assortment of devices associated with Gothic fiction, including mysterious music, shadows and whispers, witchcraft, and mesmerism, but employs them for more than simple effect. By pairing a supernatural possibility with a rational or physical explanation, Hawthorne suggests the greater import of events and images. The reader must ask: Are the Pyncheon deaths caused by a fact of nature or Maule's curse? Is the brackishness of Maule's well the result of overdevelopment of the land or Maule's haunting presence? Is the Maule ability to hypnotize an attribute of a powerful personality or the result of witchcraft? In each instance, Hawthorne leaves the question unanswered, suggesting that creative energy emerges from the tension between reason and the imagination (Michelson 77). He further suggests that such tension contributes to the development of fictional narratives.

Hawthorne also uses supernatural elements to explore the link between memory and the imagination. He describes a mirror in the house that can be manipulated by the wizardry of the Maules. The shapes of all who have gazed into the mirror appear within it. The gaze itself conveys the vanity and pride of the Pyncheons. The images reflected when the mirror is manipulated, however, portray each Pyncheon in a moment of sin or crisis. In addition to governing the reflections in the mirror, Maules are also empowered to influence people's dreams. Through the mirror and dreams, Hawthorne links the power of the Maules to the realm of the unconscious. Although his novel precedes the development of modern psychology, Hawthorne suggests that the hidden guilt of the Pyncheons will eventually come to light.

For a discussion of mesmerism see "Historical Context," Chapter 7.

HISTORICAL CONTEXT

Hawthorne derived much of the background for the conflict between the Pyncheons and the Maules from his own family history. His ancestor William Hathorne, who served as a magistrate, was known for his iron will and for meting out harsh penalties. William's son John Hathorne served as a magistrate and as a judge for the Salem witchcraft trials in the 1690s. Many suspected that accusations of witchcraft were often made to seize property, since those who admitted to or were convicted of witchcraft forfeited their lands. John Hathorne had approved the arrest and prosecution of John English and his wife for witchcraft in 1692, causing enmity between the two families. This conflict was resolved during the eighteenth century by the marriage of

Hathorne and English descendants (Cunliffe 82). Hawthorne family tradition also claimed that John Hathorne was cursed by one of the victims of the hysteria. (The curse, similar to that uttered by Maule, was spoken against another judge, Nicholas Noyes.) Some who served as judges and prosecutors during the witchcraft hysteria later repented of their actions and publicly apologized, but John Hathorne never did.

ALTERNATE READING: NEW HISTORICISM

A critic who uses a new historicist approach examines the relationship between a work of literature and the historical and cultural contexts in which it was produced and read. A new historicist argues that such contexts are not simply background information but are vital to a full understanding of the work. Contrary to the view of New Criticism that asserts that any work of art stands by itself as a unified and coherent whole, new historicists believe that a work of literature cannot be interpreted without reference to the era in which it was written. Critics who take this approach are interested in more than just the "facts" of a particular time period. They examine values and attitudes, especially as they are conveyed through language and symbols.

New historicists believe that the author of any text engages in interpretation of his or her culture and reflects that interpretation in the text. To gain a wider view of a particular era, they often look to "nonliterary" sources for insights into cultural concerns. They may examine political tracts, newspapers, advice manuals, advertisements, and illustrations as a means of identifying how people responded to issues and conflicts, how people conceived of their daily life. They also draw upon the work of theorists who have explored aspects of culture. Some, like Michel Foucault, emphasize the importance of identifying bases of power within a culture and examining how those who hold power determine what is considered true and acceptable, normal and sane. Others, like Mikhail Bakhtin, suggest that any text or discourse is dialogic, that it contains many independent voices that may be in conflict with each other. Some of these voices may be subversive, contesting the dominant ideology of the culture, whereas others defuse challenges to the culture or appear to support its codes and conventions.

Although he set *The House of the Seven Gables* a decade or so earlier than when he wrote it, many of the concerns of mid-nineteenth-century culture and Hawthorne's responses to them are evident within the text. One important issue was the role of women in American life. The Women's Rights Convention at Seneca Falls had taken place in 1848, followed by regional conventions that attempted to engage more women in social reform and the campaign for suffrage. Many of the ideas advanced in these meetings challenged prevailing views in America and called for a reordering of the relationship between men and women. As questions arose about the role of women in culture, so, too, did questions about men.

From the 1820s to the 1860s, the cult of domesticity and the cult of true womanhood were ideals that evolved to define the role of middle-class women. These principles were expressed in countless advice manuals written for women, as well as in the popular magazines aimed at a female audience. As the means of producing goods was removed from the home and men spent many hours away from the household, the home became woman's special sphere. The cult of true womanhood emphasized a woman's "natural" religious sensibility. Her role was to create domestic harmony and to maintain her husband and children's well-being before her own. A woman who embraced the values of true womanhood saw it as her duty to make the home a sanctuary from the pressures and evils of the world. Often such a woman was identified as an "Angel in the House," an image popularized in a poem by Coventry Patmore. The ideas expressed at the Women's Rights Convention and through various reform associations began to challenge this understanding of womanhood, arguing instead that women needed to take a more active role and exercise a greater voice in the public sphere.

Hawthorne's support for the traditional view of woman as defined by the cult of true womanhood is evident in his treatment of Phoebe's character. His frequent use of the term *true woman* within the narrative highlights the importance of this issue to him. Phoebe's abilities both in managing household chores and in meeting the needs of the people around her reflect her adherence to this set of principles. That she attends church regularly and engages in simple acts of devotion further enhance her piety and wholesomeness. She also achieves the ultimate goal for a nineteenth-century woman as articulated by the cult of domesticity. She makes "a home about her—that very sphere which the outcast, the prisoner . . . instinctively pines after—a home!" (472). Hawthorne links the attributes of a "true woman" to a democratic culture that rejects the aristocratic hierarchy that identifies a "lady" by birth rather than by conduct. But he remains more comfortable with the notion of a woman fulfilling her calling within the home, rather than competing with him in the public sphere.

In contrast to his support for a conventional role for women, Hawthorne seems more troubled by his culture's definitions of roles for men. The same advice literature that encouraged women to excel within the cult of domesticity encouraged men to compete in the public sphere. They were to practice planning and time management in all that they did and run their families in the same way that they ran a business, delegating duties and tasks to various members. They were to live by the work ethic and use leisure time for further enhancement of their knowledge and skills. Men were to be confident in their authority and define their successes through achievements in business and the professions.

Within *Seven Gables*, the male character who most clearly embodies these values and attributes is Jaffrey, who is depicted in a most negative light. In Chapter 18, "Governor Pyncheon," the narrator recites a list of Jaffrey's plans and ambitions and constantly emphasizes the loss of time and opportunity while Jaffrey sits dead in the chair. As he reveals Jaffrey's public accomplishments, the narrator underscores the toll this has taken on his family life. Although publicly he seems a great and admired success, privately he has been a miserable failure. Hawthorne further questions the expectations for middle-class men through his treatment of Holgrave's character. A man who has tried his hand at many trades but has no definite profession, Holgrave voices concerns about time only in terms of the weight of the past. He enjoys tending the garden and visiting with others there, using leisure for creative activity rather than to further business interests. Although he hopes for success as an artist, his ambitions do not require that he neglect or destroy others in the process. At the end of the narrative, Holgrave is rewarded with Phoebe's love and the promise of financial security, as Hawthorne advocates for greater breadth in defining masculine participation in the culture.

A second issue that troubled Hawthorne was the increasing presence of technologies that altered people's relationships to the natural and social environments. While he recognized the inevitability of change, Hawthorne expressed reservations about the pace and direction that such change was taking. Through the mention of the railroad, he indicates how advances in technology intrude on people's awareness, even from a distance, for Clifford can hear the train even when he does not see it. For Clifford the train represents the profound change in American life since he last freely moved within it. His awareness of change intensifies his feeling that he has been cut off from the present. The ride he takes with Hepzibah on the train, his second attempt to "plunge" into the stream of life, takes him nowhere. The technology cannot compensate for Clifford's inner lack of direction.

In reading *Seven Gables*, a historicist would argue that even though Hawthorne does not make these cultural concerns the central issues of his text, they are crucial to its overall import. By identifying these issues and the language that reveals their presence in the text, a new historicist demonstrates the significance of social conventions and dominant beliefs. This approach also reveals how Hawthorne endorsed some of the values and conventions of his day while questioning or resisting others.

7

The Blithedale Romance
(1852)

Drawing upon family history for *The House of the Seven Gables*, Hawthorne used his own past to shape *The Blithedale Romance*. In the preface he claims that he is not depicting the Brook Farm experiment of 1841, an attempt to found a utopian community based on Transcendentalist principles in West Roxbury, Massachusetts. His experience as a resident in this communal project, however, influences the details of the novel. During most of his career, Hawthorne associated with members of the Transcendentalist circle, a group that included Ralph Waldo Emerson, Henry David Thoreau, Margaret Fuller, and Elizabeth Peabody, among others. He lived among some of them during two different periods in Concord as well as at Brook Farm. The Transcendentalists believed that individuals should rely on their own intuition and conscience, rather than follow the dictates of society. They participated in numerous reform movements and believed in progress and in the unlimited potential for human growth. Hawthorne never fully agreed with his neighbors and friends. He was more skeptical about human nature and about the possibilities for achieving reform. In *Blithedale*, he presents both the early optimism of a utopian community and the realization of its limitations.

In the novel, Blithedale's failure grows out of the nature of its founding. The members join together out of distaste or disdain for the world as they know it. Although they claim to have united in a commitment to brotherhood and shared resources, each arrives at Blithedale with his or her own agenda and needs. Hawthorne reveals through the narrative that the bond of community cannot be imposed from outside but must evolve through the interactions of individuals and their mutual commitment, if it is to exist at all.

Critics often label *The Blithedale Romance* a failure, citing its uneven characterization and the difficulties generated by point of view. Readers, however, find the novel provocative in its treatment of the American desire to establish the community of the future, a "more perfect union." Periodically utopian movements arise in America, drawing hopeful participants to innovative communal projects. Often, these communities, such as the communes of the 1960s, have a brief life and fade from view. Some, especially those motivated by religious beliefs such as the Shaker villages, make a lasting contribution to American culture. Examining the impulses that lead individuals to attempt to define themselves and to reshape their communities, Hawthorne presents an insightful analysis of a continuing trend in American experience.

POINT OF VIEW

In *The Blithedale Romance*, Hawthorne experiments with a first-person narrative. The narrator, Miles Coverdale, participates in the plot that unfolds, although he is not an initiator of action. Instead, Coverdale reacts to what happens around him and observes the behavior of others.

The story of Blithedale is told in retrospect, as Coverdale looks back upon events that had occurred at an earlier period in his life. He identifies himself at the end as a man of middle age, "a step or two beyond the midmost point" (846), still without a sense of purpose. He narrates the Blithedale episode of his life in a melancholy tone that suggests regret. He also presents his own view of Blithedale as satirical and ambivalent from the start, creating a self-defensive posture. By doing so he is able to distance himself from the disappointment of Blithedale's failure.

Looking back on his life, Coverdale believes that he has missed out on something significant but hesitates to name it. He expresses a similar feeling while he is part of the Blithedale community. Coverdale assumes that the other characters make plans and experience pleasures that do not include him. He resents being left out but does not know how to make himself part of a group. From the beginning, when he hesitates at old Moodie's unspecified request for a favor, he shields himself from taking on responsibility that will inconvenience him. He wants the other characters to treat him as a confidant, but he does little to inspire their confidence. Retelling the Blithedale experience provides Coverdale an opportunity to identify the missing element in his life.

A problematic figure, Coverdale is often labeled an unreliable narrator. He attempts to determine the motives of other characters, even when he does not know their history. He sees only through the lens of his own anxieties and desires, engaging in conjecture when he does not know facts. Frequently, Coverdale admits to spying on others from secret vantage points, deriving pleasure from his voyeuristic acts. He analyzes other people, trying to learn their secrets, yet is dishonest in moments of introspection, rationalizing his own behavior. He also reveals ambivalence by stating one explanation, then offering an alternative that undermines the first. Coverdale's unreliability and lack of objectivity force the reader to question his interpretations and explanations.

SETTING, PLOT, AND STRUCTURE

Hawthorne uses two contrasting settings within *The Blithedale Romance*, the city of Boston and the rural Blithedale community. Often a writer uses the contrasts between city and country life to highlight differences in values and behavior. The city embodies modern values associated with progress but also generates negative qualities, such as competition, artificiality, and isolation. Rural life, on the other hand, is associated with simplicity. There individuals live in closer proximity to nature and the natural, unaffected by the artifice often engendered by city life. In his narrative, however, Hawthorne questions these contrasts by revealing that characters do not change their behaviors and values when they change locations. He implies that people shape the environment as much as the environment influences them. The name *Blithedale* means "happy valley," suggesting the hopes of those who cast their lot in this utopia. As the novel proceeds, Blithedale proves to be a misnomer in light of their experiences.

The romance begins in the city with a brief, mysterious encounter between old Moodie and Coverdale. Old Moodie steps out of the shadows and asks Coverdale to perform a favor. When Coverdale hesitates, Moodie decides not to pursue his request. Before Coverdale is fully aware, Moodie has again receded from view. Moodie's ghostly appearance evokes a sense of the supernatural, and the patch he wears over one eye suggests an attempt to conceal his identity. The unsettling circumstances of this encounter are heightened by the description of the Veiled Lady's performance, from which Coverdale is returning home. In this description, mention is made of the spirit world and the crossing of boundaries between this world and the next. At the end of the chapter, the reader is left to wonder, Who is old Moodie, and what favor does he seek? Who is the Veiled Lady, and what power does she have?

Hawthorne begins the novel as though it were a mystery, incorporating Gothic touches that recall *Seven Gables*. In the chapters that follow, he introduces the "common sense" and "light of day" elements that oppose the influence of mystery but also cannot satisfactorily explain it. These two threads coexist throughout the narrative, suggesting that something beyond the surface of the story contains its real meaning. In the opening chapter, "Old Moodie," Hawthorne also introduces a recurring motif: Characters appear out of nowhere, intrude briefly upon Coverdale's consciousness, then retreat. Coverdale makes frequent references to individuals seeming ghostly or specter-like, as though they haunt his memory but have no substance for him in time present.

The remainder of the narrative is divided into three sections, each separated by a story that provides important background or foreshadows what will follow in the plot. The first section focuses on the establishment of the Blithedale community and the developing relationships among the four main characters. The second section reveals underlying issues that are sources of tension between the main characters, often amplified by the actions of secondary figures. The last section presents open conflict, the dissolution of relationships, and the end of the Blithedale experiment.

Chapter 2, "Blithedale," records the transition from city to country. Coverdale reviews the comforts of his bachelor apartment and wonders about his decision to leave all behind for a venture he claims to doubt. In this chapter, Hawthorne introduces the motif of the journey, often used by writers to record a process of growth and change. Coverdale, however, travels back and forth between the city and Blithedale, finally remaining in the city. By structuring Coverdale's journey in this way, Hawthorne undercuts its implications of growth. He uses this pattern of travel instead to reflect Coverdale's indecision and inability to commit himself to one way of life or the other. Coverdale wavers between the benefits of either, never able to make a choice for himself. At the end of the romance, he admits that he has traveled to Europe twice and returned, still living as a wanderer looking for his place.

Coverdale's journey to Blithedale occurs in April, a month associated with renewal and rebirth. The weather during Coverdale's travels, however, is snowy and cold, a reminder of winter (though not unusual for a New England spring). This harsh weather causes Coverdale to question his decision to leave the shelter and familiarity of his city dwelling. He finds in the weather an ill omen for this venture. The weather also reinforces Coverdale's view of the world as a cold and lonely place. He moves to Blithedale to search out personal warmth and friendship, seeking an antidote to emotional coldness as much as to reform the nature of society.

Upon entering the farmhouse that will function as the initial center for the community, Coverdale encounters another of the main characters, Zenobia. Although the farm will be managed by the Fosters, Zenobia assumes the role of hostess, greeting the new arrivals. Her lively and energetic manner adds warmth to the household, a warmth reinforced by the fire blazing in the hearth of the old farmhouse. In their conversation, they discuss another of the main characters, Hollingsworth, who arrives during supper accompanied by Priscilla. While drawing them into the household, Zenobia remarks, "As we do by this friendless girl, so shall we prosper!" (658), not realizing that this statement foreshadows her own downfall. By the end of the evening, all of the main characters have been introduced, and some background on each has been revealed. The ensuing chapters recount their interactions, their initial friendships, and the growing tensions between them. Their initial meeting is marked by warmth, but Coverdale's summary of their first day, "How cold an Arcadia was this!" (664), suggests that the warmth is only temporary.

Coverdale's journey takes a toll on him. When he awakens his first morning at Blithedale, he has contracted a fevered illness that keeps him in bed. His physical illness serves as a metaphor for his psychic illness, as he confesses to Hollingsworth feelings of uselessness and lack of purpose. During his illness, Coverdale enjoys being the center of other people's attentions. His confinement in bed gives him a unique opportunity to view each of the other main characters as he or she comes before him. Since he recites the narrative in retrospect, Coverdale attempts to convey his initial interest in and enthusiasm for his new associates. Periodically, however, he interjects a sentence or two that warns the reader that these early impressions do not remain.

Once he recovers from his illness, Coverdale joins in the work of the community. He remains preoccupied with Zenobia, Hollingsworth, and Priscilla. He speculates on the nature of the relationships that exist between them, convinced that things are happening to which he should be privy. He believes that Hollingsworth exerts some dark influence upon both women and resents the fact that they are drawn to Hollingsworth rather than to himself. He also studies the interaction between Zenobia and Priscilla, attempting to decipher the nature of their connection. For Coverdale, everything remains part of a puzzle that he is trying to solve.

The society of Blithedale continues to develop, and the residents make progress in their attempts to be more workmanlike farmers. To initiate momentum toward a crisis, Hawthorne uses appearances by two outsiders who can disrupt the equilibrium. Old Moodie arrives at Blithedale, appearing once again out of the shadows. He has come to learn how Priscilla fares and to observe how Zenobia treats her. He is pleased to hear that Priscilla is happy but distressed when Zenobia puts Priscilla off as though she were a servant. Although his interest in Zenobia remains unexplained, old Moodie's gesture as he leaves, shaking "his uplifted staff" (709), foreshadows the retribution to come.

The other visitor to Blithedale also appears out of nowhere. Coverdale claims that Westervelt "had almost the effect of an apparition" (712), adding to the mystery that surrounds him. Like old Moodie, Westervelt carries a walking stick; his is carved to resemble a serpent, linking him to Satan. Westervelt has come looking for Zenobia and Priscilla. Curious as to Westervelt's business with the two women, Coverdale retreats to his "hermitage," an elevated cavity enclosed in a pine tree. From there he spies upon Westervelt and Zenobia. Although he cannot hear most of their conversation, he interprets Zenobia's gestures as signs of anger. He also surmises that there was once intimacy between Zenobia and Westervelt. Coverdale watches the pair until they move out of his view, unsure what Westervelt's visit means for Zenobia or Priscilla.

Westervelt's appearance increases the tension between the two women, made evident through Zenobia's story "The Silvery Veil." This legend functions as one of two "inset stories" that supplement the main narrative (Martin, *Hawthorne* 151). The tale that Zenobia tells in Chapter 13, "Zenobia's Legend," has two parts, both of which focus on the Veiled Lady. In the first half, Theodore, a young man who "prided himself upon his common-sense" (728), bets with his friends that he can unravel the mystery of the Veiled Lady. He attends a performance, then confronts the Veiled Lady in her dressing room. She agrees to remove her veil if he will kiss her first and become hers forever. He refuses, indicating that it is asking too much. When he reaches out to remove her veil, he briefly glimpses her beauty before she vanishes. Theodore spends the rest of his life longing for her. Through this portion of the legend, Zenobia introduces the theme of unrequited love that ultimately has an impact on her life as well as Coverdale's.

The second half of the legend entails a more sinister description of the fate of the Veiled Lady. Zenobia uses the details of Priscilla's arrival at Blithedale to connect her to the story of the Veiled Lady. She then fictionalizes her own encounter with Westervelt, describing him as a "terrible magician" (732) who warns her of a danger that the pale maiden poses. The magician gives her a veil to drape over the maiden, whom he will come to claim as his "bond-slave forever more" (733). At the conclusion of the tale, Zenobia drops a gauzy veil over Priscilla, which the listeners find a "bright idea." Priscilla, however, is shaken by the story and its implications. Although Zenobia addresses her as "my love," Priscilla senses that Zenobia will sacrifice her, should it become necessary.

Following this recitation, the relationships among the main characters become more unstable. Zenobia and Hollingsworth clash over the issue of women's rights and woman's proper sphere. Zenobia appears humbled by Hollingsworth's remarks and attempts to regain his affections. Coverdale, irritated that both women are attracted to Hollingsworth, tries to persuade Priscilla that Hollingsworth cares only for Zenobia. Priscilla rejects Coverdale's ideas and rebuffs him. The friendship between Coverdale and Hollingsworth dissolves when Coverdale perceives that Hollingsworth only wishes to make him a loyal follower, demanding all or nothing. The emotional turmoil generated by these situations causes Coverdale to depart from Blithedale, as he begins to sense that it will not provide the fellowship or love that he is seeking. Coverdale admits, "Blithedale was no longer what it had been. Everything was suddenly faded" (753), including his hopes.

Returning to the city, Coverdale again assumes a passive role. Although it is August, he sits before a fire in his hotel room, attempting to remedy the emotional coldness that he feels. As he did with his "hermitage," Coverdale uses his hotel room's position to spy upon the lives of others. He discovers that the inhabitants of one of the neighboring boardinghouses are Zenobia and Priscilla. Coverdale watches their windows and discovers that Westervelt is with them. As in the earlier episode of Coverdale's espionage, he cannot hear what Zenobia and Westervelt are saying, but he interprets their gestures. This time Westervelt discovers Coverdale's presence and alerts Zenobia. She, in one of the most pointed gestures in the novel, lowers a shade to conceal the room from Coverdale's intruding gaze.

Frustrated, Coverdale rationalizes an excuse for visiting the boardinghouse. Zenobia is civil in her greetings, but through her witty remarks and her cool gestures, she communicates that Coverdale is not someone she trusts or desires. Although he still claims to feel no attraction to her, Coverdale inwardly admits his irritation that she should find Hollingsworth preferable to him. He attempts to manipulate Zenobia's feelings by referring to Hollingsworth's interest in Priscilla. Upset to discover that Hollingsworth still has great influence over both women, Coverdale watches as he is outmaneuvered by Westervelt as well.

Finding himself "excluded from everybody's confidence" (784), Coverdale seeks out old Moodie to learn more about Priscilla. Supplying old Moodie with a glass of wine to loosen his tongue, Coverdale invites him to tell his life story. This second inset story, "Fauntleroy," creates another pause in the momentum of the plot but provides crucial details that shape the last section of the narrative. Like the first inset story, this contains two parts. The first outlines Moodie's history; the second, supplied by Coverdale, recounts an interview between Zenobia and Moodie.

Old Moodie reveals that he was once "a man of wealth" who indulged his tastes with "prodigal expenditure" (791). He had a wife and daughter for whom he held only superficial feeling, more interested in material wealth. When his expenditures had drained away his fortune, Fauntleroy, as he called himself, committed a crime to ward off his financial collapse. His crime was discovered, and he fled, leaving behind his family. His wife died shortly thereafter, leaving their daughter to be raised by an affluent uncle. Upon her uncle's death, she inherits his wealth, since no other living heir is identified.

Meanwhile, Fauntleroy emerges in another city under a different name, living in poverty. He marries again and has another daughter. When his wife dies, he cares for the child, Priscilla, speaking to her often of her stepsister, known as Zenobia. Old Moodie/Fauntleroy has hoped that Zenobia will respond to Priscilla as a sister, take her under her care, and support her. He summons Zenobia, although she does not know who he is, and charges her with this responsibility without specifying the relationship between the two women. Knowing that he is the rightful heir to his dead brother's wealth, old Moodie holds a power over Zenobia that she does not perceive. Old Moodie claims he will not use that power unless Priscilla, the daughter he truly loves, is wronged.

Once the underlying connection between Zenobia and Priscilla has been identified, the narrative can move toward resolution. This begins at a performance by the Veiled Lady that becomes a contest of wills and influence between Westervelt and Hollingsworth. As Coverdale watches, Westervelt begins his lecture and demonstration of his power over the Veiled Lady. All goes as planned until Hollingsworth steps onto the platform and beckons Priscilla to him. His steadfast gaze and calm voice break the hold that Westervelt has over Priscilla. To the audience's surprise, she throws off the veil and flees to Hollingsworth's protection.

The scene then shifts to Blithedale, where the final drama plays out. Coverdale arrives as a masquerade and celebration conclude. The revelry is only a distraction, however, as Zenobia reveals that she has been "on trial for [her] life" (819). She claims that Hollingsworth has been "judge, jury and accuser" (819). Coverdale, having missed the critical exchanges, can only guess at what has been discussed. He assumes it is the truth about Zenobia's relationship to Westervelt and her role in the plot against Priscilla. Coverdale perceives that "Zenobia and Hollingsworth were friends no longer," that their relationship had been "violently broken" (820). Coverdale witnesses the continuation of the argument, as Zenobia levels charges of her own against Hollingsworth. She confronts him with the truth about his nature, that he cares only about "self." She suspects that he has been more interested in her fortune than in her. Each has been guilty of exploiting another for personal gain. Hollingsworth denies his culpability. Zenobia confesses her guilt to Priscilla when she tells her, "You stood between me and an end which I desired. I wanted a clear path" (823–824).

Unable to envision a clear path for herself or a new identity, Zenobia commits suicide in the river. Her last confrontation with Hollingsworth has made clear to her that she has been willing to compromise her principles and compromise another person for the sake of someone who is unworthy. Her own heart has deceived her. Coverdale, having discovered signs of Zenobia's presence on the riverbank, rouses Hollingsworth and Silas Foster to help search for her in the river. In an eerie scene upon the water, the three men use poles to plumb the depths for her corpse. In his effort to draw her body to the surface,

Hollingsworth pierces her breast near the heart. This gesture symbolizes the effect that Hollingsworth's rejection had on Zenobia. When her body is brought to the surface, stiff with rigor, her hands are "clenched in immitigable defiance" (837). Her last pose represents inner turmoil and anguish rather than final rest.

Zenobia's death draws the life force from the Blithedale project. The other characters gather for her funeral, and Hollingsworth asks that she be buried in the spot once thought to be their future home. Coverdale reveals that Hollingsworth ends a broken man, weighed down by the guilt he feels over Zenobia's death. He is cared for by Priscilla, who now tries to be his protector, as he was once hers. Coverdale is once again left by himself. As his reflections on this portion of his life draw to a close, he admits that he has not found the purpose he was seeking, nor has he continued his work as an artist. His final confession, that he loved Priscilla, has provoked much irritation from readers, who find it an empty remark.

CHARACTERS

Hawthorne focuses on four main characters in this romance—Coverdale, Hollingsworth, Zenobia, and Priscilla. He develops contrasts between the two men and two women in order to highlight different aspects of human nature. Through these contrasts, Hawthorne can develop the undercurrents of tension that eventually destroy relationships between them.

As indicated earlier, Miles Coverdale serves as the narrator of the romance. At the time of the Blithedale project, he is in his early twenties, a young man without attachments. He has gained some reputation as a poet and hopes to achieve greater renown through his art. His mixed comments about the Blithedale project are difficult to evaluate, since he has the benefit of hindsight in describing his arrival and the early months of the community. At times he tries to sound more removed and analytical, frequently resorting to Latinate words when simpler Anglo-Saxon terms would do. The name *Coverdale* suggests a hidden valley and points to the self-protective aspects of his behavior.

Coverdale feels vulnerable because of his lack of attachments. He is looking for friendship and for love. He frequently reflects upon definitions of friendship as well as on the patterns of interaction between men and women. The pleasure he takes in his brief closeness with Hollingsworth highlights the importance of same-sex friendships for nineteenth-century intellectuals as well as Coverdale's fears of loneliness. His vulnerability at times brings out the negative aspects of his character, particularly when he feels threatened or neglected. He admits that his comments to Zenobia, Priscilla, and Hollingsworth are often said with malice in an attempt to create divisions between them. He is particularly sensitive to the fact that neither woman seems attracted to him. He disparages Hollingsworth's manner and Westervelt's appearance in an attempt to reaffirm his own desirability.

At the end, Coverdale makes light of his inability to commit himself and his unwillingness to extend himself to others. This trait, however, is what causes his isolation. In his opening encounter with old Moodie, he indicates a preference not to inconvenience himself. During his last scene with Zenobia, Coverdale simply stands by while she is distraught. He "leaned against a tree, and listened to her sobs, in unbroken silence" (826). He justifies his failure to respond by claiming that time would heal her grief. Although he says he identifies with Zenobia in the agony of an unrequited love, he offers no consolation. In the end, Coverdale is still a solitary figure, trying to understand the reasons for his isolation.

Hollingsworth arrives at Blithedale as a man who already has a reputation from the lecture circuit, though he has not attracted large audiences. He is about thirty but looks older, "with his great shaggy head, his heavy brow, his dark complexion, his abundant beard" (656). Before he developed an interest in philanthropic reform, he was a blacksmith. Zenobia speaks of him as a man with a "true, strong heart" (650), and initially, he seems genuinely interested in the well-being of others. His major concern is to establish a facility for the reformation of criminals. When he comes to Blithedale, he has already planned to turn the community to his own use. He assumes he can win over the other members to his project and is willing to make use of other people's resources to support his cause.

Not an intellectual, Hollingsworth is astute in terms of human psychology. He can determine what a person needs or lacks and then suggest that he can provide it. He does this when tending Coverdale during his illness. He listens to Coverdale's complaints about a lack of direction and offers to provide one for him. Later, when Coverdale admits that he cannot pledge himself unconditionally to Hollingsworth or his cause, Hollingsworth rejects him. Once Hollingsworth sees that a person offers no contribution to his mission, he has no time or place for him in his life. He does the same with Zenobia, who seeks patriarchal approval from him as much as she seeks his love. When she can no longer deliver a fortune to him to support his reform project, he turns away from her, believing that she can give him nothing else.

Hollingsworth's great fault is his single-mindedness. It narrows his vision of himself and other people. This aspect of his character is borne out in his inflexibility. He is frequently linked to images of iron, suggesting he has great strength but little give. The statements he makes about women's place and his rebuke of Zenobia during their discussion in Chapter 14, "Eliot's Pulpit," reveal his notions about a fixed order in life. In Chapter 25, "The Three Together," Coverdale compares Hollingsworth to the Puritan magistrates of old. This comparison emphasizes his strong convictions and assurance of his own correctness. It also suggests his willingness to mete out harsh punishment to those who have violated the laws he lives by. Ultimately Hollingsworth's inflexibility and inability to accept the human frailties of others lead to his great sorrow. He believes that he shares responsibility for Zenobia's death and, in the end, considers himself a criminal to be reformed.

In his treatment of the two women, Hawthorne uses the differences between dark and fair heroines typical of nineteenth-century American romance. Zenobia, the dark heroine, is energetic and lively, whereas fair Priscilla is frail and passive. Zenobia is considered by some readers to be Hawthorne's most fully drawn female character. Her physical attractiveness is complemented by her wit and her outgoing manner. Early in the novel she draws others to her through the warmth of her character. The fresh flowers in her hair and the style of her dress are chosen to set her off as unique, as an original. She has enjoyed the benefits of wealth that have allowed her to travel and to pursue avenues not open to most women in the early nineteenth century. She has found some success as a writer, and "Zenobia" is the name she uses to sign her articles, rather than her given name. This name, originally that of the Queen of Palmyra, was used in popular romances of Hawthorne's day to identify the "typical liberated woman" (St. Armand, "Love Song" 100). In choosing this name for herself, Zenobia reveals that she is conscious of creating a particular identity.

Zenobia's character appeals to current readers, and her attractive qualities make her faults less obvious. She is conscious of her ability to perform before an audience. Her legend of "The Silvery Veil" makes use of melodrama and succeeds in holding her audience's attention so that her final gesture with the gauzy veil produces the effect she desires. Her ability with language allows her to plead eloquently for redefining the relationships between men and women. When she backs away from these principles in order to maintain Hollingsworth's approval, however, Zenobia undermines her credibility. This, along with the knowledge that she has been willing to sacrifice another person for the love of someone who rejects her, leads to her despair and suicide.

The negative aspects of Zenobia's character become evident after her death. In an echo of *The Scarlet Letter*, Coverdale describes the "rank vegetation" that grows at Zenobia's gravesite. He suggests that through the weeds growing over her grave, nature reveals her deformed or hardened heart. In this passage, Hawthorne reveals what in his eyes has undermined her womanhood. For him, Zenobia is problematic because she lacks compassion. She can speak of altruism in the abstract, but she cannot enact it. She is more like Hollingsworth than she would care to admit.

If Zenobia is one of the most fully developed of Hawthorne's female characters, Priscilla is among the least. This results in part from her role as a clairvoyant and medium. To embody this role, she must have little personality of her own. Priscilla functions as a means by which the "spirit world" can reveal itself in the here and now. Priscilla is also very trusting and obedient, submissive in the areas where Zenobia is assertive. This, too, complements her role as the Veiled Lady, since an ability to resist the influence of others would interfere with her spiritual connection.

Because she lacks inner substance, Priscilla is easily manipulated by others. Hawthorne treats Priscilla as an innocent, associating her with the dove, the traditional symbol of peace and of the spirit. Priscilla's helplessness creates an opportunity for each of the other characters to respond. Hawthorne uses her to draw out underlying aspects of their natures. Zenobia's attempt to surrender Priscilla to the clutches of Westervelt initiates her own downfall. Hollingsworth's forceful intervention saves Priscilla from Westervelt's control but does not spare him later pain. In the end, it is Priscilla who becomes a caretaker of Hollingsworth, but her lack of substance limits her ability to console or protect him. For Hollingsworth and Coverdale, she represents the safe choice as a partner, one who will not challenge their superiority.

ROLE OF MINOR CHARACTERS

Hawthorne creates three important secondary characters in the romance, each with a different contribution to make. Old Moodie and Westervelt are both men of the city, and both have made use of the artifice associated with the city to create their identities. The farmer Silas Foster needs no mask when he encounters the world.

Much of old Moodie's past is revealed through the story of Fauntleroy discussed earlier. His life in time present places him at the margins of his social world. He slips in and out of scenes, attempting to pass unnoticed except when he must seek something of others. Although he was once a man of substance, he has been reduced to living off the remnants discarded by others. Coverdale compares him to "a rat without the mischief" (704). When he meets with Zenobia, however, old Moodie reveals that he has not lost the desire to exert control over life. Since he cannot compel Zenobia to care for Priscilla, he can reclaim the fortune that is legally his, thus undermining her identity and her relationship with Hollingsworth.

Westervelt, like Moodie, appears infrequently in the novel, but his presence creates turmoil. When he first visits Blithedale, Coverdale expresses intense distaste toward him, finding his quick use of the term *friend* an indication of his superficiality. Westervelt's golden teeth suggest his facility with words but also the falseness of what he says. His features and his attire, as well as his walking stick carved as a serpent, all evoke the devil. This association implies not only evil in his domination of Priscilla but also his abilities as a great deceiver. Westervelt makes his living by capitalizing on the interest in spiritualism and mesmerism that provides him a ready audience. At Zenobia's funeral, he states his belief in the possibilities of remaking the self into a new persona when an earlier one meets failure. He sees her suicide as a waste, given what she might have made herself and what he might have made of her. Coverdale sees him as an exploiter, but Westervelt also reflects the values of the cult of personality that come to dominate twentieth-century popular culture.

In stark contrast to the others, Silas Foster is a gruff man, full of "common sense." He does not create an artificial persona to hide who or what he is. His responses to people are genuine, including his expression of grief over Zenobia's end. He is not eloquent, but his simplicity of speech and his ability to function in his world reflect Hawthorne's sympathy for ordinary people. Silas may be coarse, but Hawthorne distrusts the slick or superrefined, as he reveals in the treatment of Westervelt. Silas does not use language in manipulative ways. He is often a means for Hawthorne to include verbal humor, since his directness undercuts the pretensions of others.

THEMES

Writing a romance set in his own day, Hawthorne confronts numerous issues that shaped the world of mid-nineteenth-century America. It was an age marked by enthusiasm for reform at both the individual and national levels. Many of those who embraced reform projects held an optimistic view of the potential for human beings to change. As in many of his works, Hawthorne suggests that there are some underlying aspects of human nature and behavior that remain constant, despite the outward changes in environment and culture. In addition to his questions about the possibility of reform, Hawthorne also considers the problem of public identity and the debate over gender roles and expectations.

Nineteenth-century interest in utopian communities grew out of the Romantic belief, influenced by social philosophers like Rousseau, that humans are essentially good but corrupted by their social environment. Proponents argued that if the social environment was restructured, more positive aspects of human nature would predominate. The members of the Blithedale project consciously oppose the social structure of their day. Coverdale explains that the community at Blithedale "sought our profit by mutual aid, instead of wresting it by the strong hand from an enemy, or filching it craftily from those less shrewd than ourselves . . . or winning it by selfish competition with a neighbor" (648).

The participants in Blithedale see their project as a potential model for what others could do. In this respect they are, as Hawthorne acknowledges, carrying on the tradition of New England's founding. When the Puritans arrived in the New World, they hoped to establish "a city on a hill," a more godly and righteous society than the one they left behind. In *The Scarlet Letter* and some of his short stories, Hawthorne reveals why the Puritan "errand" failed to meet its goals. He demonstrates through his characters the ways that selfishness, desire for power or wealth, jealousy, and self-deception undermine the ideals that brought the community together. Hawthorne suggests that the same is true for the utopias of his own day. The major characters in *Blithedale* carry with them the values and expectations of the world they think they are leaving behind. As he explores the nature of his characters, their motives, and behaviors, Hawthorne reveals that no utopia can emerge without profound inner change in human beings as well.

Just as he argues that changing the environment does not address the deeper issues of human failing and evil, Hawthorne asserts that many reform movements address only outward symptoms of a problem rather than underlying causes. When Coverdale returns to the city, he visits a saloon in hopes of finding old Moodie. While there, he reflects on the reasons people drink, of the way the "world will look warmer, kindlier, mellower, through the medium of a toper's glass" (784). He adds that all the efforts of the temperance movement will have no permanent effect unless the general conditions of life improve, especially for working people. He adds that "reformers should make their efforts positive, instead of negative; they must do away with evil by substituting good" (785).

In addition to his treatment of reform, Hawthorne also examines the nature of identity and the self. He is especially concerned with the ways in which a person presents a self to the world that is only a partial portrait. In developing his characters, Hawthorne poses the question, Who are these people? The stories that Coverdale relates about them and their experiences are all attempts to provide answers. Ultimately, however, Hawthorne suggests that the question is unanswerable, that it is impossible to know the true nature of others. They will always have secret selves that cannot be discovered or understood, even through spying and eavesdropping upon them.

All of the central characters in *The Blithedale Romance* have adopted masks and personas that hide their real identities. That they all do this to some degree suggests a need to avoid vulnerability and self-exposure in the exploitative culture in which they live. It also suggests a desire for privacy, a need to keep some aspect of the self a sheltered reserve. When Hollingsworth pierces Zenobia's body in his attempt to recover it, this sexually charged gesture also symbolizes his earlier penetration of her mask. He has exposed her willingness to abandon her publicly held principles to win love and approval. Once her self-constructed armor is breached, she becomes vulnerable, especially to emotional loss. Her surrender to despair indicates that some core part of her being has been affected and not just her constructed persona, as Westervelt suggests.

The Blithedale Romance also reveals the significance of gender expectations and roles in nineteenth-century America. Family life and household arrangements undergo substantial change in the first half of the nineteenth century as manufacturing, business, and professional enterprises are no longer conducted from the home. This leads to a separation of spheres for men and women, with men assigned to the public arena and women to the domestic. This separation of spheres also depends upon concepts about the inherent differences between men and women in terms of abilities and attributes. Men are socialized to embody definitions of manhood that include self-reliance, competitiveness, self-confidence, and strength of purpose. Women are encouraged to be self-sacrificing, supportive, dependent, submissive, and caring.

The participants at Blithedale talk of eliminating these divisions and definitions, which they see as restrictive. However, as with other values, they carry with them the expectations of their larger culture. When the community assembles, Zenobia comments on women's domestic duties, suggesting that they might also work in the fields. Instead, she joins the other women in the kitchen to prepare supper, even though Coverdale later reveals her talents do not include those of a cook. Zenobia also mentions woman's intuitive nature and her sensitivity to emotional truths, giving voice to the notion of essential differences between the sexes. As he is recovering from his illness, Coverdale decides it is time to emerge from his room to avoid the appearance of "effeminacy." Later he is pleased by his physical strength after days of fieldwork, since it reinforces the possibility of self-reliance. He also admits to a "masculine grossness" of thought when he contemplates the possibility that Zenobia is sexually experienced.

Gender roles and their importance shape the arguments in Chapter 14, when the main characters gather at Eliot's pulpit. Zenobia articulates her desire to speak publicly for the rights of women and for their wider liberty. She labels Priscilla an example of what man has spent centuries creating, a woman beneath and dependent upon himself. Coverdale tries to pass off her comments as a reflection of emotional turmoil following Westervelt's visit. Hollingsworth, however, reacts with an outburst of rhetoric that labels Zenobia's thoughts monstrous and that links the concept of separate spheres with a heaven-ordained order. Rather than respond to his charges, Zenobia accepts them, the first of her decisions that lead to her death. The overall argument reveals that the other three characters have accepted definitions of gender and gender roles established by the culture they claim to reject.

SYMBOLS AND METAPHORS

As in all of his work, Hawthorne develops image patterns that assume symbolic value in *The Blithedale Romance*. He also creates an extended metaphor, based upon theater and performance, to reveal aspects of life and human behavior in the novel.

One of the dominant image patterns is that of fires and hearths. From the opening chapter when Coverdale sits before his own familiar hearth to reflect, Hawthorne uses the fires and hearths to convey both mood and meaning. All of the characters in the novel are seeking a source of emotional warmth in their lives. This need draws them toward the heat and light of fires. Some offer the potential of real warmth, such as on the day of arrival at Blithedale. Others, as Silas Foster warns, are made with insubstantial brush that burns brightly with intense heat but gives out momentarily. These "false fires" are significant, for they represent the superficial quality of the bonds among the participants.

To further emphasize the difference between appearances and realities, Hawthorne creates an extended metaphor based upon the theater and performance. Through this metaphor, he conveys Coverdale's search for a role in life (Martin, *Hawthorne* 154–155). He also suggests that in public life everyone behaves as if on a stage, presenting to the world a version of the self that suits current circumstances. His use of the theater also suggests the artificiality of life in the modern world. Hawthorne supports this metaphor through the use of another set of symbolic images, the masks, veils, and pseudonyms that provide disguises for the characters at different times within the novel. These also highlight the differences between appearances and realities and suggest that individuals seldom reveal their true selves.

HISTORICAL CONTEXT

Hawthorne states in the preface that his romance is not a direct portrayal of his experience at Brook Farm. The Brook Farm community does provide background for the narrative and reveals the idealism of Hawthorne's own day. It was established in 1841 near West Roxbury, Massachusetts, under the leadership of George Ripley. One of its striking features was the number of writers, artists, and thinkers who chose to participate or to support the project. They hoped to find ways of balancing the life of work with the life of creativity. All members shared in the physical labor of running the farm, and all received similar pay. In 1843 the members decided to follow a community model called a *phalanx*, defined by French philosopher François Marie Charles Fourier. The project lasted for six years, dissolving by mutual agreement in 1847.

The Brook Farm project was not unusual in an era defined by the proliferation of reform movements. During the 1840s, America saw the rise of the women's rights movement, the temperance movement, and the early labor movement. It also witnessed the strengthening of the abolitionists, who worked to end slavery in the South. In addition to these broad social movements, Americans became interested in dietary reform, the water cure, and phrenology. They were looking for new ways to understand their world and to define their place in it. Their efforts reflected an emerging secular approach to human experience that emphasized the role of "science" and an understanding of human nature (Walters 171).

An activity that bridged the world of reform and the world of entertainment was spiritualism. Spiritualism encompassed many forms of activity, including spirit rappings, séances, and mesmerism (also known as "animal magnetism" or hypnotism). All of these were efforts to make contact with the dead, the spiritual realm or the "higher spheres." Those who pursued these activities seriously believed that the spiritual realm had wisdom to impart that would improve the quality of daily life. Some believed that they could gain answers to troubling questions or solve mysteries by working through a medium. The performances of mediums attracted large audiences, some of whom came to scoff or to challenge the truthfulness of what occurred. Hawthorne was suspicious of spiritualism and other "pseudo-sciences." He did not deny that contact with the supernatural plane was possible, making use of aspects of the supernatural in his fiction. He felt, however, that there was a high level of fraud and charlatanism, especially when such individuals were featured in public performances. Ironically, women who appeared on stage as mediums and claimed that their words were "inspired" gained a public voice that women in other reform movements were often denied.

Many notable American women gained renown through their participation in reform movements and in their claiming of a public voice. Margaret Fuller (1810–1850), an acquaintance of Hawthorne, followed such a path. Well educated and articulate, she contributed to and edited *The Dial*, a Transcendentalist magazine. She held a series of conversations to educate other women on women's rights, which she also addressed in her book *Woman in the Nineteenth Century* (1845). She wrote for the New York *Tribune* and became the first woman to serve as a foreign correspondent for an American newspaper. While in Rome she supported the struggle to create an Italian republic. Returning to America following the political turmoil in Italy, Fuller, her Italian husband, and young son drowned in a shipwreck off Long Island. Many readers believe that Hawthorne's character Zenobia is modeled on Margaret Fuller, although the extent of that portrait has been the subject of extensive critical debate (Cary).

ALTERNATE READING: MARXIST LITERARY CRITICISM

Because *The Blithedale Romance* is set during the era in which industrial capitalism is redefining American life, it offers a rich text for Marxist analysis. Marxist literary criticism examines the ways in which the economics, class structure, and ideologies (a set of beliefs and the images that reflect them) shape a culture and are revealed in its literature. Karl Marx (1818–1883), author of the *Communist Manifesto* (1848), argued that economic activity established the base of a culture and provided the foundation for its intellectual, political, and legal systems (superstructure). He asserted that the culture's ideology shapes the consciousness of human beings, so that an individual's sense of self and sense of reality emerge through social interactions.

Marxist criticism draws upon historical contexts and sociology as well as economic analysis to explore the complex nature of social relations in a given era. Marx did not see history or social relations as static. He argued that history reflected a process he called *dialectical materialism.* In this process, change occurs through the continuing struggle of opposites, including the struggle between the ruling class and the oppressed classes. For Marx, the primary struggle of the modern age lay between the capitalists (the ruling class) and the proletariat (the working and oppressed class). Their struggle ultimately focused on who would own and control the means of production, who would own and control the products of labor. Later Marxist theory also critiqued the role of the middle class, or bourgeoisie, within the culture, seeing it aligned with the interests of capital and focused on preserving the status quo.

Marxist criticism has evolved during the twentieth century into a broad range of approaches. When examining a work of literature, a Marxist critic asks questions such as: How is the economic system or power of the marketplace evident within the narrative? Who controls the means of production and/or the access to power within the culture? How are they and their ideology present and privileged in the text?

In *The Blithedale Romance*, capital is the silent but always operative factor in characters' lives. Zenobia and Coverdale enjoy a life of leisure and freedom in which they are not required to work. The sources of their income are never mentioned, but each lives on some form of inherited wealth. Since neither acknowledges other landholdings when taking up residence at Blithedale, their wealth is derived from capital enterprise. This wealth provides them with freedom and privilege within their world. Zenobia gives voice to the oppression of women within the culture, but the position she enjoys in the class structure blinds her to the intimate link between the economic structure and that oppression. Likewise, Coverdale can be seen as a "representative man of his time" who judges other people and experience "against the norms of conventional society," which he accepts as valid (Schriber 62–63). Although he joins a radical venture designed to circumvent the economic power of the day, Coverdale enjoys the material benefits of that economy and has no real desire to see it change. This, for a Marxist critic, helps to account for the mixed messages he conveys about the Blithedale endeavor.

Other characters' lives are also shaped by their relation to capital, their class status, and the changing economic structure. Hollingsworth, the former blacksmith, has abandoned his role as an artisan/craftsman who owns and controls what he produces to assume a service-oriented function in the new economy. In abandoning his earlier occupation, Hollingsworth has sacrificed his independence. Because he lacks capital to support his reform project, he now depends upon cultivating the interests of others, such as Zenobia, to gain financial backing. Although he proposes reforming individuals who have committed crimes, he, like Coverdale, accepts the values and norms of the culture as it exists. His own bourgeois sensibility governs his notions about a God-ordained role for women, and he articulates a conventional justification for maintaining the status quo.

At the bottom of the class structure and economic system reside old Moodie and his daughter Priscilla, whom he labels "the daughter of my long calamity" (800). In his earlier life as Fauntleroy, old Moodie had enjoyed power and privilege. He has never lost his sense of entitlement, and though he lives in poverty, he does not identify with the working class. Although he must scrounge for his existence, he never questions the rightness of the economic system. His revenge upon Zenobia hinges upon the power he gains when he reasserts his "rightful" claim to her wealth.

Priscilla is the figure most clearly at the mercy of the capitalist economic system. Her stitching of empty purses symbolizes her own position in the economic structure, for she has no money with which to fill them. Her father serves as the middleman who sells them, so that Priscilla does not control what becomes of the product she makes. Similarly, she does not control the use of her spiritual gifts but is held captive by another middleman who reaps a profit from her performance. Westervelt literally capitalizes on the marketability of her talents, and her natural gift has been corrupted by the commercial aspect of the stage.

The characters are also affected by the market-driven culture of the time, especially its emphasis on consumption. In this culture, even people become commodities, things that can be bought, sold, and traded in the marketplace. Zenobia has created an image of herself for public consumption, but this poses a danger because it makes her like any other commodity in the marketplace. When her value to others falls, she can be dismissed. This contributes to the collapse of her relationship with Hollingsworth. In the argument that follows her "trial," Zenobia realizes that since she can no longer deliver the fortune that he needs for his mission, she becomes disposable to Hollingsworth.

In Marxist terms, the Blithedale project itself is a superficial gesture, not a revolutionary act. Although the characters claim that they wish to share in the labor of working people, they do not truly identify with them. Their commitment is for the short term, and none of those who benefit from the capitalist system wish to see it changed in ways that alter their own privilege. The characters are unable to break through the ideology that has shaped their understanding of reality. They cannot achieve the critical distance from the culture that has shaped them so that they see its pervasive influence. Simply moving a few miles outside the city does not separate them from the values and expectations generated by capitalist ideology. Even Hawthorne as author is shaped by the ideology that governs his culture. Although he questions aspects of that culture, he also presents its values through his narrative.

8

The Marble Faun
(1860)

Eight years passed between the publication of *The Blithedale Romance* and the appearance of *The Marble Faun* in 1860. During this time, Hawthorne wrote the campaign biography of his friend Franklin Pierce, who was running for president. He also published his most popular work for children, *Tanglewood Tales* (1853), a collection of stories that continued the retelling of classical myths he had begun in *A Wonder-Book* (1852). When Pierce was elected, he rewarded Hawthorne's loyalty by appointing him U.S. consul at Liverpool, an important trade port. In 1853 Hawthorne moved his family to England, where they remained until he stepped down as consul in 1857. Before returning to America, Hawthorne traveled to France and Italy. His tour through Italy and his interaction with the American artist colony in Rome provided the background for his last complete romance.

This novel, like *The Blithedale Romance*, has been criticized as an uneven work that does not achieve the unity or cohesiveness of *The Scarlet Letter* and *Seven Gables*. It does, however, offer a fascinating account of Americans' encounters with a culture substantially different from their own. Most Americans of the early nineteenth century, including Hawthorne, knew the culture of Europe through literature and historical narrative. They were aware of the great works of European art only through engraved illustrations or later copies brought to America. The personal experience of travel and direct engagement with the culture against which Americans defined their own sensibility and values provided Hawthorne a rich subject to explore. He conveyed not only the attractive and seductive qualities of this older culture but also the confusion experienced by those who confront it and attempt to resist its influence. Hawthorne saw in this encounter the opportunity for growth and for deeper insight into the self. He also used it as a context for exploring the timeless problem of the fall from innocence into knowledge and experience.

The unsettling experiences of the American in Europe as a subject for fiction held even more appeal for the next generation of American authors, including Mark Twain and Henry James, whose opportunities to travel were greater than Hawthorne's. Given today's expanded possibilities for travel and the continuing interest in cultures that differ from our own, readers find in *The Marble Faun* fascinating insights into the ways that individuals interact with a foreign culture and how they respond to changes within themselves in light of their encounters.

SETTING, PLOT, AND STRUCTURE

The importance of his European travels becomes apparent in Hawthorne's use of Italy for the setting of *The Marble Faun*. Years earlier, he set "Rappaccini's Daughter" in Italy, but the country and the garden of that short story are stylized, based on literary accounts and images, not direct observation. The Italy that Hawthorne depicts in *The Marble Faun* is rich with detail and texture. He attempts to capture the quality of light, the air and atmosphere, the changing seasons that alter the landscape in ways more subtle than he experienced in New England. He also conveys the weight of history that affects the mood of Rome itself. He records the presence of antiquity in the ruins of classical Rome and the sense of continuity embodied in the Roman Catholic Church. He suggests that in Rome the myths and traditions that have shaped Western civilization still reverberate with a power that makes a profound impression on visitor and native alike. Throughout the narrative, Hawthorne interweaves legends, folktales, and historical allusions that add depth to and heighten the significance of place.

As he did in *Blithedale*, Hawthorne makes use of contrasts between the city and the rural countryside. He also develops contrasts within the city of Rome itself by depicting two sides of the city, one that is bathed by the golden sun of the Mediterranean, the other dark and suffused with the gloom of melancholy. The gardens especially attract his attention, and Hawthorne praises their cultivated and picturesque qualities, especially when compared to the "rude and untrained landscapes" in America (911). But the city is also crowded, teeming with life, and strange to the visitor. In a passage in his notebook, Hawthorne comments upon the "ugliness, shabbiness, un-home-likeness of a Roman street" (*French and Italian Notebooks* 56–57). His choice of the word *un-home-*

likeness reflects the displacement Americans feel in the foreignness of the Roman setting. The city is a place that confuses, with its myriad courtyards, side streets, and subterranean chambers. The weight of history can give Rome an oppressive air, compounded in the summer when the malaria, or Roman fever, drives visitors and residents alike out of town. Hawthorne also describes the catacombs, the burial chambers that evoke the constant presence of death.

The juxtaposition of light and darkness, a favorite Hawthorne motif, allows him to suggest the mixed nature of the city. It is not all good or all bad, and things are not always what they first appear to be. The contrast between light and dark also allows Hawthorne to establish the dichotomy of his characters' worlds. Miriam and Donatello, in giving way to a passionate and violent impulse, are drawn into darkness and secrecy. In contrast, Hilda and Kenyon, who deliberate and discuss everything, including their relationship, meet openly, their feelings for each other gradually revealed in the light of day.

In addition to the physical setting of Rome, Hawthorne makes use of the defining presence of the Catholic Church. Impressed by the grandeur of the Church as evidenced in its buildings, Hawthorne finds aspects of Catholic ritual and tradition engaging, particularly the emphasis on symbols and allegorical images. He enjoys the "cool, quiet beautiful place of worship" and envies the opportunity to "fling down the dark burden at the foot of the Cross" (1146–1147) to go forth from the confessional absolved of sin. He is also attracted to the unifying aspect of the Church in people's lives, the way it provides a sense of community and belonging, of shared ritual and common faith. A descendant of the Puritans, however, Hawthorne is troubled by the assertion of the dogma of the institutional church and its history of corruption. He reveals this most clearly in the scene of Hilda's confession, when the priest uses coercive tactics in an attempt to convert her. Hilda resists, asserting her own Calvinist beliefs about the soul's relationship to God.

The churches are great repositories of art, including the stained glass windows that create an aura of warmth. Hawthorne also describes numerous galleries and museums, highlighting specific works of art housed within them. He opens the narrative in the sculpture gallery of the Capitol, with its "Dying Gladiator" and other works of antiquity. Amid this collection, he notes the presence of an allegorical figure of a child accompanied by a dove and a snake, which he describes as the image of the human soul faced with good and evil. This figure forecasts the central theme of Hawthorne's narrative. It also introduces the importance of the interpretation of art, the interaction between viewer and object that complements the artistic process begun by the artist in the act of creation. Here, too, appears the "Faun of Praxiteles" (Resting Satyr), the sculpture to which Donatello is frequently compared. The encounters with art continue throughout the novel, as Hawthorne takes the reader on a tour of the monuments, palaces, and piazzas that define the city of Rome.

Although it is his longest romance, Hawthorne's plot in *The Marble Faun* follows a more linear and conventional pattern than does that of *The Scarlet Letter* or *Seven Gables*. Like *The Blithedale Romance*, *The Marble Faun* can be divided into three major sections. The first introduces the main characters and their relationships. It also describes Miriam's pursuit by the mysterious figure who emerges from the catacombs, culminating in Donatello's act of murder to eliminate this threatening presence. The first section of the novel ends with the four main characters separated from each other. Hawthorne suggests that one of the effects of Donatello's crime is the breakdown of their community. The second section explores the changes in Donatello (and to some degree in Miriam and Kenyon) following the murder. The third section focuses on the effects of the crime on Hilda and on her relationship to the other characters. It presents the reunion of the four major characters during the carnival, although their situations and relationships to each other have changed significantly. Hawthorne titles both the opening and closing chapters "Miriam, Hilda, Kenyon, Donatello," to invite comparison and to measure the degree of change that has affected them all.

Unlike Hawthorne's other romances that depend on the gradual introduction of characters, *The Marble Faun* begins with all the main characters engaged in a scene of lighthearted banter. Teasing Donatello about his resemblance to the sculpture of the Faun, the artists Miriam, Hilda, and Kenyon walk with him through the galleries of the Capitol. The mood darkens at the end of the second chapter, however, when Miriam's model appears, dogging their steps. Hawthorne conveys this change in mood by shifting the scene from the airiness of the gallery to the gloom of the catacombs. In the catacombs, the mysterious connection is established between Miriam and the model, a mystery compounded as the narrative develops by the rumors of Miriam's origins and past. The model becomes a haunting presence, and at each appearance, he unsettles Miriam, provoking the curiosity of her friends.

While he builds suspense around the model's hold over Miriam, Hawthorne includes chapters that entail visits to each artist's studio, revealing through these chapters more about their individual natures. He also describes the Anglo-American artists' colony of Rome, a group whose membership is defined by language as well as by nationality. Although on the surface this appears a congenial and supportive crowd, Hawthorne reveals the competitive and sometimes hostile interactions among the painters and sculptors. The artistic gatherings offer some respite from the solitude of the artists' studios and the isolation they feel but do not appear to be sources of many sustained friendships. Those who remain too long within this circle see "their originality die out of them" (963).

The first section of the narrative moves toward a crisis as the company of artists enjoys a moonlit stroll through the ruins of the ancient city. During their walk, Donatello professes his love for Miriam and his willingness to act in ridding her of the demon-model. The path of the artists takes them to the Tarpeian Rock, also called the Traitor's Leap, a steep precipice from which political criminals were thrown to their deaths. The party moves on, but Miriam and Donatello remain behind, where they again confront the model. In a moment of passionate rage, Donatello flings the model over the precipice. In that moment, he casts away his innocence as well. United in a bond of guilt and secrecy, Miriam and Donatello find that their relationship has been irrevocably changed. Instead of a happy union, however, Donatello experiences "the ever-increasing loathsomeness" of this partnership, "which would corrupt and grow more noisome, forever and forever" (999). Unknown to them, Hilda has returned to the scene in time to witness what transpired. She, too, finds that she no longer can look upon her friends as she once did and attempts to cut herself off from them. The closely knit group of friends unravels following the crime, though fragile threads of connection remain.

The second section of the narrative explores the aftermath of the crime and its impact upon Donatello, especially once he discovers that the man he has killed was a Capuchin monk. Instead of using inset stories to divide the sections as he had in *Blithedale*, Hawthorne uses a change in setting to delineate the middle portion of the novel. When Donatello leaves Rome, he invites Kenyon to visit him at his family estate at Monte Beni, "mount good," in the countryside of Tuscany. There Kenyon views the sylvan world that produced the innocent Donatello, a child of nature who conversed with the animals. Now cut off from the natural world, Donatello secludes himself in a dark tower that is attached to the family villa. In his tower, he broods over what he has done, and he tells Kenyon, "I am not a boy now. Time flies over us, but leaves its shadow behind" (1033). He serves Kenyon wine produced on the family estate, a vintage called "Sunshine," based on a secret family recipe. Kenyon claims that it offers those who partake "the airy sweetness of youthful hopes" (1036), but Donatello admits that he no longer savors it.

All the changes in Donatello reflect a moral gravity and a somberness, but Kenyon does not know what has caused this change. He assumes that Donatello suffers from unrequited love for Miriam in the same way that Kenyon feels distress over Hilda's reserve toward him. He attempts to probe Donatello's nature, periodically raising questions, but Donatello avoids responding. When he sculpts a bust of Donatello, Kenyon creates a "countenance [with] a distorted and violent look, combining animal fierceness with intelligent hatred"

(1078), which recalls Donatello in his act of murder. Startled by the result of his work, Kenyon refashions the clay, but his artistic insights have revealed that aspect of self that Donatello struggles to conceal from the world, although he privately broods over its existence.

Unknown to Donatello, Kenyon has discovered that Miriam is living in part of Donatello's villa. Her pallor and weakness elicit Kenyon's sympathy, as does her confessed fear of Donatello's rejection. Kenyon claims that Donatello still loves her, that she is no longer an object of horror to him, whatever had transpired between them. He promises to effect a reunion between Miriam and Donatello in the piazza at Perugia. To achieve this meeting on neutral ground and to draw Donatello out of his depression, Kenyon suggests a tour of the Tuscan countryside. While they journey together, Donatello prays at every shrine, hoping to ease his guilt, but his efforts bring him no comfort.

When they arrive in Perugia, it is market day, full of the "petty tumult" and "vivacious spectacle" of activity. In the anonymity that such a scene grants them, Donatello and Miriam meet again at the statue of Pope Julius III, whose arms are extended in a gesture of benediction. In a scene that imitates a wedding ceremony, Kenyon defines the union of Miriam and Donatello but cautions that it is "for mutual support . . . for one another's final good . . . but not for earthly happiness!" (1121). Having completed his mission in reuniting Miriam and Donatello, Kenyon returns to Rome.

Kenyon's return to the city marks the beginning of the third section of the narrative. He goes in search of Hilda, who has stayed in the city for the summer despite the dangers posed by Roman fever. Her absence from the middle section of the novel adds to its darker qualities, but even Hilda's tower has grown dim since she witnessed the scene at the Traitor's Leap. This third section of the novel forms a parallel to the second in that it explores the changes in Hilda's character and ultimately leads to the union of Kenyon and Hilda.

Although she bears no responsibility for what occurred, Hilda has also been deeply affected by the crime. Like Donatello, she was an innocent, but now she has experienced the presence of evil and the burden of human weakness. She had anticipated "a delightful summer" (1125) but finds instead that things have lost their meaning. She feels her loneliness acutely, reflecting that she is a motherless child, and seeks comfort in her devotions to the Virgin Mary, a divine Mother who understands her grief. As her transformation occurs, Hilda's perceptions of life and art undergo change. She sees "beauty less vividly" but feels "truth, or the lack of it, more profoundly" (1133). She also begins to admit her need for human companionship, especially for the devoted love that Kenyon offers.

Looking for community and for relief from the secret burden that she carries, Hilda finds herself in St. Peter's. Moved by the beauty of the building and inspired by Guido's painting of the Archangel Michael triumphing over Evil, Hilda hesitates before the confessional. Convinced that she might seek comfort there without betraying her own religious faith, Hilda pours out her anguish to the priest. When he attempts to convert her, she declines, reasserting the importance of her New England background. Hilda does find a release from her burden, however, and accepts the priest's blessing. When Kenyon confronts her about the meaning of what she has done, she reassures him that she is still a daughter of the Puritans, but she experiences a lightness of being that allows her to recapture her sense of hope.

Freed from the melancholy she had experienced, Hilda resumes her work as an artist, but she is no longer the perfect copyist. In the past she had been a type of medium, similar to Priscilla of *Blithedale*; her ethereal nature made her a vehicle for the expression of the Old Masters' ideas. Once her transformation begins, she becomes a figure of greater substance, more fully human, and can no longer "yield herself up to the painter so unreservedly as in times past" (1164). She does yield to her feelings for Kenyon, perceiving that he, too, carries a burden. Her praise of his sculpture and her insights into the meaning of his work contribute to a plane of shared vision from which their relationship grows.

Both Kenyon and Hilda have experienced some change in outlook and understanding, but they must go through a final trial before they can be united for good. Hilda, acting upon the promise she made to Miriam early in the novel, finds her way through Rome to the Palazzo Cenci to deliver a package Miriam had entrusted to her. She disappears. Instead of finding Hilda at the Vatican galleries where they had agreed to meet, Kenyon encounters first Donatello, then Miriam, who have returned to Rome. Miriam appears in the company of another mysterious stranger and simply informs Kenyon, "[W]hen the lamp goes out, do not despair" (1184). Puzzled by the strange message, Kenyon goes in search of Hilda, only to find her shrine to the Virgin in darkness. He feels a darkness descend on his own consciousness and begins to experience a loneliness similar to Hilda's summer emptiness.

The final action occurs during the carnival, amid greater confusion and activity than on market day in Perugia. Again the anonymity offered by the crowd, along with the costumes donned for the carnival, makes possible the moment of contact between Kenyon, Miriam, and Donatello. Miriam holds the key to Hilda's mysterious disappearance but hesitates to reveal all in the attempt to delay her inevitable separation from Donatello. She provides some detail about her past but does not fully recount her history. In trusting Kenyon to believe in her innocence with regard to her family's crimes, Miriam begins to rebuild the sympathetic connections that had made the four friends a community at the outset. She also reassures Kenyon of Hilda's safe return.

In a scene that recalls "My Kinsman, Major Molineux," Kenyon witnesses the parade of masked figures who appear on the Corso. The movement and confusion around him seem like a "feverish dream" (1225), but Kenyon surrenders himself to the experience. Again feeling isolated within the crowd, Kenyon's attention is drawn to a balcony, where he sees Hilda, dressed in white, smiling down on the scene below. The details of her disappearance are left in mystery, but the two are reunited and agree to wed. In a last gesture of reconnection and remembrance, Miriam sends Hilda a bracelet made of seven Etruscan gems. Although the bracelet's circle suggests closure, many mysteries remain at the end of the narrative, questions Hawthorne acknowledges but leaves unanswered.

Readers of the first edition of *The Marble Faun* found the ending unsatisfying and asked for clarifications and more explanation. For the second edition of the novel, Hawthorne prepared a "Postscript," in which he promised to explain various incidents. The postscript, however, provided little additional information other than Hilda's whereabouts during her disappearance and Donatello's prison sentence. Hawthorne, in frustrating the desire to know all the facts, seemed to remind his readers that this was within the power of the artist or romancer, who need not provide "one word of explanation" (1242). Such a response has been found insufficient by modern critics who feel that the incomplete resolution and lack of explanations are major weaknesses of the narrative.

CHARACTERS

Unlike the forced and artificial community of *The Blithedale Romance*, the four main characters in *The Marble Faun* come together out of shared interests in art and in each other. The events of the narrative, however, test the strength of their bonds and commitments as each character goes through a change or transformation. Hawthorne explores not only how such change affects the individual but also how the individual is perceived by others. He raises questions about one's ability to accept truth not only about the self but also about those who are part of one's intimate circle. As in *Blithedale*, Hawthorne compares the two women and the two men as a means of heightening their development.

In his treatment of Miriam and Hilda, Hawthorne again draws upon the dark heroine–fair heroine contrast of the romance tradition. Miriam Schaefer, the dark heroine, echoes Zenobia in both her passionate energy and her mysterious past. She, too, uses a pseudonym to conceal her true identity. The narrative gives hints of that identity, but her full story is never told. She explains that her mother was English, of Jewish ancestry, and her father from one of the princely families of southern Italy. To this mixed background she attributes her freedom of thought and her powerful will. Involved in scandal, her family had become notorious, and their name alone provokes revulsion. This scandal also remains concealed, but Miriam professes her own revulsion at the marriage contract that had been arranged for her. The secrets of her past link her to the story of Beatrice Cenci (see "Allusions" later in this chapter) whose portrait by Guido is repeatedly mentioned in the narrative.

To her friends, Miriam appears to be a talented artist but a mercurial woman. In the first section of the novel, she uses her wit and sarcasm to keep others at a distance. Implied in her knowledge of the dark side of human nature is sexual knowledge as well, and she fears her friends' rejection, should they know too much about her. Although she lives and works in a lofty space, Miriam dwells in the shadows of Rome. The gloom pervades her studio, suggesting the brooding and reflective quality of her nature as well as her secrecy. The windows of her studio are shuttered or curtained, with only a sunless portion of the sky left visible. In this studio, Miriam creates paintings that demonstrate an artistic vision both original and provocative. Based on biblical narratives that intertwine passion and vengeance, these paintings depict scenes of powerful women who have defeated threatening men. The paintings reflect Miriam's own desire to free herself from the threatening presence of the model and from her past.

Having exercised a powerful influence on Donatello in their moment of crisis, Miriam finds herself powerless to help him accept what he has become. When Donatello retreats to his tower, Miriam enters a period of mourning, grieving the loss of the one person with whom she shares a deep bond, even if it is the bond of guilt. Miriam is willing to sacrifice herself to free Donatello, but she discovers that she must wait rather than act to reconnect with him. Accepting a passive role is difficult for Miriam, but she ultimately resigns herself to it until the end. During Hilda's disappearance, Miriam plays a more active part in the turn of events but from behind the scenes.

As the fair heroine, Hilda presents a distinctly different character. Her New England idealism and faith have spared her exposure to the darker sides of human nature. She tends to see with a vision that divides life and experience into black and white, with little sense of the gray areas that entail moral complexity. She has also experienced losses in her life and as an orphan has chosen her own path to Rome and to art. Hilda does not dwell on her past, but at times she laments the absence of a mother's guidance and care. She recognizes that her innocence and inexperience cannot protect her from all of the dangers that surround her.

In her role as a copyist, Hilda willingly accepts the artistic vision of others and attempts to be true to it. Her studio, in contrast to Miriam's, sits atop a tower filled with light in the "pure transparency of air" (895). From this elevation, she tends a flock of doves and maintains a shrine to the Virgin Mary. Her association with the doves and the Virgin implies the spiritual quality of Hilda's nature, but Hilda is not perfect. Her lack of compassion and her emotional distance reveal a righteousness that must be tempered by mercy. Both Miriam and Kenyon remark that because she has no need for mercy, Hilda has difficulty appreciating that others do. In order to grow beyond her own limitations, Hilda must recognize the importance of connection to others and learn to accept their faults as well as their strengths. She also needs to experience the humanizing element of Kenyon's love to see herself more clearly, to become less confined in the image of an angel and more fully embodied as a woman. By the end of the novel, Hilda has experienced these changes. Descending from the balcony to rejoin Kenyon, she returns to the plane of ordinary human activity.

The two male characters also present striking contrasts to each other. Initially Donatello appears an insubstantial young man who floats on the surface of life, whereas Kenyon has a deeper appreciation of life's mysteries and the implications of human will and desire. In the course of the narrative, Donatello goes through the most obvious changes, but Kenyon also experiences a degree of growth through his interactions with the other characters.

As the playful companion to the three artists, Donatello exhibits attributes that link him to the figure of the Faun. In Roman mythology, fauns were woodland or rural deities associated with mischief and merriment. A faun had the head and body of a man but the horns, ears, tail, and sometimes the legs of a goat. The faun, like other woodland deities, evoked the ideal of Arcadia (see "Allusions" later in this chapter), a place where individuals lived simple lives in harmony with nature. Donatello, like the sculpture to which he is compared, lacks a "moral severity," instead reflecting a childlike honesty and simplicity. He cannot conceal his love for Miriam, since he displays all his emotions openly, without hesitation. Like Hilda, he seems to accept the world's goodness, not dwelling on the presence of evil.

The Faun's blend of man and beast also suggests a more primitive being, one that acts instinctually rather than from reason. This side of Donatello's character emerges when he senses a threat to Miriam's well-being through the actions of the demon-model. To convey this, Hawthorne uses animal metaphors to describe Donatello. Upon seeing the model again, Donatello's "lips were drawn apart, so as to disclose his set teeth, thus giving him a look of animal rage" (927). These same animal instincts surface prior to his murderous act, when Donatello has "a tiger-like fury gleaming from his wild eyes," and he evinces the "wrath of a faithful hound" (976) when he perceives Miriam's fear and desperation. These metaphors reveal the negative aspect of Donatello's fall, that he experiences a devolution toward the bestial rather than an elevation to a higher plane of being.

Startled by his plunge into the darker side of human emotion and behavior, Donatello initially blames Miriam and cannot look upon her. He anguishes over what he has done and fears the punishment that he assumes will follow. When he retreats to Monte Beni, he secludes himself in the "owl-tower." The owl is associated with night and death but also with wisdom. Gradually Donatello realizes that he must own his actions and accept who and what he is. His experiences give him a deeper knowledge of himself, and the changes in his demeanor and outlook are noticed by those around him. This knowledge makes him a new man, an individual of greater substance who appreciates moral complexity. This knowledge, however, has not been achieved without cost, including the loss of playfulness and optimism that once defined Donatello's nature. In the end, he also pays the civil price for his crime, since the postscript states that he has been sent to prison.

Of the four friends, Kenyon the sculptor remains the most constant. He is the only one who does not use a tower for his studio or as a retreat, suggesting his more grounded nature. He appears in all three sections of the narrative as a principal figure and provides a uniting consciousness for the novel. He is reflective and philosophical, but his reasoning at times follows a precision that makes him less compassionate. The only strong feelings he acknowledges are for Hilda, but he moderates expressing his love for her in light of her reserve. She finds troubling his tendency to "explain away the wonder and the mystery out of everything" (939) and to appreciate only those things that are "cold and hard" (940).

Kenyon's remarks about art reveal his emotional guardedness and reserve. This lack of warmth is also reflected in his work, which displays craftsmanship but not always the inspiration that adds fluidity to stone sculpture. Miriam teases him about his belief that "sculpture should be a sort of fossilizing process" (865), hinting at the limitations in his vision. Kenyon claims that he can resist the influence of a work of art, that he defies "any painter to move and elevate [him] without [his] own consent and assistance" (866). This statement suggests that he does not trust the responses of those who view his work. It helps to explain what Miriam notices, that in some of his work the moral lessons are conveyed too directly, as though Kenyon does not trust the work to convey its own meaning.

In the middle section of the novel, Kenyon learns as an observer rather than as an actor. He sees the evolution of Donatello's attitude and his gradual acceptance of his need for Miriam. Although Kenyon facilitates their reunion, he cannot force it to happen. By the end of his Tuscan sojourn, Kenyon has begun to see the struggles of others more sympathetically, but he remains judgmental, as his pronouncement over Miriam and Donatello reveals. In the third section of the novel, Kenyon undergoes a greater transformation as he surrenders to the experiences of life. He learns to accept what life brings and to trust the insights of others. He also learns to accept mystery and the unexplained, lessons that come to him through Hilda's disappearance and return. These lessons allow Kenyon to recognize that life has "so much human promise in it" (1237), especially in the happiness and reassurance he finds with Hilda.

ROLE OF MINOR CHARACTERS

The Marble Faun features many incidental characters who appear briefly. They contribute to the momentum of the plot or provide additional information about a character or event. These figures include Donatello's servants, many of the artists in Rome, and the priest-confessor that Hilda encounters. Only one minor character emerges as a notable presence, Miriam's model.

Hawthorne reveals little of the model's background, and his membership in the Capuchin order is not disclosed until his death. His emergence from the catacombs links him to the legend of Memmius, a man-demon who was reputed to haunt the burial chambers. Memmius had participated in the persecution of the early Christians and had entered the catacombs planning to reveal their whereabouts to the authorities. In a similar fashion, Miriam's model pursues her and has power over her connected with knowledge of her past. Their exact relationship is never explained, but he holds her in a "thralldom" in which he can command her obedience. His constant surveillance and pursuit provoke fear and hatred in Miriam. His appearance and manner make him a sinister figure of evil, and he tells Miriam that death will not end his hold over her. Even in death he has the power to unsettle Miriam and Donatello. When they approach his funeral bier, they notice that his corpse begins to bleed. Legend has it that such an event means the murderer is present, and Donatello especially shudders at this accusation from the grave.

THEMES

In *The Marble Faun*, Hawthorne draws together many of the thematic issues he addressed in earlier work. When published in England, the novel was titled *Transformation*, suggesting Hawthorne's interest in the many facets of change that affect individuals and the world around them. He again focuses on the nature of sin and guilt, as it affects not only individuals but also their relationships with others. To balance his study of the darker side of human experience, he examines the power of love to draw individuals toward wholeness and community. Throughout the narrative, Hawthorne also explores the nature of the visual arts, particularly painting and sculpture, and the role of the artist who must struggle to find balance between the ideal and the real.

In much of his fiction, Hawthorne explores the individual's movement from innocence to experience. He traces how a character gains a wider view of self and the world. He also examines how a character meets the challenge of integrating this new knowledge into his or her understanding. Those figures like Young Goodman Brown (see "Young Goodman Brown" in Chapter 3), who accept knowledge about others but reject truth about the self, often end up cut off from life and from the community around them. In *The Marble Faun*, this movement from innocence to experience shapes three of the four main characters. Only Miriam goes through little change. Her role as a more worldly woman implies that she has gone through this process prior to the novel's opening. For the other three, confronting the presence of sin (or evil) requires confronting personal limitations. Through this process Hawthorne raises questions about the possibility of the "fortunate fall," the act of corruption that leads to a greater good. Kenyon retreats from his assertion of this possibility, but Hawthorne demonstrates that his characters have gained wisdom and greater depth through the course of experience.

Many of Hawthorne's works also explore the way the burden of the past influences life in time present. Often referred to as the "sins of the fathers," events from the past shape the world in which characters function and affect the way they perceive themselves and others. In *The Marble Faun*, Hawthorne considers the weight of both the national or cultural past and the familial or personal past.

The cultural past shapes the environment of Rome, and vestiges of its existence are evident throughout the city. Physical signs of its continuing presence remain, as do the names, legends, and myths that defined earlier eras. This cultural past allows Hawthorne to examine the difference between Europeans and Americans. He suggests that Europeans are more conscious of the past's power; they accept that the past is inescapable. He intimates that Europeans have a more complex view of human failings and evil in light of this past and acknowledge the resonance of guilt and regret. Americans like Kenyon and Hilda have little sense of a cultural past to weigh them down. They live in the present and have hope for the future, but this hope can only be realized in their return to America. Hawthorne reveals that American idealism and optimism exist in part because the American scene presents fewer reminders of failure and decay/decline.

To emphasize their freedom, Hawthorne says little about Kenyon's or Hilda's family background. Familial past, however, plays a significant role in the lives of Donatello and Miriam and in the development of their characters. Donatello's family is associated with positive attributes of the past, including a simple life, a closeness to nature and to the land, and a simple faith in the goodness of creation. The "Sunshine" produced by the family vineyards underscores this harmonious relationship between people, nature, and time. When Donatello mourns his losses after the murder, one of them is this family legacy. In contrast, Miriam's family reveals the negative attributes of the past, especially the way greed and lust lead to corruption. Miriam can never free herself from the clutches of that corrupt past, although she hides her true name and attempts to create a new identity for herself. Like Zenobia in *Blithedale*, she is vulnerable to the threats posed by those associated with her past. Even at the novel's close, the dark power of Miriam's family hovers in the background, represented by her mysterious escort in the carriage. Her associations with Beatrice Cenci (see "Allusions" later in this chapter) underscore literal "sins of the father."

As in *Seven Gables*, Hawthorne moderates the darker aspects of his narrative by exploring the ways in which love and friendship draw characters out of isolation. In the aftermath of Donatello's crime, relationships fracture, leaving each of the four friends alone. Without the support of a community, each must find a way to cope with the knowledge the crime has engendered. Both Donatello and Hilda, who embody two types of innocence undone, initially retreat to their respective towers. They attempt to close out the world and the darker knowledge it brings to them. Donatello cannot accept the truth about himself, and Hilda cannot accept what she knows about Miriam and Donatello. The second and third sections of the novel focus on the integration of this new knowledge and the rebuilding of relationships, symbolically conveyed in the drawing forth of Donatello and Hilda from their respective towers.

Although the last section of the novel presents the union of Miriam and Donatello and that of Kenyon and Hilda, the changes that have occurred in their outward circumstances prevent a reestablishment of the community that they enjoyed at the beginning. Miriam knows that she must separate from Donatello. Kenyon realizes that he and Hilda will not find a suitable community to sustain them within the artist colony of Rome. Kenyon and Hilda remark upon the loneliness they feel in a city that for a brief time provided them a sense of belonging. They have come to feel that same "un-home-likeness" in Rome that Hawthorne had remarked upon in his *French and Italian Notebooks*. In an echo of another theme sounded in *Seven Gables*, Kenyon exclaims to Hilda, "[G]uide me home!" (1236), as he seeks the stability and reassurance that Rome no longer affords.

Part of Hawthorne's fascination with the works of art that he encounters in Rome relates to the way they engage his thoughts about the process of creation and interpretation. His main characters engage in numerous dialogues about the meanings of and differences between painting and sculpture. As artists, they also grapple with how others respond to their work, what others see in the finished piece compared to the ideal concept from which the artist worked.

Kenyon also expresses the artist's frustration that comes after the energy of creation is expended and dissatisfaction sets in at finding one has produced what seems another "lump of senseless stone" (1167) that cannot express a great idea. That these thoughts relate to the work of writers as well is evident in Hilda's response to Kenyon in which she explains that she has heard a great poet utter the same complaint.

Hawthorne contemplates the way art offers a sense of permanence or continuity in a rapidly changing world. Yet he also remarks upon the ravages time inflicts on art, such as the damage to frescoes that diminishes their color and vibrancy. For Hawthorne, the tension between art's timelessness and its existence within time generates a complex problem that cannot easily be resolved.

ALLUSIONS

In his references to the "Faun of Praxiteles" and to aspects of Donatello's sylvan past, Hawthorne evokes the poetic image of Arcadia. The Arcadia of classical times, a region of Greece, was isolated from the rest of the country by the mountains that surround it. The Arcadians were known for their simple lifestyle, their hospitality, and their love of music. Roman poets, such as Virgil and Ovid, drew on these qualities in creating an idealized image of Arcadia as a land of innocence and virtue. Poets in the Renaissance continued this tradition, associating Arcadia with childlike innocence and pastoral simplicity. Arcadia was untainted by the conflicts of modern, urban life. Unlike Eden, Arcadia is not associated with a fall from grace into sin but it, too, is associated with an unrecoverable golden age.

Hawthorne refers to many works of art within the narrative. One that receives frequent mention is the portrait by Guido of Beatrice Cenci. Born in Rome in 1577, Beatrice was the daughter of Count Francesco Cenci, a powerful and wealthy nobleman who had a reputation for vice and violence. During one of the frequent family disputes, the Count imprisoned Beatrice and her stepmother in a remote castle outside Rome. They were treated cruelly and failed in their efforts to escape. While held at the castle, Beatrice took her father's steward, Olimpio Calvetti, as her lover. With him, her stepmother, and two brothers, she plotted her father's murder, performed by hired assassins in 1598. One of the assassins revealed the plot, and the Cencis were arrested. Tortured, they confessed and were sentenced to death. Beatrice was denied papal clemency and was beheaded in 1599. The story of Cenci, sometimes called the "Beautiful Parricide," inspired works of art and literature, including Percy Bysshe Shelley's play *The Cenci*, published in 1819.

HISTORICAL CONTEXT

Hawthorne's travels in Italy brought him into contact with the American artists' colonies in Rome and Florence. These painters and sculptors, including William Wetmore Story, Harriet Hosmer, and Hiram Powers, were drawn to Europe to study the works of great masters and to perfect their techniques in the studios of important teachers. They had departed from the United States believing that its rapidly expanding industrial culture made little room for the appreciation of art and beauty. They chose Italy in particular as a location because of what they considered its more natural qualities of life and because of its clear differences from England and America. The artists of Hawthorne's day formed part of an expatriate movement among American artists and writers that reached its zenith in the 1920s.

ALTERNATE READING: JUNGIAN CRITICISM

In *The Marble Faun*, Hawthorne traces the transformation of individuals as they move from innocence/ignorance to experience/knowledge, ultimately bringing them to a greater sense of wholeness. In light of this focus, the novel lends itself to interpretation through Jungian criticism. Carl Jung, a psychoanalyst, was a student of Sigmund Freud, but he devised a different method of describing the nature of the individual. Instead of focusing on the ego, id, and super ego, as Freud had done, Jung discussed the conscious ego and its persona along with the unconscious psyche that includes the shadow and anima or animus. In Jungian terms, the persona, or mask, is the face we show to the world, whereas the shadow (the dark side of the self) is often denied or repressed. Each individual also possesses the anima, the female or feminine principle that complements consciousness in all males, or the animus, the masculine principle, that does so in all females. Jung theorized that these various aspects of the self must be recognized and accepted before an individual can achieve wholeness.

The persona, or mask, reflects an individual's perceptions of what society expects him or her to be. In *The Marble Faun*, Miriam appears most aware of the need to present a face to the world that it will find acceptable. Her use of a false name and the concealment of her personal history are attempts to create a self that will not be rejected by those around her. Miriam also attempts to be lighthearted and witty, but her studio and paintings reflect the brooding qualities of her nature, which are less acceptable for a woman of her time.

For a Jungian critic, Miriam's secretive disappearance into the recesses of the catacombs functions as an archetypal pattern (see below) that represents her entry into the realm of the subconscious or unconscious where the dark side of human nature resides. Although Hawthorne uses the word *shadow* for Miriam's model because he dogs her every step, the term can also be applied in the Jungian sense, since the model represents the negative aspects of Miriam's past and self that she has tried to deny or repress. The fact that the model appears wherever she does indicates that the negative aspects of the self are present, whether or not they are acknowledged. Although Donatello wishes to help Miriam escape this dark figure's influence, he cannot eliminate the dark side of Miriam's self, which she carries within her.

Like Miriam, Donatello also exhibits a persona that reflects his sense of what his companions wish to see. When they tease him about his similarity to the Faun, he consciously strikes the pose of the sculpture, indicating his wish to please by appearing playful and rustic. Yet Donatello also has another side that surfaces when his anger is aroused, the animalistic qualities that reveal his more primitive instincts. Donatello follows Miriam into the dark maze of the catacombs, indicating that he, too, is entering into the realm of the subconscious where he will confront the dark side of himself. When he throws the model over the precipice, he believes he has disposed of the figure who has become his as well as Miriam's shadow. Instead, he finds that he is haunted by his recollections of the moment and finds no peace until he accepts not only what he has done but the existence of his own dark side.

The relationship between Miriam and Donatello serves to bring out qualities in each that reflect the animus or anima, respectively. Jung associated the anima with a "chaotic urge to life" and a "secret knowledge or hidden wisdom" (315). The anima draws man into a fuller engagement with life and unleashes forces that cause him to recognize what is bad as well as what is good within himself. Miriam's influence on Donatello stimulates the power of the anima, forcing Donatello to come to terms with the nature of good and evil that resides within. Initially, Donatello resists this process, just as he avoids contact with Miriam, but he discovers that to move on with life he must reconcile with his inner state and with Miriam. Similarly, interaction with Donatello and the desire to reunite with him after the crime awaken the element of the animus within Miriam. The animus, connected to rationality and objective reality, prompts reflection and evaluation. By the end of the novel, Miriam accepts that she and Donatello cannot hide forever.

Kenyon and Hilda have less obvious encounters with the dark side of the self since neither character has a "shadow" as tangible as Miriam's model. They must, however, confront certain negative aspects of themselves in order to grow into a relationship. Kenyon and Hilda separately appear as incomplete figures. Each lacks a crucial element of character that the other can supply or draw forth, reflecting the complementarity of the anima/animus. Jung indicated that the anima can also appear as a figure of light, as Hilda does for Kenyon. She elicits from him a greater warmth of feeling, while he draws her beyond her obstinate certitude over right and wrong with regard to Miriam and Donatello. Only when they are together as a couple at the end do Kenyon and Hilda enjoy a wholeness of being.

In addition to his analysis of the "personal unconscious," Jung also explored the theory of what he termed the "collective unconscious," a repository of images and patterns that exists as a kind of primordial memory. Jung referred to these images and patterns as *archetypes*. Archetypes and archetypal stories often reflect attempts to explain natural processes and universal human experiences to which an individual responds with a sense of profound recognition and familiarity. Some literary critics have discounted the notion of a "collective unconscious" but use the term *archetype* to identify recurrent patterns of action, images, and character types that appear in a wide variety of literary forms and myths across cultures. One of the most frequently recognized archetypes is the cycle of death and rebirth.

The experiences of Miriam and Donatello as discussed earlier reflect archetypal patterns, and Donatello's transformation can be read as a version of the death/rebirth cycle, since the innocent and jovial Donatello dies away following his crime, to be replaced by a wiser and somber man. Hilda's experiences near the end of the novel also recall the death/rebirth archetype. When Kenyon comments on Hilda's lack of mercy for others because she needs none herself, Hilda thinks about her reaction to and treatment of Miriam. Kenyon's remarks literally bring Hilda down from her tower when she remembers that she has promised to deliver a package for Miriam. Going on her own journey through the mazelike streets of the city to fulfill her promise, Hilda disappears. Her figurative resurrection occurs when she reappears draped in white clothing on the balcony during the carnival. The Hilda who returns has a greater degree of compassion for others and a clearer sense of her own need for immersion in life.

In addition to archetypal patterns, Hawthorne also introduces an important archetypal image, that of the "Great Mother" in Hilda's dedicated tending of the shrine to the Virgin Mary. Pre-Christian versions of the "Great Mother" presented her as a figure of opposites, who held both benevolent and malevolent attributes. She was associated with the fertility of the fields and the cycle of the seasons but also with the coming of death. She could be contradictory and unpredictable. In the Christian tradition, the Virgin Mary possesses and embodies only the positive aspects of this archetype, associated with goodness, light, and incorruptibility. She is seen as the model of submissive virtue and has the power to comfort and console, as one who has experienced great sorrows.

Hilda treats the Virgin as a mother substitute and feels a strong identification with her. Her own lightness and moral incorruptibility connect her to the Virgin's power. Hilda, and those around her, believe that her dedicated service and personal purity have earned her special protection afforded by the Virgin.

Thus she ventures forth alone where others fear to go, trusting that nothing evil will befall her. This identification, however, removes Hilda from the realm of the mortal and everyday, and Kenyon fears that she is "unattainable" (1161). Ultimately, Hilda's experiences transform her from being a "virginal priestess" at Mary's shrine to a more earthly being. By the end of the novel, she accepts Kenyon's offer of marriage, to become "a household Saint, in the light of her husband's fireside" (1237), assuming the role of a "true woman" consistent with her New England background and the gender conventions of her day.

In *The Marble Faun*, Hawthorne's attention to the meanings behind images and to the resonant qualities of myths and legends allows him to invest his narrative with the very details that invite readers to "find a great deal more in them than the poet or artist has actually expressed" (1168). The Jungian critic might very well agree with Hilda's observation that for works of art "[T]heir highest merit is suggestiveness" (1168), especially a suggestiveness that elicits the recognition of archetypal figures and patterns of experience.

Bibliography

Note: Page numbers referred to in the text are to the following Library of America editions:

Nathaniel Hawthorne: Tales and Sketches, A Wonder Book for Girls and Boys, Tangle-wood Tales. New York: Literary Classics of the United States, 1982.
Nathaniel Hawthorne: Novels. New York: Literary Classics of the United States, 1983.

WORKS BY NATHANIEL HAWTHORNE

Fanshawe (1828)
Twice-Told Tales (1837, 1842, 1851)
Grandfather's Chair: A History for Youth (1840–1841)
Famous Old People: Being the Second Epoch of Grandfather's Chair (1841)
Liberty Tree: With the Last Words of Grandfather's Chair (1841)
Biographical Stories for Children (1842)
Mosses from an Old Manse (1846, 1854)
The Scarlet Letter (1850)
The House of the Seven Gables (1851)
True Stories from History and Biography (1851)
The Snow-Image, and Other Twice-Told Tales (1852)
A Wonder-Book for Girls and Boys (1852)
The Blithedale Romance (1852)

Life of Franklin Pierce (1852)
Tanglewood Tales for Girls and Boys (1853)
Transformation: Or, The Romance of Monte Beni [England] (1860)
The Marble Faun: Or, The Romance of Monte Beni (1860)
Our Old Home: A Series of English Sketches (1863)

POSTHUMOUS PUBLICATIONS

Pansie [a chapter from *The Dolliver Romance*] (1864)
Passages from the American Note-Books of Nathaniel Hawthorne (1868)
Passages from the English Note-Books of Nathaniel Hawthorne (1870)
Passages from the French and Italian Note-Books of Nathaniel Hawthorne (1871)
Septimius Felton; Or, The Elixir of Life [unfinished] (1872)
The Dolliver Romance and Other Pieces [unfinished] (1876)
Fanshawe and Other Pieces (1876)
The Ancestral Footstep [unfinished] (1883)
Dr. Grimshawe's Secret [unfinished] (1883)
The Complete Works of Nathaniel Hawthorne. 12 vols. Boston: Houghton Mifflin, 1883.
The Centenary Edition of the Works of Nathaniel Hawthorne. 23 vols. Columbus: Ohio State University Press, 1962– .
    I. *The Scarlet Letter* (1962)
    II. *The House of the Seven Gables* (1965)
    III. *The Blithedale Romance* [and] *Fanshawe* (1964)
    IV. *The Marble Faun: or, The Romance of Monte Beni* (1968)
    V. *Our Old Home: A Series of English Sketches* (1970)
    VI. *True Stories From History and Biography* (1972)
    VII. *A Wonder Book and Tanglewood Tales* (1972)
    VIII. *The American Notebooks* (1972)
    IX. *Twice-Told Tales* (1974)
    X. *Mosses from an Old Manse* (1974)
    XI. *The Snow-Image and Uncollected Tales* (1974)
    XII. *The American Claimant Manuscripts: The Ancestral Footstep, Etherege, Grimshawe* (1977)
    XIII. *The Elixir of Life Manuscripts: Septimius Felton, Septimius Norton, The Dolliver Romance* (1977)
    XIV. *The French and Italian Notebooks* (1980)
    XV. *The Letters, 1813–1843* (1984)
    XVI. *The Letters, 1843–1853* (1985)
    XVII. *The Letters, 1853–1856* (1986)
    XVIII. *The Letters, 1857–1864* (1987)
    XIX. *The Consular Letters, 1853–1855* (1988)
    XX. *The Consular Letters, 1856–1857* (1988)
    XXI. *The English Notebooks* (1997)
    XXII. *The English Notebooks* (1997)
    XXIII. *Miscellaneous Prose and Verse* (1994)

BIOGRAPHIES

Hawthorne, Julian. *Nathaniel Hawthorne and His Wife.* 2 vols. Boston: Osgood, 1884.

James, Henry. *Nathaniel Hawthorne.* London: Macmillan, 1879.

Mellow, James R. *Nathaniel Hawthorne in His Times.* Boston: Houghton Mifflin, 1980.

Miller, Edwin Haviland. *Salem Is My Dwelling Place: A Life of Nathaniel Hawthorne.* Iowa City: University of Iowa Press, 1991.

Stewart, Randall. *Nathaniel Hawthorne: A Biography.* New Haven, CT: Yale University Press, 1948.

Turner, Arlin. *Nathaniel Hawthorne: A Biography.* New York: Oxford University Press, 1980.

CRITICAL STUDIES OF HAWTHORNE'S WORK

Baym, Nina. "Hawthorne's Women: The Tyranny of Social Myths." *Centennial Review* 15 (1971): 250–272.

———. *The Shape of Hawthorne's Career.* Ithaca, NY: Cornell University Press, 1976.

Bell, Michael Davitt. *Hawthorne and the Historical Romance of New England.* Chicago: University of Chicago Press, 1980.

Bell, Millicent. *Hawthorne's View of the Artist.* New York: State University of New York, 1962.

Berlant, Lauren. *The Anatomy of National Fantasy: Hawthorne, Utopia and Everyday Life.* Chicago: University of Chicago Press, 1991.

Bloom, Harold. *Nathaniel Hawthorne.* New York: Chelsea House, 1986.

Bowers, Edgar. "Hawthorne and the Extremes of Character." *Sewanee Review* 102 (1994): 570–588.

Brodhead, Richard. *Hawthorne, Melville and the Novel.* Chicago: University of Chicago Press, 1976.

———. *The School of Hawthorne.* New York: Oxford University Press, 1986.

Brown, Gillian. "Hawthorne's Endangered Daughters." *Western Humanities Review* 50–51 (1997): 327–331.

Cady, Edwin H., and Louis J. Budd, eds. *On Hawthorne.* Durham, NC: Duke University Press, 1990.

Carton, Evan. *The Rhetoric of American Romance: Dialectic and Identity in Emerson, Dickinson, Poe and Hawthorne.* Baltimore, MD: Johns Hopkins University Press, 1985.

Colacurcio, Michael J. *The Province of Piety.* Cambridge, MA: Harvard University Press, 1984.

Crews, Frederick C. *The Sins of the Fathers: Hawthorne's Psychological Themes.* New York: Oxford University Press, 1966.

Crowley, Joseph Donald, comp. *Nathaniel Hawthorne: A Collection of Criticism.* New York: McGraw-Hill, 1975.

Dauber, Kenneth. *Rediscovering Hawthorne.* Princeton, NJ: Princeton University Press, 1977.

DeSalvo, Louise A. *Nathaniel Hawthorne.* Atlantic Highlands, NJ: Humanities Press, 1987.

Dryden, Edgar A. *Nathaniel Hawthorne: The Poetics of Enchantment.* Ithaca, NY: Cornell University Press, 1977.

Erlich, Gloria C. *Family Themes and Hawthorne's Fiction: The Tenacious Web.* New Brunswick, NJ: Rutgers University Press, 1986.

Fogle, Richard H. *Hawthorne's Fiction: The Light and the Dark.* Norman: University of Oklahoma Press, 1969.

Gale, Robert L. *A Nathaniel Hawthorne Encyclopedia.* Westport, CT: Greenwood Press, 1991.

Gollin, Rita K. *Nathaniel Hawthorne and the Truth of Dreams.* Baton Rouge: Louisiana State University Press, 1979.

Gupta, R. K. "Hawthorne's Treatment of the Artist." *New England Quarterly* 45 (1972): 65–80.

Herbert, Walter T. *Dearest Beloved: The Hawthornes and the Making of the Middle-Class Family.* Berkeley: University of California Press, 1993.

Hutner, Gordon. *Secrets and Sympathy: Forms of Disclosure in Hawthorne's Novels.* Athens: University of Georgia Press, 1988.

Idol, John L., and Buford Jones, eds. *Nathaniel Hawthorne: The Contemporary Reviews.* Cambridge: Cambridge University Press, 1994.

Kaul, A. N., ed. *Hawthorne: A Collection of Critical Essays.* Englewood Cliffs, NJ: Prentice-Hall, 1966.

Laffrado, Laura. *Hawthorne's Literature for Children.* Athens: University of Georgia Press, 1992.

Lee, A. Robert, ed. *Nathaniel Hawthorne: New Critical Essays.* London: Vision, 1982.

Martin, Terence. *Nathaniel Hawthorne.* Rev. ed. Boston: Twayne/G. K. Hall, 1983.

Pearce, Roy Harvey, ed. *Hawthorne Centenary Essays.* Columbus: Ohio State University Press, 1964.

Pfister, Joel. *The Production of Personal Life: Class, Gender and the Psychological in Hawthorne's Fiction.* Stanford, CA: Stanford University Press, 1991.

Ponder, Melinda M. *Hawthorne's Early Narrative Art.* Lewiston, NY: Edwin Mellen, 1990.

Roundtree, Thomas J. *Critics on Hawthorne.* Coral Gables, FL: University of Miami Press, 1972.

Smith, Allan Gardner Lloyd. *Eve Tempted: Writing and Sexuality in Hawthorne's Fiction.* London: Croom Helm, 1984.

Stewart, Randall. "Hawthorne's Contributions to the *Salem Advertiser*." *American Literature* 5 (1933–1934): 327–341.

Swann, Charles. *Nathaniel Hawthorne: Tradition and Revolution.* Cambridge: Cambridge University Press, 1991.

Wagenknecht, Edward. *Nathaniel Hawthorne: The Man, His Tales and Romances.* New York: Continuum, 1989.

Waggoner, Hyatt H. *Hawthorne: A Critical Study.* Rev. ed. Cambridge, MA: Harvard University Press, 1963.

CONTEMPORARY REVIEWS OF HAWTHORNE'S SHORT FICTION

CONTEMPORARY REVIEWS OF *TWICE-TOLD TALES* (1837, 1842, 1851)

[Benjamin, Park]. "Twice-told Tales." *American Monthly Magazine*, March 1838, 281–283.

[Duyckinck, Evert A.]. "The Loiterer: Hawthorne's Twice-told Tales." *Arcturus*, April 1842, 394.

[Fuller, Margaret]. "Record of the Month." *Dial*, July 1842, 130–131.

"Literary Notices and Criticisms." *Boston Quarterly Review*, April 1842, 251–252.

[Longfellow, Henry Wadsworth]. "Twice-told Tales." *North American Review*, July 1837, 59–73.

[Poe, Edgar Allan]. "Twice-told Tales." *Graham's Magazine*, April 1842, 254.

———. "Twice-told Tales." *Graham's Magazine*, May 1842, 298–300.

"Twice-told Tales." [Boston] *Daily Advertiser*, March 10, 1837, 2.

"Twice-told Tales." *Salem Gazette*, March 7, 1837, 2.

"Twice-told Tales." *United States Magazine and Democratic Review*, February 1842, 197–198.

CONTEMPORARY REVIEWS OF *MOSSES FROM AN OLD MANSE* (1846)

[Channing, William Henry]. "Mosses from an Old Manse." *Harbinger*, June 27, 1846, 43–44.

[Fuller, Margaret]. "Mosses from an Old Manse." *New-York Daily Tribune*, June 22, 1846, 1.

"Hawthorne." *American Whig Review* 4 (September 1846): 296–316.

[Melville, Herman]. "Hawthorne and His Mosses." *Literary World*, August 17, 1850, 125–127; August 24, 1850, 145–147.

Poe, Edgar Allan. "Tale-Writing—Nathaniel Hawthorne." *Godey's Magazine and Lady's Book*, November 1847, 252–256.

CONTEMPORARY REVIEWS OF *THE SNOW-IMAGE, AND OTHER TWICE-TOLD TALES* (1852)

"New Tales by Hawthorne." *Literary World*, January 10, 1852, 22–24.

"Review of New Books." *Graham's Magazine*, April 1852, 443.

CRITICISM OF HAWTHORNE'S SHORT FICTION

Bell, Millicent, ed. *New Essays on Hawthorne's Major Tales*. Cambridge: Cambridge University Press, 1993.

Bromell, Nicholas K. " 'The Bloody Hand' of Labor: Work, Class and Gender in Three Stories by Hawthorne." *American Quarterly* 42 (1990): 542–564.

Bunge, Nancy. *Nathaniel Hawthorne: A Study of the Short Fiction*. New York: Twayne, 1993.

Cooper, Allene. "The Discourse of Romance: Truth and Fantasy in Hawthorne's Point of View." *Studies in Short Fiction* 28 (1991): 497–507.

Frank, Albert J. von, ed. *Critical Essays on Hawthorne's Short Stories*. Boston: G. K. Hall, 1991.

Gale, Robert. *Plots and Characters in the Fiction and Sketches of Nathaniel Hawthorne*. Hamden, CT: Archon Books, 1968.

Newman, Lea Bertani Vozar. *A Reader's Guide to the Short Stories of Nathaniel Hawthorne*. Boston: G. K. Hall, 1979.

"THE GENTLE BOY" (1832, 1837)

Miller, Edwin Haviland. " 'Wounded Love': Nathaniel Hawthorne's 'The Gentle Boy.' " *Nathaniel Hawthorne Journal* 8 (1978): 47–54.

Newberry, Frederick. "Hawthorne's 'Gentle Boy': Lost Mediators in Puritan History." *Studies in Short Fiction* 21 (1984): 363–373.

Petrie, Paul R. "Hawthorne in the Time of Schism: 'The Gentle Boy' & the Second Great Awakening." *Studies in Puritan American Spirituality* 5 (1995): 149–178.

Thompson, W. R. "Patterns of Biblical Allusions in Hawthorne's 'The Gentle Boy.' " *South Central Bulletin* 22, no.4 (1962): 3–10.

Tremblay, William A. "A Reading of Nathaniel Hawthorne's 'The Gentle Boy.' " *Massachusetts Studies in English* 2 (1970): 80–87.

"MY KINSMAN, MAJOR MOLINEUX" (1832, 1852)

Bellis, Peter J. "Representing Dissent: Hawthorne and the Drama of Revolt." *ESQ: A Journal of the American Renaissance* 41 (1995): 97–119.

Colacurcio, Michael J. "Hawthorne and the Interests of History." In *New Essays on Hawthorne's Major Tales*, ed. Millicent Bell, 37–66. Cambridge: Cambridge University Press, 1993.

Collins, Michael J. "Hawthorne's Use of Clothing in 'My Kinsman, Major Molineux.' " *Nathaniel Hawthorne Journal* 8 (1978): 171–172.

Grayson, Robert C. "The New England Sources for 'My Kinsman, Major Molineux.' " *American Literature* 54 (1982): 545–559.

Herbert, T. Walter, Jr. "Doing Cultural Work: 'My Kinsman, Major Molineux' and the Construction of the Self-made Man." *Studies in the Novel* 23 (1991): 20–27.

Miller, John N. "The Pageant of Revolt in 'My Kinsman, Major Molineux.' " *Studies in American Fiction* 17 (1989): 51–64.

itzsche, J. C. "House Symbolism in Hawthorne's 'My Kinsman, Major Molineux.' " *American Transcendental Quarterly* 38 (1978): 167–175.

Shaw, Peter. "Fathers, Sons, and the Ambiguities of Revolution in 'My Kinsman, Major Molineux.' " *New England Quarterly* 49 (1976): 559–576.

Wallins, Roger P. "Robin and the Narrator in 'My Kinsman, Major Molineux.' " *Studies in Short Fiction* 12 (1975): 253–260.

"ROGER MALVIN'S BURIAL" (1832, 1846)

Beaver, Harold. "Towards Romance: The Case of 'Roger Malvin's Burial.' " In *Nathaniel Hawthorne: New Critical Essays*, ed. A. Robert Lee, 31–47. London: Vision, 1982.

Crews, Frederick C. "The Logic of Compulsion in 'Roger Malvin's Burial.' " *PMLA* 79 (1964): 457–465.

Erlich, Gloria. C. "Guilt and Expiation in 'Roger Malvin's Burial.' " *Nineteenth-Century Fiction* 26 (1971): 377–389.

Fishman, Burton J. "Imagined Redemption in 'Roger Malvin's Burial.' " *Studies in American Fiction* 5 (1975): 257–262.

Hochberg, Shifra. "Etymology and the Significance of Names in 'Roger Malvin's Burial.' " *Studies in Short Fiction* 26 (1989): 317–321.

Liebman, Sheldon W. " 'Roger Malvin's Burial': Hawthorne's Allegory of the Heart." *Studies in Short Fiction* 12 (1975): 253–260.

McIntosh, James. "Nature and Frontier in 'Roger Malvin's Burial.' " *American Literature* 60 (1988): 188–204.

Robinson, E. Arthur. " 'Roger Malvin's Burial': Hawthorne and the American Environment." *Nathaniel Hawthorne Journal* 7 (1977): 147–166.

"WAKEFIELD" (1835, 1837)

Chibka, Robert L. "Hawthorne's Tale Told Twice: A Reading of 'Wakefield.' " *ESQ: A Journal of the American Renaissance* 28 (1982): 220–232.

Enniss, Stephen C. "Told as Truth: 'Wakefield' as Archetypal Experience." *Nathaniel Hawthorne Review* 14, no.2 (1988): 7–9.

Gatta, John, Jr. " 'Busy and Selfish London': The Urban Figure in Hawthorne's 'Wakefield.' " *ESQ: A Journal of the American Renaissance* 23 (1977): 164–172.

Morsberger, Robert E. "Wakefield in the Twilight Zone." *American Transcendental Quarterly* 14 (1972): 6–8.

Perry, Ruth. "The Solitude of Hawthorne's 'Wakefield.' " *American Literature* 49 (1978): 613–619.

"YOUNG GOODMAN BROWN" (1835, 1846)

Campbell, Harry M. "Freudianism, American Romanticism, and 'Young Goodman Brown.' " *CEA Critic* 33, no. 3 (1971): 3–6.

Eberwein, Jane Donahue. "My Faith Is Gone! 'Young Goodman Brown' and Puritan Conversion." *Christianity and Literature* 32 (1982): 23–32.

Erisman, Fred. " 'Young Goodman Brown': Warning to Idealists." *American Transcendental Quarterly* 14 (1972): 156–158.

Johnson, Claudia G. " 'Young Goodman Brown' and Puritan Justification." *Studies in Short Fiction* 11 (1974): 200–203.

Keil, James C. "Hawthorne's 'Young Goodman Brown': Early Nineteenth-Century and Puritan Constructions of Gender." *New England Quarterly* 69 (1996): 33–55.

Matheson, Terence J. " 'Young Goodman Brown': Hawthorne's Condemnation of Conformity." *Nathaniel Hawthorne Journal* 8 (1978): 137–145.

Paulits, Walter J. "Ambivalence in 'Young Goodman Brown.' " *American Literature* 41 (1970): 577–584.

St. Armand, Barton L. " 'Young Goodman Brown' as Historical Allegory." *Nathaniel Hawthorne Journal* 3 (1973): 183–197.

Tritt, Michael. " 'Young Goodman Brown' and the Psychology of Projection." *Studies in Short Fiction* 23 (1986): 113–117.

"THE MAY-POLE OF MERRY MOUNT" (1836, 1837)

Drinnon, Richard. "The Maypole of Merry Mount: Thomas Morton and the Puritan Patriarchs." *Massachusetts Review* 21 (1980): 382–411.

Feeney, Joseph J. "The Structure of Ambiguity in Hawthorne's 'The May-Pole of Merry Mount.' " *Studies in American Fiction* 3 (1975): 211–216.

Joplin, David D. " 'May-Pole of Merry Mount': Hawthorne's 'L'Allegro' and 'Il Penseroso.' " *Studies in Short Fiction* 30 (1993): 185–192.

Miller, John N. " 'The Maypole of Merry Mount': Hawthorne's Festive Irony." *Studies in Short Fiction* 26 (1989): 111–123.

Pribek, Thomas. "The Conquest of Canaan: Suppression of Merry Mount." *Nineteenth-Century Literature* 40 (1985): 345–354.

Smith, Gayle L. "Transcending the Myth of the Fall in Hawthorne's 'The May-Pole of Merry Mount.' " *ESQ: A Journal of the American Renaissance* 29, no.2 (1983): 73–80.

Weltzien, Alan O. "The Picture of History in 'The May-Pole of Merry Mount.' " *Arizona Quarterly* 45 (1989): 29–48.

"THE MINISTER'S BLACK VEIL" (1836, 1837)

Barry, Elaine. "Beyond the Veil: A Reading of Hawthorne's 'The Minister's Black Veil.' " *Studies in Short Fiction* 17 (1980): 15–20.

Carnochan, W. B. " 'The Minister's Black Veil': Symbol, Meaning, and the Context of Hawthorne's Art." *Nineteenth Century Fiction* 24 (1969): 182–192.

Coale, Samuel. "Hawthorne's Black Veil: From Image to Icon." *CEA Critic* 55, no.3 (1993): 79–87.

Colacurcio, Michael J. "Parson Hooper's Power of Blackness: Sin and Self in 'The Minister's Black Veil.' " *Prospects* 5 (1980): 331–411.

Franklin, Rosemary F. " 'The Minister's Black Veil': A Parable." *American Transcendental Quarterly* 56 (1985): 55–63.

Freedman, William. "The Artist's Symbol and Hawthorne's Veil." *Studies in Short Fiction* 29 (1992): 353–362.

German, Norman. "The Veil of Words in 'The Minister's Black Veil.' " *Studies in Short Fiction* 25 (1988): 41–47.

Newman, Lea Bertani Vozar. "One Hundred and Fifty Years of Looking at, into, through, behind, beyond, and around 'The Minister's Black Veil.' " *Nathaniel Hawthorne Review* 13, no.2 (1987): 5–12.

"THE BIRTH-MARK" (1843, 1846)

Eckstein, Barbara. "Hawthorne's 'The Birthmark': Science and Romance as Belief." *Studies in Short Fiction* 26 (1989): 511–519.

Gatta, John. "Aylmer's Alchemy in 'The Birthmark.' " *Philological Quarterly* 57 (1978): 399–413.

Rosenberg, Liz. " 'The Best That Earth Could Offer': 'The Birth-mark,' a Newlywed's Story." *Studies in Short Fiction* 30 (1993): 145–151.

Rucker, Mary. "Science and Art in Hawthorne's 'The Birth-mark.' " *Nineteenth-Century Literature* 41 (1987): 445–461.

Scheer, Thomas F. "Aylmer's Divine Roles in 'The Birthmark.' " *American Transcendental Quarterly* 22 (1974): 108–109.

Youra, Steven. " 'The Fatal Hand': A Sign of Confusion in Hawthorne's 'The Birth-Mark.' " *American Transcendental Quarterly* 60 (1986): 43–51.

"EGOTISM; OR, THE BOSOM-SERPENT" (1843, 1846)

Arner, Robert D. "Of Snakes and Those Who Swallow Them: Some Folk Analogues for Hawthorne's 'Egotism; or, the Bosom Serpent.' " *Southern Folklore Quarterly* 35 (1971): 336–346.

Barnes, Daniel R. " 'Physical Fact' and Folklore: Hawthorne's 'Egotism; or, the Bosom Serpent.' " *American Literature* 43 (1971): 117–121.

Monteiro, George. "A Nonliterary Source for Hawthorne's 'Egotism; or the Bosom Serpent.' " *American Literature* 41 (1970): 575–577.

Schechter, Harold. "The Bosom Serpent: Folklore and Popular Art." *Georgia Review* 39 (1985): 93–108.

Wohlpart, A. James. "Allegories of Art, Allegories of Heart: Hawthorne's 'Egotism' and 'The Christmas Banquet.' " *Studies in Short Fiction* 31 (1994): 449–460.

"THE ARTIST OF THE BEAUTIFUL" (1844, 1846)

Bassil, Veronica. "Eros and Psyche in 'The Artist of the Beautiful.' " *ESQ: A Journal of the American Renaissance* 30 (1984): 1–21.

Berthea, Dean Wentworth. "Heat, Light, and the Darkening World: Hawthorne's 'The Artist of the Beautiful.' " *South Atlantic Review* 56 (1991): 23–35.

Billy, Ted. "Time and Transformation in 'The Artist of the Beautiful.' " *American Transcendental Quarterly* 29 (1976): 33–35.

Idol, John L. " A Show of Hands in 'The Artist of the Beautiful.' " *Studies in Short Fiction* 22 (1985): 455–460.

Liebman, Sheldon W. "Hawthorne's Romanticism: 'The Artist of the Beautiful.' " *ESQ: A Journal of the American Renaissance* 22 (1976): 85–95.

Wohlpart, A. James. "The Status of the Artist in Hawthorne's 'The Artist of the Beautiful.' " *American Transcendental Quarterly*, n.s., 3 (1989): 245–256.

"RAPPACCINI'S DAUGHTER" (1844, 1846)

Baris, Sharon Deykin. "Giovanni's Garden: Hawthorne's Hope for America." *Modern Language Studies* 12, no.4 (1982): 75–90.

Chappel, Charles. "Pietro Baglioni's Motives for Murder in 'Rappaccini's Daughter.' " *Studies in American Fiction* 18 (1990): 55–63.

Davis, Joe. "The Myth of the Garden: Nathaniel Hawthorne's 'Rappaccini's Daughter.' " *Studies in the Literary Imagination* 2 (1969): 3–12.

Hallissy, Margaret. "Hawthorne's Venomous Beatrice." *Studies in Short Fiction* 19 (1982): 231–239.

Kloeckner, Alfred J. "The Flower and the Fountain: Hawthorne's Chief Symbols in 'Rappaccini's Daughter.' " *American Literature* 38 (1968): 323–336.

Miller, John N. "Fideism vs. Allegory in 'Rappaccini's Daughter.' " *Nineteenth-Century Literature* 46 (1991): 223–244.

Ross, Morton L. "What Happens in 'Rappaccini's Daughter.' " *American Literature* 43 (1971): 336–345.

"ETHAN BRAND" (1850, 1852)

Davison, Richard A. "The Villagers and 'Ethan Brand.' " *Studies in Short Fiction* 4 (1967): 260–262.

Eisen, Kurt. "The Tragical History of Ethan Brand." *Essays in Literature* 19 (1992): 55–60.

Harris, Mark. " A New Reading of 'Ethan Brand': The Failed Quest." *Studies in Short Fiction* 31 (1994): 69–77.

Klingel, Joan E. " 'Ethan Brand' as Hawthorne's Faust." *Studies in Short Fiction* 19 (1982): 74–76.

Liebman, Sheldon W. "Ethan Brand and the Unpardonable Sin." *American Transcendental Quarterly* 24 (1974): 9–14.

McElroy, John. "The Brand Metaphor in 'Ethan Brand.' " *American Literature* 43 (1972): 633–637.

Vanderbilt, Kermit. "The Unity of Hawthorne's 'Ethan Brand.' " *College English* 24 (1963): 453–456.

THE SCARLET LETTER (1850)

CONTEMPORARY REVIEWS

Brownson, Orestes. "Literary Notices and Criticisms." *Brownson's Quarterly*, n.s., 4 (October 1850): 528–532.

[Duyckinck, Evert A.]. "Nathaniel Hawthorne." *Literary World*, March 30, 1850, 323–325.

"Literary Notices." *Boston Post*, March 21, 1850, 1.

"The New Romance." *Boston Transcript*, March 15, 1850, 4.

"The Scarlet Letter." *Christian Inquirer*, May 25, 1850, 2.

"The Scarlet Letter." *Christian Register*, April 13, 1850, 58.

"*The Scarlet Letter.*" *Salem Gazette*, March 19, 1850, 2.

"The Scarlet Letter Prefix." *Salem Register*, March 21, 1850, 2.

Tuckerman, Henry T. "Nathaniel Hawthorne." *Southern Literary Messenger* 17 (June 1851): 347–348.

CRITICISM

Baym, Nina. The Scarlet Letter: *A Reading*. Boston: G. K. Hall, 1986.

Bell, Millicent. "The Obliquity of Signs: *The Scarlet Letter*." *Massachusetts Review* 23 (1982): 9–26.

Bensick, Carol M. "Dimmesdale and His Bachelorhood: 'Priestly Celibacy' in *The Scarlet Letter*." *Studies in American Fiction* 21 (1993): 103–110.

Bercovitch, Sacvan. *The Office of the Scarlet Letter*. Baltimore, MD: Johns Hopkins University Press, 1991.

———. "*The Scarlet Letter*: A Twice-Told Tale." *Nathaniel Hawthorne Review* 22, no.2 (Fall 1996): 1–20.

Clark, Michael. "Another Look at the Scaffold Scenes in Hawthorne's *The Scarlet Letter*." *American Transcendental Quarterly*, n.s., 1 (1987): 135–144.

Colacurcio, Michael J. *New Essays on* The Scarlet Letter. Cambridge: Cambridge University Press, 1985.

———. " 'The Woman's Own Choice': Sex, Metaphor, and the Puritan 'Sources' of *The Scarlet Letter.*" In *New Essays on* The Scarlet Letter, ed. Michael J. Colacurcio, 101–135. Cambridge: Cambridge University Press, 1985.

Cottle, Samuel. "*The Scarlet Letter* as Icon." *American Transcendental Quarterly*, n.s., 6 (1992): 251–262.

Egan, Ken, Jr. "The Adultress in the Market-Place: Hawthorne and *The Scarlet Letter.*" *Studies in the Novel* 27 (1995): 26–42.

Elbert, Monika. "Hester on the Scaffold, Dimmesdale in the Closet: Hawthorne's Seven Year Itch." *Essays in Literature* 16 (1989): 234–255.

———. "Hester's Maternity: Stigma or Weapon?" *ESQ: A Journal of the American Renaissance* 36 (1990): 175–207.

Gerber, John C. *Twentieth Century Interpretations of* The Scarlet Letter. Englewood Cliffs, NJ: Prentice-Hall, 1968.

Hoffman, Elizabeth Aycock. "Political Power in *The Scarlet Letter.*" *American Transcendental Quarterly*, n.s., 4 (1990): 12–39.

Johnson, Claudia Durst. "Impotence and Omnipotence in *The Scarlet Letter.*" *New England Quarterly* 66 (1993): 594–612.

———. *Understanding* The Scarlet Letter. Westport, CT: Greenwood Press, 1995.

Kesterson, David B. *Critical Essays on Hawthorne's* The Scarlet Letter. Boston: G. K. Hall, 1988.

Martin, Terence. "The Power of Generalizations in *The Scarlet Letter.*" *Nathaniel Hawthorne Review* 21, no.2 (1995): 1–6.

Moers, Ellen. "*The Scarlet Letter*: A Political Reading." *Prospects* 9 (1984): 49–70.

Pimple, Kenneth D. " 'Subtle but Remorseful Hypocrite': Dimmesdale's Moral Character." *Studies in the Novel* 25 (1993): 257–271.

Powers, Douglas. "Pearl's Discovery of Herself in *The Scarlet Letter.*" *Nathaniel Hawthorne Review* 16, no.1 (1990): 12–15.

Railton, Stephen. "The Address of *The Scarlet Letter.*" In *Readers in History: Nineteenth-Century American Literature and the Contexts of Response*, ed. James L. Machor, 138–163. Baltimore, MD: Johns Hopkins University Press, 1993.

Scharnhorst, Gary. *The Critical Responses to Nathaniel Hawthorne's* The Scarlet Letter. Westport, CT: Greenwood Press, 1992.

Schiff, James A. *Updike's Version: Rewriting* The Scarlet Letter. Columbia: University of Missouri Press, 1995.

Walters, James. "The Letter and the Spirit in Hawthorne's Allegory of American Experience." *ESQ: A Journal of the American Renaissance* 32 (1986): 36–54.

THE HOUSE OF THE SEVEN GABLES (1851)

CONTEMPORARY REVIEWS

[Duyckinck, Evert A.]. "The House of the Seven Gables." *Literary World*, April 26, 1851, 334–335.

"The House of the Seven Gables." *Salem Register*, April 14, 1851, 2.

[Mayo, Amory Dwight]. "The Works of Nathaniel Hawthorne." *Universalist Quarterly*, July 1851, 273–293.

"Review of New Books." *Graham's Magazine*, June 1851, 467–468.

[Ripley, George]. "The House of the Seven Gables." *Harper's New Monthly Magazine* 2 (May 1851): 855–856.

CRITICISM

Baym, Nina. "Hawthorne's Holgrave: The Failure of the Artist-Hero." *Journal of English and Germanic Philology* 69 (1970): 584–598.

Bellis, Peter J. "Mauling Governor Pyncheon." *Studies in the Novel* 26, no.3 (1994): 199–217.

Benardete, Jane. "Holgrave's Legend of Alice Pyncheon as a *Godey's* Story." *Studies in American Fiction* 7 (1979): 229–233.

Buitenhuis, Peter. The House of the Seven Gables: *Severing Family and Colonial Ties.* Boston: Twayne/G. K. Hall, 1991.

Burns, Rex S. "Hawthorne's Romance of Traditional Success." *Texas Studies in Language and Literature* 12 (1970): 443–455.

Cox, Clara B. " 'Who Killed Judge Pyncheon?' The Scene of the Crime Revisited." *Studies in American Fiction* 16 (1988): 99–103.

Cunliffe, Marcus. "*The House of the Seven Gables.*" In *Hawthorne Centenary Essays*, ed. Roy Harvey Pearce, 79–101. Columbus: Ohio State University Press, 1964.

Davis, Sarah I. "The Bank and the Old Pyncheon Family." *Studies in the Novel* 16 (1984): 150–166.

Emery, Allan. "Salem History and *The House of the Seven Gables.*" In *Critical Essays on Hawthorne's* The House of the Seven Gables, ed. Bernard Rosenthal, 129–149. New York: G. K. Hall, 1995.

Fogle, Richard H. "Nathaniel Hawthorne: *The House of the Seven Gables.*" In *Landmarks of American Writing*, ed. Hennig Cohen, 111–120. New York: Basic Books, 1969.

Gable, H. L., Jr. "Kaleidoscopic Visions: Images of the Self in *The House of the Seven Gables.*" *Arizona Quarterly* 48 (1992): 109–135.

Gallagher, Susan Van Zanten. "A Domestic Reading of *The House of the Seven Gables.*" *Studies in the Novel* 21 (1989): 1–13.

Goddu, Teresa. "The Circulation of Women in *The House of the Seven Gables.*" *Studies in the Novel* 23 (1991): 119–127.

Gray, Richard. " 'Hawthorne: A Problem': *The House of the Seven Gables.* In *Nathaniel Hawthorne: New Critical Essays*, ed. A. Robert Lee, 88–109. London: Vision, 1982.

Harris, Kenneth Marc. " 'Judge Pyncheon's Brotherhood': Puritan Theories of Hypocrisy and *The House of the Seven Gables.*" *Nineteenth-Century Literature* 39 (1984): 144–162.

Johnson, Claudia D. "Unsettling Accounts in *The House of the Seven Gables*." *American Transcendental Quarterly*, n.s., 5 (1991): 83–94.

Michelson, Bruce. "Hawthorne's House of Three Stories." In *Critical Essays on Hawthorne's* The House of the Seven Gables, ed. Bernard Rosenthal, 76–90. New York: G. K. Hall, 1995.

Millington, Richard H. "Reading *The House of the Seven Gables*: Narrative as Cultural System." *Prospects* 15 (1990): 39–90.

Olesky, Elzbieta H. "Hawthorne's Monstrous Doubles: Metonymic Links between *The House of the Seven Gables* and *The Marble Faun*." *Nathaniel Hawthorne Review* 18 (1992): 15–19.

Ragan, J. F. "Social Criticism in *The House of the Seven Gables*." In *Literature and Society*, ed. Bernice Slote, 112–120. Lincoln: University of Nebraska Press, 1964.

Rosenthal, Bernard, ed. *Critical Essays on Hawthorne's* The House of the Seven Gables. New York: G. K. Hall, 1995.

Schoen, Carol. "The House of the Seven Deadly Sins." *ESQ: A Journal of the American Renaissance* 19, no.1 (1973): 26–33.

Scoville, Samuel. "Hawthorne's Houses and Hidden Treasures." *ESQ: A Journal of the American Renaissance* 19, no.2 (1973): 61–73.

Tharpe, Colman W. "The Oral Storyteller in Hawthorne's Novels." *Studies in Short Fiction* 16 (1979): 205–214.

Thomas, Brook. "*The House of the Seven Gables*: Reading the Romance of America." *PMLA* 97 (1982): 195–211.

THE BLITHEDALE ROMANCE (1852)

CONTEMPORARY REVIEWS

"*The Blithedale Romance*." *American Whig Review*, November 1852, 417–424.

"False Tendencies in American Literature." *Literary World*, August 1852, 139–140.

"*The House of the Seven Gables* and *The Blithedale Romance*." *North American Review*, January 1853, 227–248.

"New Publications." [New York] *Tribune*, July 22, 1852, 6–7.

"Review of New Books." *Graham's Magazine*, September 1852, 333–334.

CRITICISM

Anhorn, Judy Schaaf. " 'Gifted Simplicity of Vision': Pastoral Expectations in *The Blithedale Romance*." *ESQ: A Journal of the American Renaissance* 28 (1982): 135–153.

Bales, Kent. "The Allegory and the Radical Romantic Ethic of *The Blithedale Romance*." *American Literature* 46 (1974): 41–53.

Baym, Nina. "*The Blithedale Romance*: A Radical Reading." *Journal of English and Germanic Philology* 67 (1968): 545–569.

Berlant, Lauren. "Fantasies of Utopia in *The Blithedale Romance*." *American Literary History* 1 (1989): 30–62.

Brodhead, Richard H. "Veiled Ladies: Toward a History of Antebellum Entertainment." *American Literary History* 1 (1989): 273–294.

Canaday, Nicholas, Jr. "Community and Identity at Blithedale." *South Atlantic Quarterly* 71 (1972): 30–39.

Cary, Louise D. "Margaret Fuller as Hawthorne's Zenobia: The Problem of Moral Accountability in Fictional Biography." *American Transcendental Quarterly*, n.s., 4 (1990): 31–48.

Christophersen, Bill. "Behind the White Veil: Self-Awareness in Hawthorne's *The Blithedale Romance*." *Modern Language Studies* 12 (1982): 82–92.

Egan, Ken, Jr. "Hawthorne's Anti-Romance: Blithedale and Sentimental Culture." *Journal of American Culture* 11 (1988): 45–52.

Fogle, Richard H. "Priscilla's Veil: A Study of Hawthorne's Veil Imagery in *The Blithedale Romance*." *Nathaniel Hawthorne Journal* 2 (1972): 59–65.

Gable, Harvey L., Jr. "Inappeasable Longings: Hawthorne, Romance and the Disintegration of Coverdale's Self in *The Blithedale Romance*." *New England Quarterly* 67 (1994): 257–278.

Griffith, Kelley, Jr. "Forms in *The Blithedale Romance*." *American Literature* 40 (1968): 15–26.

Hume, Beverly. "Restructuring the Case against Hawthorne's Coverdale." *Nineteenth-Century Literature* 40 (1986): 387–399.

Justus, James H. "Hawthorne's Coverdale: Character and Art in *The Blithedale Romance*." *American Literature* 47 (1975): 21–36.

Kay, Donald. "Five Acts of *The Blithedale Romance*." *American Transcendental Quarterly* 13 (1972): 25–28.

Levy, Leo B. "*The Blithedale Romance*: Hawthorne's 'Voyage through Chaos.' " *Studies in Romanticism* 8 (1968): 1–15.

McGuire, Peter J. "Dante's Inferno in *The Blithedale Romance*." *English Language Notes* 18 (1980): 25–27.

Millington, Richard H. "American Anxiousness: Selfhood and Culture in Hawthorne's *The Blithedale Romance*." *New England Quarterly* 63 (1990): 558–583.

Pearce, Roy Harvey. "Day-dream and Fact: The Import of *The Blithedale Romance*." In *Individual and Community: Variations on a Theme in American Fiction*, ed. Kenneth Baldwin and David K. Kirby, 49–63. Durham, NC: Duke University Press, 1975.

Ross, Donald, Jr. "Dreams and Sexual Repression in *The Blithedale Romance*." *PMLA* 86 (1971): 1014–1017.

St. Armand, Barton L. "The Love Song of Miles Coverdale: Intimations of Eliot's 'Prufrock' in Hawthorne's *Blithedale Romance*." *American Transcendental Quarterly*, n.s., 2 (1988): 97–109.

Schriber, Mary Suzanne. "Justice to Zenobia." *New England Quarterly* 55 (1982): 61–78.

Sprague, Claire. "Dream and Disguise in *The Blithedale Romance*." *PMLA* 84 (1969): 596–597.

Stay, Byron L. "Hawthorne's Fallen Puritans: Eliot's Pulpit in *The Blithedale Romance*." *Studies in the Novel* 18 (1986): 283–290.

Stock, Irvin. "Hawthorne's Portrait of the Artist: A Defense of *The Blithedale Romance*." *Novel: A Forum on Fiction* 11 (1978): 144–156.

Stone, Edward. "The Spirit World of *The Blithedale Romance*." *Colby Library Quarterly* 14 (1978): 172–176.

Strychacz, Thomas F. "Coverdale and Women: Feverish Fantasies in *The Blithedale Romance*." *American Transcendental Quarterly* 62 (1986): 29–45.

Tanner, Laura E. "Speaking with 'Hands at Our Throats': The Struggle for Artistic Voice in *The Blithedale Romance*." *Studies in American Fiction* 21 (1993): 1–19.

Waite, James J. "Nathaniel Hawthorne and the Feminine Ethos." *Journal of American Culture* 11 (1988): 23–33.

Weldon, Roberta F. "Tyrant King and Accused Queen: Father and Daughter in Nathaniel Hawthorne's *The Blithedale Romance*." *American Transcendental Quarterly*, n.s, 6 (1992): 31–45.

Wershoven, C. J. "Doubles and Devils at Blithedale." *American Transcendental Quarterly* 58 (1985): 43–54.

THE MARBLE FAUN (1860)

CONTEMPORARY REVIEWS

"Contemporary Literature/Belles Lettres, *Transformation*." *Westminster Review* [England], April 1860, 624–627.

[Lowell, James Russell]. "The Marble Faun." *Atlantic Monthly*, April 1860, 509–510.

"Nathaniel Hawthorne." *Atlantic Monthly*, May 1860, 614–622.

"*Transformation*." *Athenaeum* [England], March 3, 1860, 296–297.

"Transformation." *Examiner* [England], March 31, 1860, 197.

CRITICISM

Baym, Nina. "*The Marble Faun*: Hawthorne's Elegy for Art." *New England Quarterly* 44 (1971): 355–376.

Beidler, Peter G. "The Theme of the Fortunate Fall in *The Marble Faun*." *ESQ: A Journal of the American Renaissance* 47 (1967): 56–62.

Bercovitch, Sacvan. "Of Wise and Foolish Virgins: Hilda versus Miriam in Hawthorne's *Marble Faun*." *New England Quarterly* 41 (1968): 281–286.

Carton, Evan. The Marble Faun: *Hawthorne's Transformations*. Boston: Twayne/G. K. Hall, 1992.

Dryden, Edgar A. "The Limits of Romance: A Reading of *The Marble Faun*." In *Individual and Community: Variations on a Theme in American Fiction*, ed.

Kenneth Baldwin and David K. Kirby, 17–48. Durham, NC: Duke University Press, 1975.

Hall, Spencer. "Beatrice Cenci: Symbol and Vision in *The Marble Faun*." *Nineteenth-Century Fiction* 25 (1970): 85–95.

Gollin, Rita K. "Painting and Character in *The Marble Faun*." *ESQ: A Journal of the American Renaissance* 21 (1975): 1–10.

Greenwald, Elissa. "Hawthorne and Judaism: Otherness and Identity in *The Marble Faun*." *Studies in the Novel* 23 (1991): 128–138.

Howard, David. "The Fortunate Fall and Hawthorne's *The Marble Faun*." In *Romantic Mythologies*, ed. Ian Fletcher, 97–136. New York: Barnes & Noble, 1967.

Janssen, James G. "The 'Grim Identity' in Hawthorne's *Marble Faun*." *Studies in the Novel* 15 (1983): 108–121.

Johnson, Claudia D. "Resolution in *The Marble Faun*: A Minority View." In *Puritan Influences in American Literature*, ed. Emory Elliott, 128–142. Urbana: University of Illinois Press, 1979.

Kesterson, David B. "Journey to Perugia: Dantean Parallels in *The Marble Faun*." *ESQ: A Journal of the American Renaissance* 70 (1973): 94–104.

———. "*The Marble Faun* as Transformation of Author and Age." *Nathaniel Hawthorne Journal* 8 (1978): 67–77.

———. *The Merrill Studies in* The Marble Faun. Columbus, OH: Charles E. Merrill, 1971.

Levy, Leo B. "*The Marble Faun*: Hawthorne's Landscape of the Fall." *American Literature* 42 (1970): 139–156.

Liebman, Sheldon. "The Design of *The Marble Faun*." *New England Quarterly* 40 (1967): 61–78.

Morris, Margaret Kissam. "Rhetoric in a Romance: An Unstable Synthesis in *The Marble Faun*." *American Transcendental Quarterly*, n.s., 2 (1988): 207–221.

Moss, Sidney P. "The Problem of Theme in *The Marble Faun*," *Nineteenth-Century Literature* 18 (1964): 393–399.

———. "The Symbolism of the Italian Background in *The Marble Faun*." *Nineteenth-Century Fiction* 23 (1968): 332–336.

Schiller, Emily. "The Choice of Innocence: Hilda in *The Marble Faun*." *Studies in the Novel* 26 (1994): 372–391.

Schneider, Daniel J. "The Allegory and Symbolism of Hawthorne's *The Marble Faun*." *Studies in the Novel* 1 (1969): 38–50.

Scrimgeour, Gary J. "*The Marble Faun*: Hawthorne's Faery Land." *American Literature* 36 (1964): 271–287.

Shumaker, Conrad. " 'Daughter of the Puritans': History in Hawthorne's *The Marble Faun*." *New England Quarterly* 57 (1984): 65–83.

Smith, Judy. "Fall into Human Light: Hawthorne's Vision of Love." In *American Declarations of Love*, ed. Ann Massa, 17–34. New York: St. Martin's Press, 1990.

Stern, Milton R. *Contexts for Hawthorne*: The Marble Faun *and the Politics of Openness and Closure in American Literature*. Urbana: University of Illinois Press, 1991.

Vallas, Stacey. "The Embodiment of the Daughter's Secret in *The Marble Faun*." *Arizona Quarterly* 46 (1990): 73–94.

RELATED SECONDARY SOURCES

Bakhtin, M. M. *The Bakhtin Reader: Selected Writings of Bakhtin, Medvedev, and Voloshinov*. Ed. Pam Morris. London and New York: E. Arnold, 1994.

Boyer, Paul, and Stephen Nissenbaum. *Salem Possessed: The Social Origins of Witchcraft*. Cambridge, MA: Harvard University Press, 1974.

Buell, Lawrence. *New England Literary Culture*. Cambridge: Cambridge University Press, 1986.

Foucault, Michel. *The Foucault Reader*. Ed. Paul Rabinow. New York: Pantheon Books, 1984.

Gilmore, Michael T. *American Romanticism and the Marketplace*. Chicago: University of Chicago Press, 1985.

———. *The Middle Way: Puritanism and Ideology in American Romantic Fiction*. New Brunswick, NJ: Rutgers University Press, 1977.

Herzog, Kristin. *Women, Ethnics, and Exotics: Images of Power in Mid-Nineteenth Century American Fiction*. Knoxville: University of Tennessee Press, 1983.

Karlsen, Carol F. *The Devil in the Shape of a Woman: Witchcraft in Colonial New England*. New York: W. W. Norton, 1987.

Madison, Charles. *Book Publishing in America*. New York: McGraw-Hill, 1966.

Melville, Herman. *Letters of Herman Melville*. Ed. Merrell R. Davis and William Gilman. New Haven, CT: Yale University Press, 1960.

Porte, Joel. *The Romance in America: Studies in Cooper, Poe, Hawthorne, Melville and James*. Middletown, CT: Wesleyan University Press, 1969.

Reynolds, David S. *Beneath the American Renaissance: The Subversive Imagination in the Age of Emerson and Melville*. New York: Knopf, 1988.

Swift, Lindsay. *Brook Farm*. 1900. Reprint. Secaucus, NJ: Citadel Press, 1961.

Walters, Ronald G. *American Reformers, 1815–1860*. New York: Hill and Wang, 1978.

Woidat, Caroline M. "Talking Back to Schoolteacher: Morrison's Confrontation with Hawthorne in *Beloved*." *Modern Fiction Studies* 39 (1993): 527–546.

Index

Garland, Hamlin, 18
"The Gentle Boy," 3, 24–27, 77
Georgiana ("The Birth-mark"), 49, 50, 51, 60
Godwin, William, 2
Goethe, Johann Wolfgang von, 65
Goodrich, Samuel, 3
Gothic, 16–17, 19, 104, 111
Grandfather's Chair: A History for Youth, 11
"The Gray Champion," 44
The Great Awakening, 41–42
The Great Deceiver, 36, 37, 121. *See also* Devil; Satan
Guasconti, Giovanni ("Rappaccini's Daughter"), 59, 60, 61, 62

Hathorne, John, 2, 104, 105
Hathorne, Nathaniel, 1
Hathorne, William, 2, 104
Hawthorne, Elizabeth, 2
Hawthorne, Elizabeth Manning, 1
Hawthorne, Julian, 6, 7
Hawthorne, Louisa, 7
Hawthorne, Nathaniel: boyhood, 1–2; courtship and marriage, 4–8, 7, 12; development as writer, 9; employment (non-literary), 5, 6, 67; travels in Europe, 7–8, 129; U.S. consul in Liverpool, 7, 12, 129
Hawthorne, Nathaniel, works of. *See names of individual works by Hawthorne*
Hawthorne, Rose, 7
Hawthorne, Sophia Peabody, 4, 5, 7, 24
Hawthorne, Una, 6, 7, 8
Herkimer, George ("Egotism; or, The Bosom-Serpent"), 52, 53
Hibbins, Old Mistress (*The Scarlet Letter*), 76, 78
Higgins, Ned (*The House of the Seven Gables*), 92, 101

Hilda (*The Marble Faun*), 137–38; relationship to other characters, 139–40; relationship to plot, 131–136; relationship to themes, 141–143; as seen through Jungian criticism, 145–147
Holgrave (*The House of the Seven Gables*), 97–98, 107; relationship to plot, 92–96; relationship to themes, 101–103; relationship with Phoebe, 99
Hollingsworth (*The Blithedale Romance*), 118–119, 120; relationship to plot, 113–117; relationship to themes, 122–123; as seen through Marxist criticism, 127–128
Holmes, Oliver Wendell, 6
Hooper ("The Minister's Black Veil"), 42–44, 45, 54
Hosmer, Harriet, 8, 144
The House of the Seven Gables, 6, 11, 14, 15, 89–107, 109, 111; and Gothic elements, 16, 104, 111; relationship to other works by Hawthorne, 10, 35, 53, 54, 69, 142
Hovenden, Annie ("The Artist of the Beautiful"), 55, 57
Hovenden, Peter ("The Artist of the Beautiful"), 54, 55, 56, 57
Howells, William Dean, 18
Hutchinson, Anne, 74, 79, 84

Ilbrahim ("The Gentle Boy") 24–26, 27, 77
Ingersoll, Susan, 3

James, Henry, 18–19, 130
Jewett, Sarah Orne, 18
"The Jolly Corner" (James), 18
Jung, Carl, 144
Jungian criticism, 144–147

Kemble, Fanny, 6

About the Author

MELISSA McFARLAND PENNELL is Associate Professor of English at the University of Massachusetts Lowell. She specializes in the American novel prior to 1900 and has published numerous articles on American literature. Her current research interests include a book-length critical appraisal of the work and career of Mary Wilkins Freeman.